THE BIBLE PROJECT

Published by Herminia Fonseca
For any comments, concerns or to purchase additional
copies go to amazon.com

Dedicated to my children
Julie, David
And
My Grandson, Brandon

The Front Cover

On the cover of this book I have given samples of the cross stitching of a few of the several frames I have given away.

Words of Acknowledgment

I want to thank Martin Lopez for sharing with me so many of the books he has read, and for phoning me regularly. Martin's encouragement helped me to finish this book. Thank you Arnulfo Cortes, you started these friendships at a Crete Safety meeting years ago. Arnulfo and Martin understand and share my passion for reading, and healthy discussions. We still manage to have so much fun with these heated conversations in conference calls. Juan Manuel "Willie" Ruiz and Fabian, and others of the "notorious nine," cared enough to share their lives with me. They took the time to invite me to dinners. I know what a hassle it is in time, limited parking space, not to mention extra energy it takes when driving a big rig. Thank you for the invitations to Crete's Christmas dinners and for keeping me in the loop with a culture I fell in love with. It certainly makes new memories, and brings back so many old ones.

Since truck driving was so much a part of my life, I want to thank all those wonderful truck drivers across the country. Who among other things, certainly added color to my life. We spent many hours in passionate and energetic discussions among so many controversial topics. I mentioned some in Part II called Truck Stop Chatter.

I especially want to thank those who shared similar beliefs and defended me against the others who didn't. I felt less alone. This also helped to reinforce my faith in humanity and in God.

I also want to thank Charlie who was the inspiration for the poem I wrote, which I share with you in this book. I don't even know what Charlie looked like, but the impression he made on me will affect and stay with me forever. Charlie set an example of how kind words from a complete stranger can affect another life.

To this phantom voice on the CB radio more than 30 years ago and all the people in my life who have helped me throughout the years: It is my hope this book will somehow pay it forward.

Very few can understand the life and culture of a truck driver without having driven a truck for several years. The poem "The Long Haul" is a glimpse of what truck drivers had to endure before cell phones, and computers. Technology gives the transportation industry another set of problems. Such is life, and as my son says, "It's all good." My prayers go with all great trucking companies such as Crete, and if someone is still alive to remember, Sam Tanksley out of Cape Girardeau Missouri. Sam Tanksley, like Crete knows the value of its drivers and treats them very well. I know because I worked for many of the major trucking companies which didn't.

I want to thank my very dear friend Louise Olson, whom I mention in this book, and her husband Lionel, who I consider lifelong friends. They opened their home to me with I applied for jobs in Wisconsin. Louise and Lionel are a blessing from God.

I want to thank my best friend Angela Howard. Anyone would be blessed to have you in their life. Thank you for being in my life all these years. Thank you for sharing, your children, (Hi Chalisa), and your mom Doris, and now Philip Juel's new baby. Thank you Angela for allowing me to call him my grandson.

I want to thank each of my family members and their spouses: My brothers and sisters but also their children and their spouses. I also want to thank all my wonderful cousins. It is an absolute privilege to know you. All of you are such wonderful people. I found the God I craved for, in each of you. You are, and continue to be the training ground for my spiritual journey. Thank you.

Thank you Gil Sanchez for taking the time to read the manuscript. I truly hope this book is worthy of your comments. This is especially comforting, since I have known you so many years and most of these topics we have "driven to the ground."

Thank you Ashley Knabe for your encouraging comments. Without some sort of feedback, I would have no way of knowing if what I wrote was of any value. You were the angel on my shoulder. Thank you again.

Thank you Brock, Ben, Deb, Alex, Ken, Cindy and others at the Advanced Learning Library for your angelic patience. Your vast amount of knowledge was invaluable. You helped me make this book a reality, thank you.

Thank you God for all your blessings throughout my life even when I didn't feel so blessed at the time.

Table of Contents

Part III

In The Beginning

Part IV

The Physical Process

"A journey of a thousand miles begins with a single step."
— Ancient Chinese saying

The Door of a Forest

I take a deep breath, and I close my eyes.
I leave behind the world's morbid lies.
With no sight I can be,
Because without the world it sets my soul free.

Within the darkness, there is no ground.
I gain footing, yet there is no land to be found.
I maintain a purpose for each faithful step.
Leaving a trail of tears that were painfully wept.

A desperate man, who walks alone.
Thoughts of a new life promised to be shown.
Ever so further into the night,
The impatient soul fought so much to fight.

Without a reason, the anger wasn't there.
Neither could anything else be found anywhere.
Simple thoughts for simple minds.
Insanity, little by little, slowly dies.

From my tears I could see
A thought that said, the key comes from me.
The wisdom that emanates burns in my head.
Giving life to what I thought was dead.[1]

---

[1] Part one of a poem by David Voth, entitled True Beginnings: The Door of a Forest. Published with permission from my son, David.

"Insanity, little by little, slowly dies."
— David Voth

Part I

Bible Verses I Love

God,
Make me an instrument of thy peace,
Where there is hatred, let me sow love;
Where there is injustice, pardon;
Where there is doubt; faith;
Where there is despair, hope;
Where there is darkness, light;
Where there is sadness, joy.

Oh Divine Creator,
Grant that I may not so much seek to be consoled as to console;
To be understood as to understand;
To be loved as to love;
For it is in giving that we receive;
It is in pardoning that we are pardoned;
And it is in dying that we are born to eternal life.

— Saint Francis of Assisi

How the Bible Project Begins

In 1971 I was renting a house in the south side of Wichita, Kansas. After negotiating with the landlord for a few cans of paint and several garage sales later, I managed to make it a nice home for my daughter and myself. I took pride in the inside, but I could not say as much for the outside. It would be sometime before I could save enough money to buy a nice shed and plant bright colored flowers.

However, there was one problem that took top priority: Every time it rained I would have to jump from my porch to the sidewalk over an area packed with slippery mud. This can be especially difficult when one is dressed for church.

One day I decided I had had enough: I grab a few pieces of 2 by 4's which had been left by the fence line, I dig out my Black and Decker hand saw, a hammer and some nails, and I form a square 36" by 36". Now all I need is a trip to buy the cement. Mixing it would be a no brainer: As a child I had seen my brothers and sisters pour cement. Just add water to the consistency of cake batter. A few hours later, there it was. I stood back and thought, *All I have to do it let it dry.* And if it had not been for my artistic and creative nature, I would have left it alone. But there it was, a blank canvas just begging for something: But what? I needed to come up with something fast because it was drying. It had to be something I would not get tired, or bored with easily. Then I remembered a bible verse I especially liked. On an impulse, I run inside, grab a kitchen knife, and rush outside to carve the verse on the blank slab.

A few months passed, I was coming out of my door and I spot two white haired ladies walking down the sidewalk toward the house. They stop at my gate.

Assuming they had come on business, I ask, "May I help you?"

One lady replies in a grateful tone, "My friend and I often walk down this sidewalk and make it a point to stop and read your verse."

It was hard for me not to feel some pride with each of her kind words.

Into the future, and a few states later, I end up near the old neighborhood.

One day I get the bright idea that I need a quiet place to think. Never mind I now live alone. This time I not only want a shed, but a Gazebo. For the foundation on my shed, I could now afford to hire a contractor.

I finally decide on a gazebo with curtains and mosquito netting. I move it several times, and finally decide on a permanent place on a corner, safe from tree branches.

To help reduce the out-of-pocket expense, I want to use as many materials that were left behind by the previous owner. I lay out the foundation with some large bricks I found. I change the pattern several times until I finally settle on one I liked. However, for what I had in mind, it lacks 36 inches on each side. I talk to the contractor. But of course, since it is such a small area, he tries to convince me it would be better to forget the bricks. But I already had my mind set on using the large 12×12 square, light green, and light red bricks. I level and prepare the foundation, and make the forms I will need to fill in with cement for the reminding area.

With my previous cement experience under my belt, I go to Home Depot and once again grab a few sacks of ready mix concrete.

I roll out my trusty wheel barrel and start mixing to the consistency of cake batter, reaffirmed by my friend Leroy at Home Depot. I start pouring, and there it is, another blank Slab. Ah, but this time I am ready. I remember the verse. But just to make sure of the chapter, I go to my library and pull off my Strong's Exhaustive Concordance and double check my copy of

King James. To my surprise, the chapter and verse (4:8) is my grandson's birthday. How great is that? I would now be able to remember the reference. Obviously the whole verse would not fit on the slab, so I abbreviate like I had years prior. Instead of the repetitions, I place comas and finish it off with the bible chapter and verse. It turned out great. It is a nice reminder to watch my thoughts. It reads:

> Whatsoever things are true,
> honest, just, pure, lovely, and
> of good report, if there is any
> virtue, or praise, think on
> these things. — Phi'p. 4:8.

I would latter make a narrow sidewalk, which runs up to the Gazebo, there would be many more blank slabs just begging for special something. This time I carefully plan each of the seven slabs on large pieces of white construction paper and write the letters so they are all uniform. I put flowers and vines around what I write. On the top slab I write:

> I set before you
> life and death:
> Choose Life.
> — De. 30:19.

My mind could not help think about the reference on the verse I carved twice over the years: Philippians 4:8. I start to wonder what bible verse I will find under my birthday. A personal message from God to me, so-to-speak. This is how this bible project begins.

I look up my birthday, my daughter, my son, my niece and her husband Frank, and my nephew's birthday. Then I got the bright idea to cross-stitch their verses on satin pillow cases with the colors according to their bedroom decor. I buy all the materials, pick out a verse I liked which matched their birthday, crossed stitched the verses, and before I realized it, I was memorizing verses. I sent out six satin pillows for Christmas.

Then I got the bright idea, (Not again!) I would find a nice verse I could give to every person on the planet! It seemed like a good idea at the time. However, my goal was firmly cemented. (No pun intended.) I was on a mission from God.

I can't quit even if I want to. I am determined to find a special message for each of the 366 days of the year, which includes leap year. The cross stitching evolves from pillows, to 5×7 inch frames, and from 18 inch gauge squares, to 14 inch gauge squares (The higher the number the smaller the squares). This is how my adventure goes from cross-stitching to this book.

My Feelings about the Bible

The first thing I want to do is clarify my feelings about the bible. The reason this idea can work is because of the way the King James Bible is laid out. It fits nicely with the months and days of the year. I have several different translations of the bible. However, I prefer the King James Version because it has been the most commonly used, and to me, it has a certain poetic Shakespearean appeal I like. However, when I had to break the verses down for the required space, I used the New American Standard Bible and/or a combination of several others and because of the need for space; I sometimes use contractions, colons, and semi colons.

My main objective was to keep the original meaning in relation to space and make it a personal message to myself.

The bible has gotten a bad rap over the centuries. For example: "Jesus freaks," or "bible thumpers" are just a few of the derogatory terms which have made their way into our culture. I realize people have strong views about the bible. I especially notice the adverse reactions of some of my friends when I mention it. For example: I had a friend, who was a preacher's kid (PK) who had a drinking problem. I started to tell him what the bible said about drinking. I pressed on when he tried to stop me. I think he thought I was going to preach to him. I told him to just wait until I finished and I promised I would then listen to him. I told him the bible says a man who drinks would never be rich. (Proverbs 21:17) He looked at me with a blank face, hesitated as if he was processing the words, and then said, "Well, that's obvious." And the conversation ended there. It took him a few years to get sober, by then he had lost his job as a systems analyst, divorced his wife, and finally ended up in a halfway house.

The bible has so much wisdom. But unfortunately, because like the PK and many others, it was probably strongly indoctrinated by a "holier than thou attitude". No one likes to be admonished. My guess is at some stage people just turn it off. The bible had the opposite effect on my son because curiously enough he learned to read and write Hebrew.

Some people lose common sense when it comes to religion. I like what Buddha said, "I point to the sun and you worship my finger."[2] To say the same thing in a different way: The Old Persian saying goes, "A bridge is for crossing, not for building a house on."[*3]

Some religious cults have used it as an excuse for self-mutilation, punishing others, and to justify burning

---

[2]This is taken from a wonderful book called "Old Path White Clouds" written by Thich Nhat Hanh. This book is taken directly from 24 Pali, Sanskrit, and Chinese sources partly from the eyes of Svasti, "the buffalo boy," one of his student followers and partly from Buddha himself. It is retold beautifully by Hanh.

[3] From Vedanta Heart of Hinduism by Hans Torwesten

"witches" or "heretics" at the stake. It seems like every religion has skeletons in its closet. But as history would confirm, there was often greed or fear involved. Even in this "modern age" with the same motives, some religious "zealots" have used the bible as a reason for government interference with civil rights such as racism, separation of the races, and preventing miscegenation. In my humble opinion, this is beautifully illustrated in the movie Loving, which is based on true story of the Supreme Court case.

As early as the 1900's, religions have insisted the government interfere with regulations on what a person can do or not do with their own body. They attack the rights to groups of people. Their present target being homosexuals: You can fill in the rest.

Unless people are hurting themselves and others they should be left alone. Some laws are outdated. I suppose we can find a verse in the bible to justify just about anything. For example Matthew 9:16-17; Mark 2:22; and Luke 5:37-38, warn against recycling:

"No one puts a patch of new cloth on an old garment; for the patch pulls away from the garment, and a worse tear results" — Luke 5:38.

To save money and as necessity i.e.[4] poverty demanded, I would use old clothes to make new ones and used new thread on old cloth. Like it or not, things change over the centuries. New technologies make changes not only in the way materials are made, but also how our food is processed.

Fortunately laws change: I am sure some alcoholics are glad we no longer stone them to death. (Deuteronomy 20-21.)

I know of a few people who get information from the bible second hand and actually believe it. I

---

[4] i.e. (id est) is Latin for 'that is'.

remember a recent conversation with the security guard. This is how he quoted what he believed was a bible verse:

"Do to others what they **want** to do to you."

I told him it was an old joke also went:

"Do unto others **before** they do it unto you."

The actual verse is called the "Golden Rule" or The "Law of The Prophets" and is found in many forms, for example Matthew 7:12 and in Luke 6:31. The way I learned it makes basic common sense. It reads:

"Do unto others **as** you would have them do unto you."

And just so we are perfectly clear, the verse that advises us to turn the other cheek (Matthew 5:39 and Luke 6:29) is not referring to your butt cheeks.

Some people think the bible is the infallible word of God, and take it as their solemn duty to convert everyone to what they belief. Yet there are so many belief systems or religions have come out of the same bible. They also conveniently forget the Golden Rule.

My goal with this book is to simply share something I found quite wonderful. I am not trying to convert anyone. I believe everyone is on his own spiritual journey. As it turned out, this is mine. I believe truth needs no defense: Either it speaks to you or it doesn't. For me:

1. The bible is a history book.
2. The bible is a book of evolutionary generations.
3. These generations are simply trying to find a better way to live; oftentimes in very difficult circumstances.
4. This bible, like all the others, can be used as a guide to rule governments, however, to me, it is a self-help book with an emphasis on self.

In my misspend youth, I tried to change people's opinions. But the more I read, the more I realize people are smart enough to figure things out for themselves. If they don't, they can always serve as a bad example of what not to do.

My only responsibility is to my beliefs. I am to use each day to become a better person, enjoy whatever life remains, and constantly look for the truth in myself, not in someone else. The bible however, does not tell us to remain silent:

"Warn and teach all men wisdom." — Colossians 1:28

One day I was in Kansas City waiting to get on to an elevator. There was a lady who I had never met, waiting there with me, for what seemed like an ungodly amount of time. For some reason, God put it in my heart to ask her if she had ever heard of Joyce Meyer.[5]

No sooner than the words came out of my month, she lit up and said, "YES! Don't you just love her?"

We talked and talked for the full ride. It was one of the most extraordinary, pleasant, surprising, experience in my life. I know some people do not agree, but I personally like the way Joyce presents the bible. She continually teaches us to take responsibility for our lives.

I used to love it when people challenged my beliefs. I no longer try to challenge theirs. I try instead to see the attraction, in that particular aspect of their religion, so I can better understand them.

For example: A Vietnamese family I know, placed a plate of fruit in the kitchen area before they moved into their new house. They were excited as I entered their new residence recently. The husband told me he did not believe in the custom, and thought it was silly. He speaks English, although he has not been in the United

---

[5]Joyce Meyer is a Pentecostal evangelist who has a television ministry; writes books; has prison ministry; and helps people all over the world. I listen to her every chance I get.

States long, and I suspect this has a lot to do with changing his old customs.

I think the placing of the fruit is a wonderful gesture because it places one's heart in the right place. I can't speak Vietnamese well enough to find out if the offering is to pacify spirits; bless their deity; or for prosperity: Probably all three. It does not matter, as long as their hearts are in the right place. What also matters is our mutual love and respect: I like what the bible says:

"We wrestle not against flesh and blood, but against principalities." — Ephesians 6:12

I like to think it is much better to be a good example and leave it there. I have not yet reached sainthood. But like my little brother said to my big brother while on a paddle boat, "I am paddling as hard as I can."

I have to laugh when I think back to the time I tried to get out of jury duty. I told the judge the reason I could not be on the jury was because, "I could not throw stones."[6] I heard a few brief chuckles, as the judge hesitated. I half way wondered if he expected me to make the conscientious objector argument. I also felt like he was trying to decide if I was joking.

All I knew was I getting deep into something I was not comfortable with and I was very relieved when he finally told me to remain seated.

I did not want to be there because the trial was about a guy with three DUI's (Driving under the influence) who was headed for prison on the 'three strikes and

---

[6]This is in reference to what Jesus told the people when they were going to stone Mary Magdalene: "He that is without sin let him cast the first stone." — John 7:8. After searching their conscience they dropped the stones and walked away.

you're out' rule. I was quite serious about not wanting to be there. While generally I would have welcomed the challenge, I knew the defendant was facing a very heavy jail term. At the time, the political climate was such, in which there was public pressure on repeat offenders: Thus 'the 3 strikes and you're out' rule of law. It could have very easily been friends, family or even me.

Later in the proceedings the judge asked if any family member had ever been affected by alcohol. I raised my hand again. When he pressed for more details, I told him it cost us a lot of money. Everyone laughed uneasily, especially the lawyers, so I guessed it wasn't the details he was after. I ignored the laughter for fear this time the judge would get angry with me for sure. When the judge asked who it was (I think he half expected it was me), I told him I got my husband help, and he had been clean for 15 years.

While waiting to be called the next day, we were told we could go home. I asked the clerk what had happened. I was thankful the case went through mediation and the guy got help instead of going to jail. Maybe, just maybe, my comments made a difference.

I am getting better at setting a good example, especially with people who disagree with me; attempt to hurt my feelings; or bruise my ego. Whether I like it or not, everyone or anything I face throughout the day is my teacher.

"I learned to be content whatever the circumstances."
— Philippians 4:11

I have worn out a book by a lady Unity Minister,

Terry Brooks,[7] titled: "<u>What You Think of Me Is None of My Business</u>." The title speaks for itself.

When people try to take advantage of me, I now realize it is always my choice, not theirs. Not only are they teaching me about myself, but more and more, I am realizing it has nothing to do with them. If my ego is hurt, it has something to do with my past. This is something I can change only in my mind. After all, isn't this where the past is?

The Process for the Bible Project

I am fortunate to have a lifelong friendship, (since 1978) with a wonderful person. Louise Olsen moved to Wisconsin years ago, but by some miracle, we manage to stay in touch. The thing I enjoy about Louise is that she periodically rattles off a bible verse. I thought it was so wonderful because whatever she quotes always makes sense. Many times I wished I could do the same. I guess I needed to be careful what I wished for.

Years ago, after reading a couple of books: The <u>Pilgrims Progress</u>[8] and <u>The Way of the Pilgrim</u>.[9] I got the idea I should also 'attempt to pray without ceasing'. I have a bit of an obsessive compulsive nature, both a

---

[7]A different Terry Brooks, the male writer wrote, <u>The Sword of Shanara</u> and their sequels. One day, feeling frustrated, I asked God how I could get through to my teenage son. We started reading these wonderful books together, and subsequently had many wonderful discussions, and beautiful memories.

[8]John Bunyan was an English Preacher who lived from 1628 until 1688. He was in and out of jail for 12 years. The first time it was because he preached without a license. He wrote the classic <u>Pilgrim's Progress</u> while in jail.

[9]<u>The Way of the Pilgrim</u> and <u>The Pilgrim Continues His Way</u>, (Author unknown) were found in a Monastery at Kazan. They were printed in 1884, and translated from Russian by R. M. French in 1930. The author questioned how he could pray unceasingly, when he had to go and make a living.

blessing and a curse.

"Pray without ceasing." — I Thessalonians 5:17

I attempted to always put God first, by training my mind. The idea for the bible verses probably took root here.

For this project I look for inspirational, instructive verses I want to memorize and repeat several times, and verses which will "do no harm". And will help me when I need them. The "who begets who" verses, obviously have no value to me for this project: Neither do any controversial, violent verses with cruelty. I want to follow what Philippians 4:8, alludes to: Think only good thoughts.

I am fortunate to have so many friends with many different belief systems. I pick very general verses which give good instruction no matter what religion, so I use the word "God" instead of the word "Lord", because to me, the word "Lord" implies a more earthly authority.

The verse in Corinthians says it best:

"By one Spirit are we all baptized into one body, whether we be Jews or Gentiles, whether we be bond or free; and have been all made to drink into one spirit."
—I Corinthians 12:13
My modification reads:
"No matter the religion: Everyone has the same Spirit."
— I Corinthians 12:13
In other words:
"We being many are one..." —I Corinthians 10:17

In the beginning of this project, there was great concern about changing any verse. Consider this verse in Genesis:

"I pray thee, thou art my sister; that it may be well with me for thy sake; and my soul shall live because of thee."
— Genesis 12:13.
I modified it as:
"You are my sister, my soul lives because of you."
— Genesis 12:13

This is what a brother is saying to his step-sister, (who is also his wife) so she will lie to the king and save his life. To me the message is basically the same. I am asking my sister to tell people only the good things about me, so I may "live". Considering of course omission is still a lie.

If you notice for 12:13, I worked up two verses: First Corinthians 12:13 and Genesis 12:13. I found the love for my sister(s) in one and my love for all religions in the other.

By the same token, consider the verse:

"Rejoice in Albimelech, and let him also rejoice in you."
— Judges 9:19.
I wrote it down as:
"Rejoice in one another." — Judges 9:19.

To me the message is the same, and even though I don't know anyone whose name is (King) Albimelech, I didn't think "Rejoice in one another" was offensive or took away from what the verse was trying to say.

It was the same with this following verse:

"Do that which is right in the sight of the Lord."
— Deuteronomy 12:25
Because of the allotted space, I tweaked it to say:
"Do what is right in the eyes of God."
— Deuteronomy 12:25

I changed fear to awe because a minister said it

was the same. Just to make sure, I looked it up in the dictionary for verification. I also changed preacher to teacher; preach to show; commandments to laws; guidance to counsel; and righteous to morally right or upright, depending on what would fit. I think:

"The wise will understand." — Daniel 12:10.

I read somewhere we are not supposed to change the Bible. However, what we have today is has been translated so many times and indeed we have so many versions of it. My feeling is it would give people a guide to look up the verse and get it for themselves.

There is a verse I often quote:

"The thing that I fear the most is upon me." —Job 3:25

I like this verse because it is a reminder that anything which happens to me which is considered "bad", I am ultimately doing it to myself. Consciously or unconsciously, I alone am responsible for it.

According to the Book of Job, (pronounced 'Jobe' with a long 'o') God and the devil are wrestling for Job's soul. God told the devil, you can do what you want to him, but don't kill him. And if it had not been for this little tiny verse, the credit for all of Job's misery would have been attributed to the devil: Or even God for allowing it.

One fear kept going through my mind was I would not be able to find a verse for everyone in the planet.

Well my fear came true: I could not find any verses on 8:30 I liked.

Strangely enough, later I did find a couple I did like. They are as follows:

"I was by Him; I was daily His delight rejoicing always before Him." — Proverbs 8:30.

28

And:
"Whom He justified he also glorified." — Romans 8:30

However in the beginning, filling a self-fulfilling prophecy (Job 3:25), I could only find:

"Know the truth and the truth will set you free."
— John 8:32.

Verse, John 8:32, is one of my favorites, and even though I found the other verses, and since I had already made the pillow a year back, I kept it. I felt like I was ultimately doing this for myself. But it played on my conscience until I read the verse again and later found another verse which eased my conscience. It reads:

"The day of rest was made for man: Man was not made for the day of rest." — Mark 2:27

In writing verse 8:32, I place ellipses (...) to show there were some words missing in between the verses.
I felt this would justify using the verse and keeping the integrity of what I was trying to do. For example I sewed the verse as:

"...Know the truth and the truth will set you free."
— John 8:30...

Read your verse, look it up then memorize any you wish.
When I hand the framed bible verse to the person, I say something like, "If it's something you don't like, it's okay to give it away or even throw it away. It is yours to do with what you wish."
Most of the persons who received a frame seemed to love the idea. Most everyone likes to receive a free gift.

One gray haired lady cried and told me it was beautiful. After getting over my initial embarrassment, (She thought I was doing it for her.) it was the encouragement I needed to push me onward to complete this project. Every time I think of quitting something like this happens and I find myself once again asking, "When is your birthday?"

The results were sometimes amusing: I once did a frame for a lady who works for Shelter Insurance, and ironically her office is next door to State Farm Insurance whose slogan is: "Like a good neighbor—State farm is there." Her verse reads:

"Don't harm your neighbor: He lives beside you."
— Proverbs 3:29

Sometimes the results were almost like a personal message to the person I was giving it to.

For example: There was a lady clerk at Ace Hardware, and after I asked her for her birthday and others in her family, it turned out her mother had recently died.

Two days later I handed her three frames, the one for her mother ironically read:
"She was purified and returned home."
—II Samuel 11:4

I know Andrea is too young now to understand the value of the message which was on the frame I made for her:

"God gave me the power to lay it down or pick it up again." — John 10:18

I chose this verse because it seems to speak to me personally. I try to remember the verse I made for little Andrea, when I want to continue work. Oftentimes,

I will be doing something and someone calls and interrupts me. In the past I would, get so angry and I would feel like my whole day was ruined.

I would get angry when those inconsiderate, pesky people would interrupt my concentration. Especially the telemarketers. I tried to personalize them, reminding myself they were just people trying to feed their families. Now I just pick up whatever I am doing, and it is like there is no interruption at all. I don't have to get into the mood or "f-e-e-e-l" like going back to work.

I am now able to work through interruptions so beautifully I am amazed I hadn't realized how much I had been fighting it.

I was recently in line at Home Depot, when the man in front of me, got a call. He then turns around with an irritated expression on his face and says, "I hate those robot calls."

"They're good practice," I told him.

"What do you mean?"

"Well, it's good practice for things you can't control. I count to three then calmly hang up." I can't have some robot controlling my moods." Unfortunately they are overdoing this practice so I no longer bother to answer calls which are not tagged.

He paid, looked back and with a nice smile he told me, "Have a good day."

I used to frequent a cafe called Fat Ernie's. I would go there so often, I made frames for the waitresses and a few of the regulars. One day I presented the manager with a frame:

"The beasts in the field will be at peace with you"
— Job 5:23

For some reason I just like the way the verse reads. I told him I picked the verse selfishly because of my love for animals. It was not until a small conversation afterwards I realized how apropos the verse is. As it turned out, he lives on a farm and over the years he has raised horses, goats, a donkey, dogs, and presently two house cats, something I did not know about him.

I run out of neighbors so I find sales persons, and finally complete strangers. Even if you work at the Burger King drive through, you were not safe from me asking you for the month and day you were born. A day or two later, I would present you and your family members with the frames. Some would volunteer more birthdays. I didn't care if it was a family member or not, or even if they were being greedy.

One day, out of the blue, my daughter, who works for Hospice asks for 35 verses. This was great! I need as many birthdays as I can get. When I have people to sew for, it helps to motivate me, and since I turn on the television while I sew, I think all I really want to do, is to have an excuse to watch Person of Interest or Murdoch Mysteries.

A week after I send my daughter the 35 verses, I get a call from her with another request. When I think of it, I have to laugh. I think I broke out in a cold sweat. She asked if I could make a verse for an upcoming wedding anniversary. I tried to explain to her it did not work that way. But quickly realized it was futile to explain to her it might be hard to find a verse which would be suitable for the occasion.

I can't just make up a verse; I had to be able to find it in the bible. I could not believe my good luck when I found one with their anniversary date that would actually be appropriate:

"They sang together giving thanks to God."
— Ezra 3:11

This was close enough. It was one of those "Oh,

thank God," moments, and in the back of my mind, I was saying to myself:

"Oh yee of little faith," — Matthew 6:30.

My efforts did not go unrewarded. I recently received a visit from my daughter. She handed me a thank you card from the lady, whose husband who has since passed away. The card reads:

Thank you for the bible verses that were made using Rick's birth date and also one using our anniversary date. That is such a wonderful idea. I have started giving others a verse according to their date of birth. I just print them and frame them, not nearly as nice as the ones you made. I have been blessed looking up the verses.

The Rick Gravitt Family

I live for moments like this!

After two years I have it down to a science; most of the time it would take me only two hours of DVD's to get one frame done. I would take a picture, file it in my computer, and the process would begin again. I love it. One verse I loved so much I kept it: It wasn't even my birth date. (Luke 5:28)

I am memorizing verses partly because I am associating them with certain people. However, so many people had the same birth date and the verses were getting repetitive. Cross stitching the same verse several times probably had more to do with being able to retain the verses in my memory. Although, associating them with a certain person helps. Repetition also helps save time knowing where to start counting the squares.

By the time I realized it, I had given away over 350 frames. I love giving them away. I think this is the best part of this project, and maybe why I became obsessed with the idea of "One verse for every birthday".   My motto became: Remember the person, remember the verse. Although, I could barely remember the person, I remembered more and more verses. This project seems to be taking a life of its own.

Not only am I memorizing verses:

1. My memory is improving.
2. My mind is thinking better thoughts.
3. I am feeling good about myself.
4. I have a purpose.

One thing is definitely clear, if I am depressed all I have to do is think about somebody other than myself. Every time I tried to quit, I would find myself, asking, "When is your birthday?" I would say to myself, "*Oh no, here I go again, I hope I can find a verse.*"

At times I had the opposite problem, there were so many beautiful verses I was forced to choose.   The higher numbers were a problem: The verses tend to run out around Hebrews. At times I want to quit, especially when I realized it is no longer about memorizing the verses.

Since my goal was about getting anything for a particular birthday, I made it easier on myself by not trying to find people with all the different days of the year. This is when I got the idea to write this book.

Here are the verses I picked, and are ready to cross stitch.   If you want to try your hand at cross stitching these verses: The instructions, a sampler, and the abbreviations are in back of the book in the section entitled "The Physical Process".   In this section the small subscript numbers are also explained. Just to be safe, please recheck my numbers. I also took the liberty of putting in some of the other verses I did not work up. They are in the back of the book. (Page 280)   If you are having a bad day, all you have to do is read them. I just know they will help.

The project is fun and inexpensive. I hope you enjoy this project as much as I did, but be careful, it can be addictive.

Happy Birthday Everyone!

"Everyone is born of God."
— I John. 2:29

1. [34]Grace [24]and peace [20]be unto you. — II Th. 1:1[20]
2. [23]I wish you [21]prosperity, [22]and health. — II Jo. 1:2[21]
3. [20]Whatsoever [25]you do, you [20]will prosper. — Ps. 1:3[20]
4. [16]God comforts [15]us to comfort [15]others. — III Jo. 1:4[15]
5. [22]If you lack [30]wisdom [23]ask God. — Jas. 1:5[22]
6. [13]He has [18]begun a good [13]work in you. — Ph'p. 1:6[13]
7. [21]God did not [12]give me a Spirit [12]of fear. — II Ti. 1:7[12]
8. [26]Laws are [20]good if used [20]lawfully. — I Ti. 1:8[20]
9. [29]Be strong: [29]God is [20]with you. — Jos. 1:9[20]
10. [9]Give me [18]wisdom and [23]knowledge. — II Ch. 1:10[9]
*11. [11]Don't fellowship [28]with the [10]unfruitful work [10]of darkness. — Eph. 1:11[10]
12. [3]Wisdom, knowledge, [4]riches wealth and [3]honor are yours. — II Ch. 1:12[4]
13. [24]I gave my [27]heart to [19]seek wisdom. — Ec. 1:13[19]
14. [8]The grace of God [22]is generous [3]with faith and love. — I Ti. 1:14[8]
*15. [18]I talked to my [18]heart: It had [3]great wisdom [13]and knowledge. — Ec. 1:15[13]
16. [24]Of God's [24]fullness all [17]have received. — Jo. 1:16[17]
17. [24]I gave my [27]heart to know [20]wisdom. — Ec. 1:17[24]
18. [22]If wronged: [25]Give that [11]account to God. — Ph'm. 1:18[11]
19. [5]Be swift to hear, [15]slow to speak, [5]and slow to anger. — Jas. 1:19[5]
20. [33]All the [11]promises of God [11]are in us. — II Co. 1:20[11]
21. [20]Keep yourself [26]in the love [20]of God. — Jude 1:21[20]
22. [6]People that have [6]compassion make [6]a difference. — Jude 1:22[6]
23. [14]Peace and love [17]with faith be [14]yours.—Ph'p. 1:23[10]
24. [13]You were given [13]the power and [13]wisdom of God. — Co. 1:24[13]
25. [6]I have confidence [9]and will be with [6]you in your joy. — Ph'p. 1:25[6]
26. [10]If a man can't [10]hold his tongue, [10]religion is vain. — Jas. 1:26[10]
27. [9]Conduct yourself[20]in a dignified [30]manner. —Ph'p. 1:27[19]
28. [27]Warn and [27]teach all men [34]wisdom. — Col. 1:28[17]
29. [24]God saves [30]me from [30]any distress. — I Ki. 1:29[20]
30. [12]Don't be afraid [17]God will fight [17]your battles. — De. 1:30[12]
31. [14]God saw what[20]He made: It [12]was very good.— Ge. 1:31

1. [26]My heart [30]rejoices [33]In God. — I Sa. 2:1[15]
2. [10]As the soul lives, [21]God will not [16]leave you. — I Ki. 2:2[16]
3. [12]God is with you [21]in weakness [23]and fear. — I Co. 2:3[12]
4. [24]God is rich in [14]mercy and has [5]great love for me. — Eph. 2:4[5]
5. [31]Walk in [27]the light [31]of God. — Isa. 2:5[20]
6. [18]Kindness and [24]truth are [10]required of you. — II Sa. 2:6[13]
7. [27]God has blessed [23]all the works [17]of your hand. — De. 2:7[17]
8. [32]In you [13]the true light [13]shines. — I Jo. 2:8[13]
9. [31]You will [21]understand [13]the good path. — Pr. 2:9[13]
10. [26]My heart [19]rejoiced in all [27]my labor. — Ec. 2:10[16]
11. [24]God knows [18]not man, but [18]his spirit. — II Co. 2:11[18]
12. [21]Blessed are [30]all that [18]trust in God. — Ps. 2:12[18]
13. [19]Compare the [16]Spiritual with [24]the Spiritual. — I Co. 2:13[16]
14. [3]Things of the Spirit [15]are Spiritually [15]discerned. — I Co. 2:14[15]
15. [25]Don't love [17]the things of [23]this world. — I Jo. 2:15[17]
16. [15]Avoid profane [28]and vain [24]babblings. — II Ti. 2:16[15]
17. [21]Honor all men [8]love your brother, [12]be in awe of God. — I Pe. 2:17[8]
18. [27]The Good [19]hand of God [19]is upon me. — Ne. 2:18[19]
*19. [14]God said: I will [11]pledge you upon [15]me forever in [11]loving kindness. — Hos. 2:19[11]
20. [30]God will [29]prosper [21]me. — Ne. 2:20[18]
21. [28]Practice [35]what [20]you preach. — Ro. 2:21[20]
*22. [5]He revealed the [19]deep secret [11]things: and the [8]light in me. — Da. 2:22[6]
23. [16]God has given [24]me wisdom [22]and power. — Da. 2:23[16]
24. [28]Be gentle [20]to all: Teach [12]and be patient. — II Ti. 2:24[12]
25. [29]God has [20]respect for [21]His children. — Ex. 2:25[15]
26. [15]God gives man [4]wisdom and knowledge [4]and joy. — Ec. 2:26[4]
27. [19]I choose the [17]straight and [17]narrow path. — De. 2:27[17]
28. [23]Live in God [27]and have [23]confidence. — I Jo. 2:28[17]
29. [27]Everyone[32]is born [31]of God. — I Jo. 2:29[17]

1.^{15}Rejoice in God, ^{8}don't be grievous, ^{8}you are safe.
— Ph'p. 3:1^{8}
2.^{23}A long life ^{21}and peace ^{22}will be yours. — Pr. 3:2^{21}
3.^{13}You are with ^{7}the Spirit of God: ^{17}The living God.
—II Co. 3:3^{7}
*4.^{8}A time to weep, ^{8}a time to laugh; ^{8}A time to mourn, ^{8}A time to
dance. — Ec. 3:4^{8}
5.^{14}May your heart ^{10}be directed into ^{10}the love of God.
— I Th. 3:5^{10}
6.^{24}The letter ^{15}kills: The Spirit ^{28}gives life. — II Co. 3:6^{15}
7.^{31}We are ^{22}comforted ^{13}by your faith. — I Th. 3:7^{13}
*8.^{8}A time to love, ^{8}a time to hate; ^{8}a time of war, ^{8}a time of peace.
— Ec. 3:8^{8}
9.^{20}They which ^{20}be of faith ^{19}are blessed. — Ga. 3:9^{19}
10.^{18}I ask God to ^{14}let me know ^{14}Him personally. — Isa. 3:10^{14}
11.^{16}God has made ^{22}everything ^{26}beautiful. — Ec. 3:11^{16}
12.^{9}I have given you ^{7}an understanding ^{7}heart. — J'g. 3:12^{12}
13.^{31}Forgive^{23}as you are ^{27}forgiven. — Col. 3:13^{19}
14.^{15}Whatever God ^{18}does, He does ^{15}forever.— Ec.3:14^{15}
15.^{15}I will feed you ^{12}with knowledge^{7}and understanding.
— Jer. 3:15^{7}
16.^{24}A long life,^{4}riches and honor^{12}are yours.—Pr. 3:16^{12}
17.^{23}Your ways ^{40}are ^{20}pleasant. — Pr. 3:17^{24}
18.^{22}Let God do^{13}what he thinks^{13}is good. — I Sa. 3:18^{13}
19.^{26}Know God's^{19}love and you^{19}will be filled. — Eph. 3:19^{19}
20.^{7}I will stretch^{16}out my hand^{7}with all my wonders.
— Ex. 3:20^{7}
21.^{21}Keep sound^{18}wisdom and^{18}discretion. — Pr. 3:21^{18}
22.^{30}Ask and^{28}you will ^{22}receive. — Jo. 3:22^{15}
23.^{25}Your foot ^{31}will not ^{29}stumble — Pr. 3:23^{15}
24.^{22}The Spirit^{19}entered into^{16}me and spoke. — Co. 3:24^{16}
25.^{34}God is^{19}good to them^{22}that wait. — La. 3:25^{15}
26.^{30}God will^{30}be your,^{24}confidence. — Pr. 3:26^{20}
27.^{19}If you have^{15}the power to^{14}do good: Do it.—Pr. 3:27^{14}
28.^{18}I will give you^{21}the morning^{18}star. — Re. 3:28^{18}
29.^{11}Don't harm your ^{20}neighbor: He ^{11}lives beside you.
— Pr. 3:29^{11}
30.^{24}Don't be in^{14}conflict without^{11}good reason. — De.3:30^{11}
31.^{21}Don't envy^{8}bullies, nor want^{8}their ways. — Pr. 3:31^{8}

1. [12]He teaches you[18]laws to do, so[20]you may live. — De. 4:1[12]
2. [18]You have not [29]because [23]you ask not. — Jas. 4:2[18]
3. [12]Keep the unity [17]of the Spirit [12]bound in peace. — Eph. 4:3[12]
4. [32]Rejoice [34]in God [30]always. — Ph'p. 4:4[15]
5. [14]Walk in wisdom [30]toward those [6]that are without. — Col. 4:5[6]
6. [13]Let your speech [24]be always [21]with grace.— Col. 4:6[13]
7. [5]Get wisdom, and [8]in getting, get [11]understanding. — Pr. 4:7[5]
8. [4]Whatsoever [13]things are good[11]think on these things.
— Ph'p. 4:8[11]
9. [16]Use hospitality [13]one to another [7]without grudging. — I Pe. 4:9[7]
10. [10]Humble yourself [10]and God will lift [10]you up. —Jas. 4:10[10]
11. [12]I learned to be [2]content whatever [2]the circumstances.
— Ph'p. 4:11[6]
12. [25]If we love[19]one anther[19]God is in us. — Jo. 4:12[19]
13. [11]All things are[20]possible: God[11]strengthens me.
— Ph'p. 4:13[11]
14. [2]Whoever drinks the [1]water of the Spirit [2]will never thirst.
—Jo. 4:14[2]
15. [12]Avoid it, don't get[19]near it, keep[12]away from evil.
— Pr. 4:15[12]
16. [12]God's scripture[13]is inspirational,[13]and profitable
— II Ti. 4:16[13]
17. [21]God stands [20]with me and [10]strengthens me.
— II Co. 4:17[10]
18. [19]Perfect love [34]casts [27]out fear. — I Jo. 4:18[20]
19. [31]God will [28]supply all [25]my needs. — Ph'p. 4:19[15]
20. [19]God's kingdom[16]in not in word[16]but in power. —II Co. 4:20[16]
21. [16]He that loves[18]God loves his[16]brother.—I Jo. 4:21[16]
*22. [18]God is life to [10]those that find [18]Him: Health to [10]their   flesh.
— Pr. 4:22[10]
23. [23]Be renewed[16]in the Spirit[16]of your mind. — Eph.4:23[16]
24. [13]Heed what you[27]hear and[22]measure it. —Mic. 4:24[13]
25. [16]He that has:[23]to him will [16]be given. — Ph'p. 4:25[16]
26. [14]If a man can't[13]hold his tongue,[13]religion is vain. — Jas. 4:26[10]
27. [24]Break off [15]your sins by[8]rightmindedness.—Da. 4:27[8]
28. [21]We are the [23]children of [21]promise. — Ga. 4:28[21]
29. [27]Seek God[14]with all your[11]heart and soul.—De. 4:29[11]
30. [10]The mother said: [16]As God lives I[6]will not leave you.
— I Ki. 4:30

1.[10]Be free don't be[16]entangled in[10]bondage. — Pr. 5:1[10]

2. [6]Hate kills the fool;[22]jealosy kills[20]the silly one.— Job 5:2[6]

3.[24]Tribulation[25]works out[28]patience. — Ro. 5:3[20]

4.[31]Feed on[17]the strength[17]of God. — Mic. 5:4[17]

5.[33]We are[24]all children[20]of the light. — I Th. 5:5[20]

6.[28]Seek God[39]and[21]you will live. — Ec. 5:6[20]

7.[8]Cast your cares[14]upon God: He[8] loves you. — I Pe. 5:7[8]

8.[18]Stay absent[22]in body, and[13]present in God. — I Co.5:8[13]

9.[16]Blessed[30]are the[16]peacemakers. — Mt. 5:9[16]

10.[16]He that loves[21]silver won't[19]be satisfied. — Ec. 5:10[16]

11.[4]Comfort yourselves[28]and edify [19]one another.
— I Th. 5:11[4]

12.[14]The sleep of a[11]laboring person[11]is sweet.—Ec. 5:12[11]

13.[38]The wise[29]will keep[29]silent. — Am. 5:13[15]

14.[29]You are[17]the light of[17]the world. — Mt. 5:14[17]

*15.[13]The candlestick[18]gives light to[13]everyone in the[13]house.
— Mt. 5:15[13]

16.[30]Let the[20]light in you[20]shine. — Mt. 5:16[20]

17.[28]Happy is[15]the man whom[15]God corrects. — Job 5:17[15]

18.[42]In[22]everything[20]give thanks. — I Th. 5:18[20]

19.[20]Make melody[17]in your heart[17]to God.— Eph. 5:19[17]

20.[21]The Father[37]loves [20]His son. — Jo. 5:20[20]

21.[25]Hold on to[22]that which[22]is good. — II Th. 5:21[15]

22.[10]The fruit of the[18]Spirit is love,[10]joy, peace... — Ga. 5:22[10]

23.[14]The beast of[3]the field will be[3]at peace with you. — Job 5:23[3]

**24.[20]Let it be. — II Sa. 5:24[15]

25.[19]We live in the[6]Spirit, let us walk[19]in the Spirit. — Ga. 5:25[6]

26.[7]Praise and thank[14]God for all the[6]wonderful things. — Lk. 5:26[6]

27.[27]Listen to[24]what God[28]tells you. — De. 5:27[20]

28.[27]I left all,[20]rose up and[17]followed God. — Lk. 5:28[17]

29.[27]Obey God[33]rather[24]than man. — Ac. 5:29[20]

30.[24]Don't seek[19]your will, but[19]God's will. — Jo. 5:30[19]

31.[24]The healed[19]don't need a[19]physician. — Lk. 5:31[19]

*1. [2]Be content before[11]the mountains: [11]and let the hills [5]hear your voice. — II Th. 6:1[5]

2.[37]I am[25]weak, heal[25]me God. — Ps. 6:2[20]

3.[22]May you be[22]well and live[6]long on this earth.— Eph. 6:3[6]

4.[32]Walk in[19]the newness[19]of life. — Ro. 6:4[19]

5.[9]Don't argue with[18]persons with[14]corrupt minds. —I Ti. 6:5[14]

6.[29]Do God's[29]will with[29]love. — Ph'p. 6:6[15]

7.[17]With goodwill[15]do service to[17]God, not men.— Eph. 6:7[15]

8.[10]God knows what[11]you need before[10]you ask. — Mt. 6:8[10]

9.[29]Don't be[26]weary of[25]well doing. — Ga. 6:9[20]

10.[7]God won't forget [4]your labors of love [4]and good works. — Heb. 6:10[4]

11.[31]Give us[25]this day[11]our daily bread. — Mt. 6:11[11]

12.[26]Fight the[23]good fight[23]of faith. — I Ti. 6:12[15]

13.[12]May you be well[20]and live long[17]on this earth. — Eph. 6:13[12]

14.[31]God will[10]keep His promise[7]and will bless you. — Heb. 6:14[7]

15.[27]Diligently[14]obey the voice[14]of God. — Zec. 6:15[14]

16.[12]Fear not, there[13]is more for you [7]than against you. — II ki. 6:16[7]

17.[24]He that is*([17]) joined with God[13]is one Spirit.— I Co. 6:17[13]

*18.[18]Do it for God[11]in secret and He[11]will reward you [11]openly. — Mt. 6:18[11]

19.[32]Lay up[32]a good[22]foundation. — I Ti. 6:19[15]

20.[22]Glorify God[19]in your body[19]and Spirit. — I Co. 6:20[19]

21.[24]What you[3]treasure, there will[3]your heart be also. — Mt. 6:21[3]

22.[28]The light[20]of the body[20]is the eye. — Mt. 6:22[20]

23.[21]Whatsoever[21]you ask you[19]will be given.—Mk. 6:23[19]

24.[27]The Lord[25]bless and[25]keep you. — Nu. 6:24[17]

25.[28]You are[37]more[18]than a body. — Mt. 6:25[18]

26.[19]May God look[5]lovingly on you and[5]give you peace. — Nu. 6:26[5]

27.[12]Which of you by[23]worry can make[23]it better?—Mt. 6:27[12]

*28.[20]Consider the[23]lilies of the[11]field, how they[11]toil not... — Mt. 6:28[11]

29.[11]Go from injustice[30]and return to the[30]confidence of God. — Job 6:29[20]

30.[31]Give to[24]every man[14]that asks you. — Lk. 6:30[14]

1. ^{26}The Glory^{23}of God fills^{23}this house. — II Ch. 7:1^{15}
2. ^{24}Keep God's^{26}laws and^{24}live. — Pr. 7:2^{15}
3. ^{23}Do what is^{11}in your heart for^{11}God is with you.—I Sa. 7:3^{11}
4. ^{17}Stay close to^{6}wisdom and closer^{6}to understanding. — Pr. 7:4^{6}
*5. ^{12}It is better to^{8}hear the rebukes^{9}of the wise than^{8}the songs of fools. — Pr. 7:5^{8}
6. ^{31}God will^{21}comfort me^{9}when I am down. — II Co. 7:6^{9}
7. ^{2}Ask: It will be given.^{8}Seek: You will find.^{6}Knock: It will open. — Mt. 7:7^{6}
8. ^{2}Ask: It will be given.^{8}Seek: You will find.^{6}Knock: It will open. — Mt. 7:8^{6}
9. ^{20}Anger rests^{20}in the bosom^{20}of fools. — Ec. 7:9^{15}
10. ^{14}My defense is^{14}God, who saves^{14}the upright. — Ps. 7:10^{14}
11. ^{13}God being good,^{7}can give you more^{7}of what you ask. — Mt. 7:11^{7}
12. ^{13}Do unto others^{6}as you would have^{6}them do unto you. — Mt. 7:12^{6}
13. ^{13}He will love you,^{4}bless you and cause^{4}you to prosper. — De. 7:13^{4}
14. ^{18}You are filled^{9}with wisdom and^{9}understanding. — I Ki. 7:14^{9}
15. ^{12}Refuse the evil^{21}and choose^{12}the good. — Isa. 7:15^{12}
16. ^{30}I have^{19}confidence in^{11}you in all things. — II Co. 7:16^{11}
17. ^{20}A good tree^{14}produces good^{14}fruit. — Mt. 7:17^{14}
18. ^{10}Don't be afraid; ^{15}remember all^{10}God can do. — De. 7:18^{10}
19. ^{31}Wisdom^{29}strengthens,^{29}the wise. — Ec. 7:19^{15}
20. ^{18}All will know^{15}you by what^{15}you do. — Mt. 7:20^{15}
21. ^{21}Don't be^{13}afraid for God^{13}is with you. — De. 7:21^{13}
22. ^{22}I delight in^{11}God's law after^{10}the Spirit in me. — Ro. 7:22^{10}
23. ^{20}Blessed is he^{22}that is not^{8}offended by God. — Lk. 7:23^{8}
24. ^{31}Don't judge^{10}appearances but^{10}right judgments. — Jo. 7:24^{10}
25. ^{19}My heart is^{18}set to know^{18}true wisdom. — Ec. 7:25^{18}
26. ^{19}I was made^{19}higher than^{19}the heavens. — Heb. 7:26^{19}
27. ^{16}His messenger^{11}will prepare the^{11}way for you.— Lk. 7:27^{11}
28. ^{34}I was^{8}strengthened by^{8}the hand of God. — Ezr. 7:28^{8}
29. ^{23}God bless^{23}this house^{23}forever. — II Sa. 7:29^{15}
30. ^{29}An angel^{25}appeared^{25}to him. — Ac. 7:30^{15}
31. ^{35}God's^{23}voice came^{23}to him. — Ac. 7:31^{20}

1. [7]Wisdom cries out; [12]understanding[7]raises its voice. — Pr. 8:1[7]
2. [14]The law of the[25]Spirit has[17]made me free. — Ro. 8:2[14]
3. [27]Man does[23]not live by[20]bread alone. — De. 8:3[20]
4. [11]God's law will be[3]filled in us who walk[3]in the Spirit. — Ro. 8:4[3]
5. [11]He has crowned[13]you with glory[11]and honor. — Ps. 8:5[11]
6. [19]There is only[19]one God, and[19]we are in Him. — I Co. 8:6[19]
7. [24]My mouth[25]will speak[23]truth. — Pr. 8:7[20]
8. [18]My words are[9]sincere, without[9]doubt or falsehood. — Pr. 8:8[9]
9. [18]Today is holy[36]don't[13]mourn or weep. — Ne. 8:9[13]
10. [14]Bless God for[21]all He has[14]given you. — De. 8:10[14]
*11. [7]Wisdom is better[19]than rubies,[7]nothing compares[7]to it.
— Pr. 8:11[7]
12. [7]Wisdom lives with[5]caution and finds[5]witty inventions.
— Pr. 8:12[5]
13. [20]As you have[15]believed, so be[9]it done unto you. — Mt. 8:13[9]
14. [21]Sound wisdom[12]is understanding[12]and strength. — Pr. 8:14[12]
15. [31]To be in[16]awe of God is[16]to hate evil. — Pr. 8:15[16]
16. [5]The Spirit itself is[4]witness that you[3]are a child of God.
— Ro. 8:16[3]
17. [21]I love them[16]and they love[16]me. — Pr. 8:17[16]
18. [17]God gives you[16]the power to[16]get wealth. — De. 8:18[16]
19. [23]God's fruit[13]is better than[13]gold and silver. — Pr. 8:19[13]
20. [14]God's gift can't[17]be purchased[14]with money.— Ac. 8:20[14]
21. [19]Spread your [15]hands toward[15]heaven. — I Ki. 8:21[15]
22. [22]God said: I[9]have confidence[9]in you. — II Co. 8:22[9]
23. [24]Walk with[19]God in your[19]heart. — I Ki. 8:23[15]
24. [14]God repressed[17]the wind, and[11]there was calm.— Mk. 8:24[11]
25. [14]Hope for what[9]you don't see: Be[9]patient and wait. — Ro. 8:25[9]
26. [14]God repressed[17]the wind, and[11]there was calm. — Mk. 8:26[11]
*27. [8]Search the heart[20]and you will[16]know the mind[20]of the Spirit.
— Ro. 8:27[8]
28. [14]All things work[8]for good to them[8]that love God. — Ro. 8:28[8]
29. [30]God has[30]not left[30]me. — Jo. 8:29[20]
30. [5]...Know the truth[11]and the truth[5]will set you free. — Jo. 8:30[5]
31. [5]...Know the truth[11]and the truth[5]will set you free. — Jo. 8:31[5]

1. [38]I will[35]praise[42]God. — Ps. 9:1[20]
2. [22]Be of good[12]cheer, your sins[12]are forgiven. — Mt. 9:2[12]
3. [18]The works of[30]God will[14]manifest in me. — Jo. 9:3[14]
4. [8]You are wise in [2]heart and mighty[2]in strength. — Job 9:4[8]
5. [4]Bless God Forever:[14]Blessed be His[4]glorious name.—Ne.9:5[4]
6. [30]Forsake[24]the foolish[24]and live. — Pr. 9:6[15]
7. [23]Happy are[10]those that hear[10]your wisdom. — Ch. 9:7[10]
8. [22]He made all[16]grace abound[16]in me. — Co. 9:8[16]
9. [24]God will be[19]a refuge for[13]the oppressed. — Ps. 9:9[13]
10. [14]The awe of God[12]is the beginning[12]of wisdom.—Pr. 9:10[12]
11. [26]He healed[12]those that had[12]need of healing. — Lk. 9:11[12]
12. [10]The strong and[5]well have no need[5]of a doctor. — Mt. 9:12[5]
*13. [20]Turn to God[16]that you may[21]understand[16]the truth.
— Da. 9:13[16]
14. [10]God does what[10]is morally right[10]and just. — Ne. 9:14[10]
*15. [12]Thanks be unto[23]God for His[20]unspeakable[12]gift of grace.
— II Co. 9:15[12]
16. [26]Wisdom is[19]better than[19]strength. — Ec. 9:16[19]
17. [31]God will[20]not forsake[20]you. — Ne. 9:17[20]
18. [7]Wisdom is better[12]than weapons[7]of war. — Ec. 9:18[17]
***19. [31]He was [10]strengthened. — Ac. 9:19[19]
20. [20]I was given[18]a good Spirit[11]to instruct me. — Ne. 9:20[11]
*21. [5]I took your sin:[5]made it as dust,[5]then cast it into[5]a brook.
— De. 9:21[5]
22. [22]Your faith[22]has made[22]you whole. — Mt. 9:22[22]
23. [17]All things[8]are possible to[8]those that believe. — Mk.[8]
24. [26]I believe: [29]Help me[14]when I don't. — Mk. 9:24[14]
25. [12]What profit to[14]gain the world[6]and lose yourself?
— Lk. 9:25[6]
26. [8]You will be called[15]a child of the[8]living God. — Ro. 9:26[8]
*27. [26]I will not[8]complain; will let[8]burdens go; and[8]comfort myself.
— Job 9:27[8]
28. [10]Unto them that[20]seek Him, He[20]will appear.— Heb. 9:28[10]
29. [18]According to[24]your faith[18]be unto you. — Mt. 9:29[18]
30. [30]God has[24]opened my[24]eyes. — Jo. 9:30[15]

1. ^{19}A wise child^{6}makes a glad^{16}parent. — Pr. 10:1^{16}
2. ^{17}Treasures of^{22}wickedness ^{12}profit nothing. — Pr. 10:2^{12}
3. ^{10}Though you walk^{8}in the flesh, don't^{8}war after it.
— II Co. 10:3^8
4. ^{6}Arise, this matter^{19}is God's: Have^{6}courage and do it.
— Ezra 10:4^6
5. ^{11}Practice what^{16}is right and^{11}live by it. — Ro. 10:5^{11}
6. ^{9}God is great and^{23}His name is^{9}great in might. — Jer. 10:6^9
7. ^{27}Let it be^{34}God is^{27}with you. — I Sa. 10:7^{15}
8. ^{24}Freely you^{15}have received, ^{15}freely give. — Mt. 10:8^{15}
9. ^{29}He that^{15}lives uprightly^{15}has confidence. — Pr. 10:9^{15}
10. ^{7}A dull blade needs^{12}more force: Let^{7}wisdom guide you.
— Ec. 10:10^7
11. ^{29}Don't be^{21}ashamed to^{16}believe in God. — Ro. 10:11^{16}
12. ^{29}It's not^{10}wise to compare^{4}yourself to others.
— II Co. 10:12^4
13. ^{8}If the house be^{7}worthy, let your^{2}peace come upon it.
— Mt. 10:13^3
14. ^{14}The wise store^{17}knowledge: The^{12}fool invites ruin. — Pr. 10:14^{12}
15. ^{12}How beautiful is^{10}the foundation that^{10}preaches peace.
— Ro. 10:15^{10}
16. ^{13}What is kept^{8}from you will be^{8}revealed in time. — De. 10:16^8
17. ^{28}We being^{36}many^{28}are one. — I Co. 10:17^{20}
*18. ^{12}God gave me the^{16}power to lay it^{16}down or pick it^{12}up again.
— Jo. 10:18^{12}
19. ^{27}Fear not:^{19}Be at peace^{14}and be strong. — Da. 10:19^{14}
20. ^{13}The tongue of^{12}the just is like^{12}choice silver.— Pr. 10:20^{12}
21. ^{7}He hid things from^{17}the wise, and^{7}reveals to babes.
— Lk. 10:21^7
22. ^{18}Draw nearer^{20}to God with^{18}a true heart. — Heb. 10:22^{18}
23. ^{28}A man of^{14}understanding^{14}Has wisdom. — Pr. 10:23^{14}
*24. ^{4}Many desire to see^{13}and hear what^{16}you have seen^{4}and heard.
— Lk. 10:24^{16}
25. ^{28}Fear not^{8}be strong and^{8}of good courage. — Jos. 10:25^8
26. ^{15}The earth and^{22}it's fullness^{15}is God's. — I Co. 10:26^{15}
27. ^{27}With God ^{27}everything^{19}is possible. — Mk. 10:27^{19}
28. ^{23}Fear not, they^{21}cannot kill^{13}your soul. — Col. 10:28^{13}
29. ^{12}The way of God^{21}is strength^{12}to the upright.—Pr. 10:29^{12}
30. ^{6}The righteous will^{9}never be apart^{6}from God.— Pr. 10:30^6
31. ^{10}The mouth of ^{15}the just brings^{10}wisdom. — Pr. 10:31^{10}

*1.[3]I will put my trust[7]in God, say to my[5]soul, flee as a bird [6]to your mountain. — Ps. 11:1[5]

2.[9]Pride comes with[13]shame: Humility[13]with wisdom.— Pr. 11:2[13]

3.[14]The integrity[14]of the upright[14]will guide them.— Pr. 11:3[14]

4.[30]She was[13]purified and[13]returned home. — II Sa. 11:4[8]

5.[31]God will[21]direct your[21]way. — Pr. 11:5[20]

6.[18]Nothing will be[17]kept from you: [17]Just imagine it. — Ge. 11:6[17]

7.[16]It's pleasant[12]for the eyes to[12]behold the sun.— Ec. 11:7[12]

8.[16]The righteous[12]is delivered out[12]of trouble. — Pr. 11:8[12]

9.[11]Rejoice in youth: [9]Walk in the ways[9]of your heart. — Ec. 11:9[9]

10.[6]Take sorrow from[12]your heart, for[6]youth is vanity . — Ec. 11:10[6]

11.[15]The Spirit of[15]life from God[7]entered into you. — Lk. 11:11[7]

12.[10]Woman is of man[5]man is by woman[5]but all is of God. — I Co. 11:12[5]

13.[15]Love God with[18]all your heart[15]and soul. — De. 11:13[15]

14.[28]Don't let[7]unjust acts dwell[7]in your hands. — Job 11:14[7]

15.[20]Lift up your[29]face and[11]and don't be afraid.— Job 11:15[11]

16.[8]Forget your misery,[13]remember it as[13]water passing. — Job 11:16[13]

17.[19]You will shine[24]and will be[13]as the morning.— Job 11:17[13]

18.[21]Sow justice[16]and a reward[16]is guaranteed. — Pr. 11:18[16]

19.[26]I will put[20]a new Spirit[26]with you. — Ez. 11:19[20]

20.[20]You believed[15]and turned to[15]God, He is with you. —Ac. 11:20[15]

21.[26]The hand[30]of God is[25]with them. — Ac. 11:21[15]

22.[15]Love God, walk[17]in his ways and[11]don't let Him go. —De. 11:22[11]

23.[4]Say without doubt[11]and believe and[11]you will have it. — Mk. 11:23[11]

24.[4]Say without doubt[11]and believe and[11]you will have it. — Mk. 11:24

25.[24]Those who[17]believe in God[17]will live. — Jo. 11:25[17]

26.[14]As you forgive[25]you will be[14]forgiven. — Mk. 11:26[14]

27.[6]He that diligently[7]seeks good[6]gets favor. — Pr. 11:27[6]

28.[15]Riches will fail[5]your righteousness[5]will not. — Pr. 11:28[5]

29.[20]The gifts of God[30]are without[30]regard to what we do .— Ro. 11:29[20]

30.[11]My bond is easy[11]and my burdens[11]are light. — Mt. 11:30[11]

1. ^{11}I will trust and^{8}not fear, for God^{8}is my strength.—Isa.12:1^8
2. ^{12}Be transformed^{9}by the renewing^{9}of you mind.— Re. 12:2^9
3. ^{14}The wise shall^{10}shine as bright^{10}as stars. — Ps. 12:3^{10}
4. ^{15}With God^{15}your burdens will^{15}be made lighter.—I Ki. 12:4^{15}
5. ^{34}All we,^{21}being many,^{31}are one. — Ro. 12:5^{10}
6. ^{12}Though I desire^{11}for glory I will^{12}not be a fool.—II Co. 12:6^{13}
7. ^{26}Be still so^{15}that God may^{10}reason with you. — I Sa. 12:7^{10}
8. ^{18}Speak to the^{10}earth and it will^{10}teach you. — Job 12:8^{10}
9. ^{22}Let love be^{10}genuine: Hold on^{10}to what is good. — Ro. 12:9^{10}
10. ^{32}Be kind^{33}to one^{28}another. — Ro. 12:10^{20}
11. ^{16}To follow vain^{4}people is to be void^{4}of understanding.
— Pr. 12:11^4
12. ^{10}The Spirit will^{8}teach you what^{10}you should say. — Lk. 12:12^8
13. ^{7}You are my sister^{14}my soul lives^{12}because of you.
— Ge. 12:13^{12}
$^+$13. ^{14}No matter the^{9}religion: Everyone^{6}has the same Spirit.
— I Co. 12:13^6
14. ^{10}Be in awe of God,^{15}obey His voice,^{10}obey His laws.
— I Sa. 12:14^{10}
15. ^{5}No matter what a ^{9}part says, it is^{6}part of the body.
— I Co.12:15^6
16. ^{34}God is^{26}strength^{21}and wisdom. — Job 12:16^{15}
17. ^{12}Provide things^{14}honest in the^{8}sight of all men.— Ro. 12:17^8
18. ^{23}As much as^{21}you can live^{5}peaceable with all.—Ro. 12:18^5
*19. ^{9}I will say to my^{15}soul: Take ease,^{11}eat, drink, and^{11}be merry.
— Lk. 12:19^{11}
20. ^{25}There are^{15}many persons,^{15}yet one body. — I Co. 12:20^{15}
21. ^{10}Be not overcome^{4}with evil; overcome ^{4}evil with good.
— Ro. 12:21^4
22. ^{27}All parts^{9}matter however^{9}insignificant. — I Co. 12:22^9
23. ^{21}I will teach^{18}you the good^{13}and right way.— I Sa. 12:23^{13}
24. ^{33}Praise^{39}and^{20}give thanks. — Ne. 12:24^{20}
25. ^{28}Do what^{26}is right in^{23}God's eyes. — De. 12:25^{20}
26. ^{9}When one suffers^{6}all suffer: When one^{4}rejoices, all rejoice.
— I Co. 12:26^4
27. ^{12}The nature of ^{9}the persistent^{9}is precious. — Pr. 12:27^9
28. ^{21}In the way^{15}of the morally^{15}right is life. — Pr. 12:28^{15}
29. ^{26}An angel^{26}spoke to^{26}him. — Jo. 12:29^{15}
30. ^{10}Love God with all^{16}your heart, soul,^{10}and strength.
—Mk. 12:30^{10}
31. ^{12}Seek the kingdom^{4}of God, and all will^{4}be added unto you.
— I Co. 12:31^4

Part II

My Training Ground

"I have never let my schooling interfere with my education."— Mark Twain

How Things Work

I describe one of my sisters as coming out of the womb cleaning her body. I on the other hand, came out of the womb pointing at everything and asking, "What's that?" My sister is a neat freak; I have a curious nature. She became a nurse. I became...well...aha..., "I'm not done yet." I heard a comedian recently say, "The doctor knocked on his mother's womb and said, 'You've got five minutes 'til curtain call'." Ironically, he was describing one of my brothers.

He and I were basically saying the same thing, sometimes we are born with certain proclivities, traits or pulls toward certain things.

In my library I have a book called The Way Things Work by David Macaula. The book is beautifully illustrated, and not only tells why things work but how they work. In the book, you can find anything from abacuses to zippers. Along with other books, I often refer to these illustrations when I am curious about something or want to make small repairs around the house.

I read somewhere that we are curious creatures and that a monkey will forgo food and sex to find out what is behind a door. I guess maybe there might be some people who are more curious than others.

My curiosity has often gotten me into trouble: For example, around the age of twelve I once tore apart a typewriter just to see how it worked.

When I was seventeen, I was the next in line for the hand me down family car. It was a blue over blue, 1956, ford Mercury. One day the car would not start. The car, as it turned out, had a bad starter. I drew a picture, took out the part; took it to the parts shop; bought the same part; and then I followed the recipe (the picture). When I turned the key, the car actually started. To this day I vividly remember how the neighborhood kids jumped up and down as they cheered and hollered. I don't know who was more surprised or excited, me, or the neighborhood kids?

David Macaula's book certainly helps people like me: People who have come into this world asking, "How? Why? What? When? And where?"

Where does one go when one is curious? My cheeky answer is: "Everywhere". I was told at the age of two my maternal grandmother used to tie me to the bed. This sounds rather harsh unless you consider the era, culture, and/or the particular circumstances. Now-a-days parents put harnesses on kids. And I suppose there might be many mothers who wished they had. But if there is one thing I want to remember from doing time in academia (college) is that we need to get as many facts as we can before we can come to a reasonable conclusion. This is called 'critical thinking'.

For as long as I remember, I was attracted to books. I remember laughing at my seventeen year old. Out of nowhere came my son's curious remark, "She can smell the book bindings from here." It was then I noticed the bookstore on the opposite side of the mall. My son has a unique sense of humor.

With an insatiable curiosity, my attraction to books would naturally follow.

Asking questions is okay when it comes to things in which we use our sensory apparatus, but what about things you can't perceive with the five senses?

From my past, I remember one day in particular: The family was cramped into the car on the way to church. My mother turned toward the back seat and told us we had to go to confession. Since I was ten at the time, I was exempt. Nevertheless, this did not stop me from innocently asking, "Why do we have to tell the priest? Why can't we just tell God?" I knew I was in trouble when the car got unusually quiet. I was fortunate the silence only lasted for a brief moment in time. I suspect from that day forward, why people react to God the way they do, would fascinate me. This might also explain why other things happened to me at this age.

I once asked my son around the age of three, "David, who is God?" I observed that he was obviously irritated at what seemed to him, so obvious. "I don't mean to upset you," I pressed, "But what is God to you?" He once again showed his irritation at such a stupid question then blared out, "Why, you and dad of course!"

To my recollection I had never mentioned God to him. His answer, I concluded, made perfect sense. We, were who, and where our son received love; food; water; and shelter. I was glad to have had an elevated raise in status no matter how temporary. At any rate, I knew he would eventually grow out of it and left it there.

But where does a grownup go when he wants to find out, "Who is God?"

I look back over the years to this wonderful journey I call my life. There is so much I still have to learn. For instance, why mushrooms keep coming into my head! Apparently, I am guided to write about them. Mycelium are fascinating.[10] Did you know if you place food on one end of a complicated maze, they will find the quickest route? Is that not cool? It seems like everything even the lowest of the low has a purpose; is connected; is important; and wants to survive.

Did you know some mushrooms breakdown highly toxic radioactive elements and make it safe for humans to handle? These mushrooms are much like our service men and policemen. Yes, it seems to me people are a lot like mushrooms: There are so many different kinds. Each kind with its own specialized trait.

Unlike mushrooms, some people become lost;

---

[10]Mycelium Running: How Mushrooms Can Save the World by Paul Stamets pages 7-103.

they don't know which direction to turn; and don't know what they are. Some don't know where to look or are looking in all the wrong places.

I often refer to this story to make this point:

It was dark outside when a man looked out his window and saw his neighbor searching through the grass. He decided to go and help him look, "What are you looking for?" He asked.

"I've lost my keys." He replied.

After sometime searching, the man asked, "Are you sure you lost them here?"

"No, I lost them over there, but this is where the light is."

When I want to learn about mycelium I get books on mushrooms. When I want to find out about what I am. I want to get to the source. I found this will inevitably lead me back to God. When I want to know about God, a good place to start is the bibles.

Some say prostitution is the oldest profession, but shamanism is the oldest profession. The belief in a power greater than us, is as old as the caveman. I suspect it was either his fear of death, or when he realized he had no power over it. Nevertheless, the search for something greater than us, for whatever reason, has been going on forever. In their own way, all the bibles have tried to answer the question who or what is God? If God is not a person than what is it? Does God even exist? Apparently it has comforted many people over the centuries to believe or not believe in a superior being. All cultures, in some way have tried to explain away the unexplained.

These mysteries have been called by many names: The sixth sense, the paranormal, miracles, love, and child birth. I will call them all God. So the question once again is, "What is God?" The truth is:

1. I can only answer this question in this space in time.

2. I can answer only what God is to me. My conclusions are in this book.

Like I said in the beginning I am not trying to convert anyone. Everyone is on their own spiritual journey. This portion of the book is what I am learning in my journey. I sincerely hope what I have learned gives you some insight into yourself.

Definitions

Although definitions are riddled throughout this book, in this section I want to make sure we are on the same page on five main topics: God; sin; love; charity; and what is meant by the word repent.

I understand there are several ways each of these words can be interpreted. I simply want to give you an idea of what goes on in this head of mine. And while I am on this particular subject, I hope I do not offend anyone when I refer to God as Him. Him is a reference to man, a substitute for humanity. Every time I refer to God: I strive to be reverent of the Spirit in all of humanity.

Also while this book was mostly for selfish reasons, kindly forgive so many repetitions.

What is God?

Raised as a Catholic, I was taught God is in everything. And even if other religions give different names to each different attribute of the unknown and the mysterious, I think they are essentially worshiping only one God.

Even in Greek mythology there is usually one god which stands out above all the others. The same pattern is revealed in all the religions that practice polytheism.[11]

_____

[11]The worship or belief in more than one god.

"God is God for everyone." — Romans 3:29

In many ways and throughout the bible, it is repeatedly saying there is only one God. In the book of Revelation God said:

"I am the Alpha and the Omega, the beginning and the ending, that which is: which was; and which is to come."" — Revelation 1:8

"Woman is of man, man is by woman, BUT ALL IS OF GOD. "(*My emphasis*) — I Corinthians 11:12

"God is above all, through all, and in all."
— Ephesians 4:6

If you believe the bible, then God is also in us.

"We dwell in God: He is in us.
He has given us of His Spirit." — I John 4:13

Read what Jesus says in Matthew and John; first between God and everyone; then between God and himself, and finally between himself and everyone else.

"(God) shall answer...I say unto you, in as much as you have done it unto one of the least of these my brethren, you have done it unto me." — Matthew 25:40.

"I and my Father are one." — John 10:30

"The works that I do, (you) will do also; and greater works than these (you) will do." — John 14:12

The message is very consistent. God is in everything and everyone. The connection is made between me and God and everyone else. WE ARE ALL

CONNECTED. How cool is that? To say it another way, I am the center of the universe with everyone else. I put myself first: I put everyone else first.

There are many visual concepts which say the same thing. I like to think of it a single cell in the body of God. This is much like a single cell would be in my body. Or I can think of the same thing in microscopic terms: The nucleus of a single cell is the center of this universe.

The first commandment tells me my part in relation to the whole:

"I am the Lord thy God...thou shall have no other gods before me." — Exodus 20:2-3

I need to put God first in my life and if I don't, I will never be satisfied and I will feel alone. The reason for this is because in reality we are all connected: Like a team, or family.

If I become a better person I bring everyone else with me. But how do I become a better person? Well, in reality I can't! This is because as a child of God, I am already there. And just because I don't know what I really am, does not make it less so. If I am "lost" it does not mean I'm not already there. Remember, it's all connected and God is already perfect. We all are part of the whole.

"All parts matter however insignificant."
— I Corinthians 12:22

Wait! If God is perfect and we are a part of the whole, then why is the world in such a mess? But more importantly, why am I in such a mess? I used to bristle up when Christians would tell me I was born a sinner. I would tell them, "Maybe **you** were, but not me!" I had heard I was "born a sinner" so many times from Christians, I thought it was a bible verse. The closest I found was in parentheses in I Kings 8:46: "(for there is no man that does not sin.)" and Romans 3:23 "...all have sinned..." There are others, however John 3:6 made more sense about how we are born:

"That which is born of the flesh is flesh; and that which is born of the Spirit is spirit." — John 3:6

Notice how in the bible, one Spirit is capitalized and the other is not.

In Genesis 2:21, God put Adam into a deep sleep, but nowhere in the bible does it say Adam ever woke up. We, descendants of Adam, are still trying to wake up. Within this dream, we can do anything with all God gives us. Within our dream we have freewill to do whatever we can dream up.

Now the other verses made more sense to me:

"For we know that the law is spiritual: but I am carnal, sold under sin." — Romans 7:14

If as humans, we all sin then it would be wise to know what we are talking about.

What is sin?

Sin, according to any dictionary, is an error or mistake. Is that all? I make mistakes all the time. If I don't make mistakes, how will I learn they were mistakes? The bible also tells us (while we live on this earth), we are of the flesh and that it is all vanity:

"Vanity of vanities; all is vanity." — Ecclesiastes 1:2

This is consistent with all the rest of the verses in relation to sin. We know vanity can manifest in people who are excessively vain, conceited or have a distorted preoccupation with their appearance.

John 3:6 suggests we are born with two spirits. With a degree in Psychology, I prefer to call my fleshly spirit "ego". The two spirits (Ego and Spirit) seem to always be in constant conflict.

"For the good that I wish to do, I do not: But the evil which I wish not to do, that I do." — Romans 7:19

Paul alludes to this fight in Romans 7:19. What is this fight about? What happens when you love God with all your heart and all your soul? The ego dies or loses power and control. However, the ego is not going down easily, because it is literally fighting to stay alive. When the ego knows it is losing the battle, it will use deception.

It knows it has to maintain a certain comfort level in order to keep us from going to the "deep end". If it goes too far, in desperation we might turn our attention to God. It knows to keep the stress balanced. For the ego, the two extremes are bad. I think this is why the bible is telling us the two extremes (in working toward God) are good:

"Because you are lukewarm, and neither cold nor hot, I will spit you out." — Revelation 3:16

If the ego does not maintain a certain comfort zone, we will eventually get the message that it, (the ego) is of no real value. It will start losing its grip on our Spirit. The closer we come to Spirit, (God) the closer the mind and body identify with it. When this happens the ego gets scared. Its very existence depends on identifying with the body and this earth. It tries to cleverly control the mind. It will use all kinds of deception. Distractions as insidious as frustration, self-pity or depression, manipulations, gossip, jealousy, or pride. These are generally its first line of defense. After it gets us hooked, it might resort to bigger and better things: Addictions;

the fear of losing what we have gained; or the fear of physical death. It uses anything it thinks is necessary to stay in the fight. It creates a "catch 22": I am damned if I do, and damned if I don't. It confuses our motives, goals, and attitudes. We get burned out on doing any good works. We are more concerned with ego than with our Spirit.

"Let us not be weary in well doing, for in due season we will reap, if we faint not." — Galatians 6:9

Our ego, and the ego of many preachers alike, tries to convince us God wants a sacrifice in time, energy, money, or even our flesh. The ego tries to convince us if we turn our lives over to God, we will die.

"Don't be afraid of God." — Deuteronomy 3:2

In reality God does not need or want anything from us. God gives us unconditional love with no strings attached.

Another common deception is that ego wants us to believe that God is magic. And then when the magic does not work, we are disappointed.

There is nothing magic about God; it is hard work to understand ourselves, invest in self-discipline, and learn to be closer to the Spirit (God).

The real magic is in our power to want to turn to God (Love). The closer we come to God the more power our ego loses, and the more Spiritual power we gain. It is the ego which loses it power, not us. I think this is what all the great teachers were getting at with their teachings.

"One's obedience can make many righteous."
— Romans 5:19

God is what our ego is trying to keep from us. Our

greatest fear is unconditional love. This is the death the following verses refer to:

"...seek (God) and you will die in your sins (ego)..."
— John 8:21

"...to die is gain." — Philippians 1:21

"Know the truth and the truth will set you free."
— John 8:32

The real magic is when we realize all we have to do is turn our lives over to God (love) and at the very least lessen our fears.

"Perfect love removes all fear." — I John 4:18

"He that loves not knows not God; for God is love."
— I John 4:8

In the verse above, (I John 4:8) states God is love. So now the question leads us to the definition of love.

What is love?

The bible gives approximately 309 references to the word "love." Yet all we need to do, is look at our lives to realize how little we understand it. Some people know what it is not. Some say love is like beauty, "I'll recognize it when I "see it".

I once wrote:

Love is a word which can't be described
  Because it's a feeling deep inside.
The feeling I get when I see you smile
  Knowing you're happy at least for a while.

What can I say? I was young (Seventeen?) when I

wrote it. Love is not a seeing nor a feeling, yet this is the only way most of us can relate to it. Love is an experience.

If I attempt to describe what mangoes taste like, I might say they taste like peaches. If the person has never tried peaches, I have another problem. If the person I am trying to love has never felt the kind of love, friendship, or generosity I am capable of giving, then I have a similar problem. This is when we describe what love is not. Any time there is fear (John 4:18) it is not perfect love.

We can't even love ourselves how can we be expected to truly love others. The conundrum, puzzle, cosmic joke, is that we are all connected: To love others is to love ourselves.

The bible says the love of money is an addiction which produces greed based on fear:

"The love of money is the root of all evil." — I Titus 6:10

The following verse I found baffling. How can you hold on to more than you make? It might be talking about being a hoarder, a recluse or some other form of spiritual poverty?

"If you hold on to more than you make, it will lead to poverty." — Proverbs 11:24

This verse is more in line with what I can understand:

"He that loves silver will not be satisfied with silver; nor he that loves abundance with increase: this is also vanity." — Ecclesiastes 5:10

In Matthew 19:24 it states it is easier for a camel to get through the eye of a needle than it is for a rich man to find God. I think this is saying, it is harder for a person to choose God, over what he thinks he has gained here on earth. If the fear is excessive then it becomes greed. The opposite of greed is charity.

What is Charity?

Instead of hording money (among other things), it is freely given. It has its foundation in love (security).

"Though I have the gift of prophecy, and understand all mysteries, and all knowledge, and though I have all faith, so that I could remove mountains, and have not charity, I am nothing." — I Corinthians 13:2

If God is love, than evil is hate. Hate has its basis in fear. Therefore there are only two basic emotions: Love and fear.

Greed and charity are expansions of these two emotions. The war in this world is with greed (insecurity) and charity (security). Charity does indeed begin at home. It begins in our heads with our thoughts. Only I have direct access to my thoughts.

How is God charitable?

"Whatever you ask it will be given." — Mark 6:23

Is this generous or what? God will give us anything we ask because God's love is unconditional. Unfortunately, in the world man created, love is conditional.

When Paul wrote the verse in Romans 7:19, he is fighting his sinful nature. He is fighting his ego which cunningly tries to control the mind. When I know I am doing what, "I wish not to do", it is at this point I will want to repent.

What is repent?

At this point I will probably lose you. The word "repent" has often been shouted to some from the pulpits over the years with such anger and menacing gestures by preachers with good intentions. However, the word "repent" merely means: To turn around; to change our minds; or to change our mental GPS (Global Positioning System) directions. You know, the feeling you get when the pesky GPS tells you to turn around and you don't feel like it? This is the same feeling I get when I know I am going the wrong way. I continue going the wrong way for a long time, and pray for a miracle. Yet the fact remains: I'M GOING THE WRONG WAY!

The word repent is "bad" primarily because of its connection to sin which is also supposedly a "bad" thing. As previously mentioned, sin is simply an error or mistake. Any mistake (sin) according to the bible can be forgiven with the exception of one.

"He that blasphemes against the Holy Spirit will never have forgiveness, but is in danger of eternal damnation."
— Mark 3:29

Have you ever wondered why this is? Just think of it, any despicable crime a person can come up with can be forgiven by God with the exception of one: Blasphemy of the Holy Spirit. But as Mark says in chapter 3:29, he is in danger. This means there is still a chance to be "redeemed" (to save himself). To blasphemy is to speak of something sacred as if it means nothing. When we do this we don't have a clue of what God is. In other words blasphemy is not having respect for the Spirit: Blasphemy is ignorance about what God is. Blasphemy is hate or fear or anything which cuts us off from the Spirit. This makes perfect sense: How can God get through to us, if we close ourselves off from Him? How can we forgive ourselves if we put up a wall between us and our transmitter to God? Our good self can't get through to our bad self because of this wall. Nothing can get through to us unless we start dismantling the wall. We can begin by understanding how it functions, and what is happening to us. Maybe then we can come to terms with our fears. And if all else fails remember:

"He that is dead is freed from sin." — Romans 6:7

Time to Wake up

Put God first and the other nine commandments are irrelevant. Because, if we think about it, do the first one, and we won't find a need to kill, steal, lie, covet, etc. Unfortunately, we forget to place God first in our lives, so the rest of the commandments are there for our protection. They are the first phase (kindergarten) to learning. To put our Spirit or the Spirit in others first, is the first step to waking up. The solution(s) to waking up to what we really are, has varied from schools of thought. The views on waking up have taken us from astrology, philosophy and finally to full blown religions.

It is interesting that Jesus was asked by his apostles who they thought he was. "You are the Christ," They answered him. Christ means anointed, or messiah, which is Hebrew for "Deliverer." When Siddhartha was asked who he was: He answered, "I am awake." His answer became his name: Buddha.

When we start to wake up, after some adjustment, things around us get better. Getting out of our comfort zone might feel funny at first. Especially if our life before had been a total nightmare. We lose some of our fears, and start enjoying life more. The wonderful part about this is we start to realize once again we are not alone. We start recognizing others with similar struggles and ideas. There are so many remarkable people around us, I meet them every day.

Unfortunately, sometimes I turn off the alarm or hit the snooze button, and go back to sleep. Nevertheless, the book of Job as I mentioned in page 14, suggests God is not going to leave me at the mercy of "Satan". Because like all the stories and books in the bible, Job is a metaphor for all of humanity. The Spirit with which we are born becomes ego (spirit), and although the ego goes by many names, for example, Beelzebub, Satan, the devil, the trickster, etc., one friend calls her ego "Tricksy". The name "evil" is given depends on the degree of destruction at a particular point in time.

The more fearful we become, the more destructive we become, and the deeper we are into the dream/nightmare. This means we will continue to suffer proportionally. The dream/nightmare becomes the norm. The dreamer will continue to suffer the consequences forever until he wakes up.   I   tweaked some of the verses I used in the beginning of this project. I changed the 's' to a capital 'S' because I wanted to clarify which spirit I was referring to: The Spirit of God, or my ego. I changed the capitals on some of the words in these verses for the same reason:

"God is life to those that find H̲im and health to their flesh." — Proverbs 4:22

"God be with your S̲pirit. Grace be with you." — Titus 4:22

"I that have ears will listen to the S̲pirit." — Revelation 4:22

The bible tells us, while we live on this earth, it's all vanity: Vanity is another word for "ego". Evil (ego) will blame the victim, (his Spirit self or others) to take the attention off of the real architect, itself. As long as we let our egos run amok, we will continue to suffer and continue to have others around us suffer. This will continue until we learn to stop blaming other egos and do something about our own.

How do we recognize ego? Why would we want to minimize it? Where is it showing up? All these questions are an individual's responsibility, and a way to recovery (waking up). Which makes sense to me. It would be, like me going over to your house and rearranging your furniture because it suited me. A person has to decide he is sick and then decide if he needs help. It is totally up to each individual unless, of course, he is destructive to himself and others. There are so many choices, conditions and situations too numerous to mention.

Perfect Love will always show a person's true Spiritual nature. It looks deeply in to all things and overcomes ignorance. Ignorance causes the drives and impulses. I am reminded of a story I read in a book mentioned earlier (<u>Old Path White Clouds</u>)[12]. In the story Buddha is confronted by a ruthless serial killer. This in my humble opinion is my very condensed version:

***

The killer yells at the monk to stop, but the Buddha keeps walking and says "Angulimala, I stopped a long time ago. It is you who have not stopped." Since the monk knew his name, Angulimala realizes the monk knew who he was and knows of the hundred atrocities he had committed, and wonders why the monk is not scared? He also wants to know what he meant with what he said. Buddha tells him, "I stopped committing acts which cause suffering...you have not. All living beings want to live. All fear death. We must nurture a

---

[12] This story is found on page 352. This book is has so many wonderful stories. I strongly recommend it.

heart of compassion and protect the lives of all beings...It is never too late to stop traveling the road of hatred and violence." After experiencing Buddha's love, and lack of judgment, Angulimala felt as if his heart was ripped open...he bowed down and sobbed...and became a follower.

* * *

How do we nurture a heart of compassion and dwell in perfect love? There are as many ways as there are people but we all have one major obstacle: We all have to deal with our egos. The bible says:

"Get behind me Satan; you don't savor the things of God, but the things that are of men."— Matthew 8:33

"A house divided cannot stand." — Matthew 12:25

"...if Satan cast out Satan, he is divided against himself; how shall then his kingdom stand?" — Matthew 12:26

By turning our thoughts toward God (putting love, or others first) we can leave evil behind us. In this way we can conquer and divide. If I pit spirit against Spirit, the evil will stand out like a sore thumb, and make it easier to know what I am dealing with.

"Don't believe every spirit, but try the spirits whether they are of God." — I John 4:1

In the book, The Art of War by Sun Tzu, (400-320 BC), translated by Samuel B. Griffith, in my opinion, it tells how battles are won. I thought it was interesting to note that the actual author(s) of this book are not known or even if they existed. It is suspected it was a series of authors. The first translation (In French.) of 'The Art of War' was in 1772 by Father J.J. M. Amiot, a Jesuit. I thought it odd that a man of the cloth would be

68

interested in the subject of war. I understood after I read the book.

I think that what it is saying is that one way to win is at all costs, and the other is to use balance, and stealth. The later will be less "expensive in blood, sweat and tears. No one is interested in elaborate complicated strategies". We all want to win intelligently. To win the war against the ego will not be obvious at times. Ego uses many kinds of deception specifically targeted to each individual. It will attack you where you are most weak. We can all be heroes to this bad movie, and in this lifetime and see evil, or fear for what it really is.

"Know your enemy and know yourself and you can fight 100 battles without disaster." — Sun Tzu

"Know the truth and the truth will set you free."
— John 8:32

Always remember the battles with the ego are about principalities not the flesh (Ephesians 6:12): So don't do anything stupid. And remember: If you are in an airplane and the air masks drop down, administer the oxygen to yourself first, otherwise you will be of no use to anybody.

To summarize what I believe so far: I know God is love, and will give us whatever we want, and we can do with it what we wish. We can create whatever sweet dreams or nightmares we wish to create. But God will never leave us at the mercy of fear. There are two emotions: Love and fear. Fear goes by many names depending on the degrees of destruction. I use the word "ego." The ego will put up a fight because its existence is at stake. It is cunning with its use of deception. Know the truth about your true Self. The battle, here on earth, is about principalities. It is not about anything tangible:

"Lay up for yourselves treasures in heaven, where neither moth nor rust doth corrupt, and where thieves do not break through nor steal." — Matthew 6:20

I learned the intangible things like good thoughts, knowledge, and good habits, are things no one can take it away from me. These are the things which can make my life easier, more secure, and less fearful. I also know that whenever I try to change anything there will be some resistance from the ego. How much resistance will depend on how I approach it. If I use balance and stealth, it is better than a huge fight.

Over the years there has been a lot of research on learned responses. One I remember is in the great self-help book Psycho-cybernetics, (1960) Maxwell Maltz, M.D. In my take on this book, a plastic surgeon, noticed it took his patients twenty one days to get rid of the "phantom limb" and adjust to an amputation. What this means to me, it that if I can change anything; an attitude; a bad habit; etc., for twenty one days, I can get out of the Spiritual death I am in. And if you are like me, you will wonder why you ever put up with it as long as you did. Or, you might even wonder, what was the big deal in the first place? If nothing else, I learn something of value that can help me become a better person. It can help me deal with other bad habits, addictions or relationships.

One good way to learn something is to teach it.

"In teaching, you teach yourself: Practice what you preach." — Romans 2:21

So here is something I would like to share with you. It is how I like to create a habit. Though people are basically the same, their methods of learning may vary: Some learn best if they see it, others if they hear it, but all learning is by actually doing it. Muscles have to be exercised: This is especially noticeable in learning a new language. With any skill set, it is a matter of practice, practice, and more practice. It is retraining the mind first, the body's Muscles second.

My method starts out with a 3×5 card and small stickers.

Remember when you were a little kid and how glad you when your teacher put a star on your paper? Well I decided to do the same thing to myself every time I wanted to accomplish something. I draw a calendar on a 3×5 card, label it, and every day I do what the card says. When I do, I place a star or happy face for that day. You will be surprised how much this little sense of accomplishment will mean to you. I use it for so many things.

"Do your duty according to day as required." – Ezra 3:4

Here is an example of one of my cards I started on October the 26th:

25 Exercise - October stairs						
Sun	Mon	Tue	Wed	Thu	Fri	Sat
	1	2	3	4	5	6
7	8	9	10	11	12	13
14	15	16	17	18	19	20
21	22	23	24	25	☺	☺
☺	☺	☺	☺			

I realized long ago I have to sneak up on it. So I will do 25 steps each day for a month. Climbing 25 stairs a day won't put a strain on my legs. The following month I will do more. I decide how much is right for me. I strongly advise you to go easy on yourself. Because, I have to tell you, it was not my legs which were affected. It was my groin area. After doing the 25 for a month with ease, I decided I could do 50 for the following

71

month. However, on the 3rd day, I was in so much pain, I had to take aspirin. It did not hurt while doing the exercise; it was when I tried to walk. I certainly did not see that one coming!

In hindsight maybe a bit more gradually (30?) would have been better. I continued with the 50, and the pain went away after the third day. But fair warning: Do these at your own pace. Only you know what your pace is. You might even consider starting out with just one. You will start seeing progress. You don't have to rush into it.

A similar card system has been around since the 1940's. It has many uses. I let my receipts get behind, (I tend to procrastinate with some things) so now I have a card. It seems all my mind wants is an excuse to begin the chore, because after I start, it becomes fun. I decide when to stop.

Without the card system, lists, schedules, or routines in general, I make excuses for not doing what I decide I want to change. The "reward" of the happy face simply gives me an added incentive. I keep the card in a file to push me forward. It becomes fun to see all my accomplishments however small.

I like it because it is very versatile. It can also serve as a plan. This is especially great for people who have trouble making decisions. I am more resistant to somethings than others. If a few days go by, I can decide there is too much resistance and tear up the card. This is so I don't feel guilty about not doing what is in the card.

I used to post it on the refrigerator as a family menu planning guide for the whole month: "What's for dinner?" Became, "Oh is this what we are having for dinner."

It can be used to reinforce or reduce any good or bad habit. The count can be in amounts or in minutes. I have used it for a variety of things: Practicing the piano, practicing a language, or other chores like cleaning, and organizing anything. Break up the habit(s) into small amounts of time or increments so it can be a fun thing and so you won't be overwhelmed by it.

I first learned of another somewhat more elaborate system in 1980 when I attended a seminar by Pam Young and Peggy Braken for sloppy housewives. Their company and book by the same title, Sidetracked House Executives (SHE), has its own version. Their card system uses cards for doing daily chores, (brushing teeth etc.) to monthly, yearly or seasonal chores. The cards can also serve as reminders, like changing filters in air conditioners. Both sisters have written several books. It goes without saying: It can save time and money.

When I think I have a problem or bad habit, I ask God to help me find the source of the pain or irritation.

For example, when I started to wake up with a pain in my neck one morning, I started experimenting with pillows. A pillow with goose down was my favorite, I could shape it anyway I wanted. Unfortunately, one day I left it behind in a motel somewhere during my travels. But this helped me to realize all pillows work the same as long as they support my neck.

The second pain I noticed, had to do with the way I was sleeping, the pain was in my lower back. Any firm pillow worked if they are strategically placed. I learned through trial and error, I needed to place the pillow between my legs so my hips could remain aligned. When I didn't do this the pain would come back the next day. It became part of my nightly sleeping routine.

The third pain was on my right shoulder. I noticed the same thing that was happening to my hips was happening to my shoulders. I now hug a good firm pillow so my elbow has a place to rest.

I once noticed my knees were starting to hurt so I kept wrapping them up in ace bandages in cold weather and the pain went away. Not every pain is the same, sometimes it is about fasting, staying away from sugar, or rubbing magnesium gel on the affected area. Magnesium gel worked for me. It can be found in any health food store. My body really does tell me what it needs. The trick is to listen to it.

"...have dominion...over every living thing that moves upon the earth." — Genesis 1:28

"Everyone should know how to possess his vessel in sanctification and honor." I Thessalonians – 4:4

As a truck driver, I could not take the chance of losing my job by failing a random drug test so I kept away from any drugs. However, I also had to fall asleep when I wanted. So I had to learn how to do it without drugs. This is how I finally got control over my body's sleeping habits:

1. I put on a sleep mask to reduce visual stimuli. I found the mask not only keeps light out, but also keeps my eyes from drying out and watering the next day.

2. I put in ear plugs to reduce physical stimuli.

3. I take a deep breath, tighten up, then release my body, and tell it: "You've done a great job today, but now it's time to relax."

4. I thank each body part for all the hard work it did during the day. "I love you, but it is time for you to relax." This keeps me from taking my body for granted.

The first three are the triggers tell my body my intentions. Even now when I want to go to sleep, I will go through this routine so my body will know it is time to shut down.

I start with my toes, then go to my feet, ankles, calves, knees, legs, abdomen, all the organs inside, up to my diaphragm. I skip to my fingers, hands, wrists, forearms, elbow joints, upper arms, shoulders, back, down my spinal cord, to the tail bone, and up in line with my diaphragm. Then I go to my lungs, heart, clavicle bone, neck, lower jaw, eyes and sinus area, then the top on my head. (Good for you if you did not fall asleep during this paragraph.)

Sometimes I name a few of the organs specifically, like the liver, kidneys, stomach. I only do this if I sense a problem area.

This will give you a general idea, so you can create a mental routine which will serve you best. I know I can't always go to sleep at the same time every day. I found out my body will do what I tell it day or night. It didn't work as well in the beginning but now it works like a charm. Most of the time I'm asleep before I get started. Which is okay because my goal was to fall asleep not to bless the different parts of my body. I try to do this during the day. At first, it used to take a bit more discipline, because my mind tended to wander, or race. This is okay unless it keeps me awake. When it does, I continue where I left off. If nothing else this gives me a reference point as to what I am trying to accomplish. The best thing about this method is I don't use any drugs.

"I will lay down in peace and sleep: For you God, makes me live in safety." — Psalms 4:8

"The sleep of a laboring person is sweet."
— Ecclesiastes 5:12

I learned I could control different aspects of my body with my mind when I worked in a "freezer" packing bacon. My hands were so cold I could not stand it, but I could not afford to quit, (I was putting myself through college.) so I asked God to help me. I imagined tiny electrodes extending to my fingers and imagined they were radiating heat. And by golly it worked!

In the end, I know if I become a better person with all these little training gimmicks, however long it takes, I set a good example for others. And since we are all connected, if I become a better person, everyone benefits. There are many examples of how this works: An alcoholic sobers up, everyone in his family benefits.

"With the offense of one many die: With grace by one, many live." — Romans 5:15

Although, we often feel very uncomfortable with the newness of any change: Keep at it. Often it seems "The devil we know, is better than the devil we don't know." It is not.

In the same way one person can affect a family for the better; one person can affect an entire community.

And to expand on this: There are people like Moses, Jesus, Buddha, and Mohammed, who made the world a better place.

And while I'm on the subject, and although I will write more on this in **The Evil That Men Do.** So much of the hatred toward Islam is generalized.

This is like thinking all Christians are snake handlers. It never ceases to amaze me, how stupid some people can be. In Rwanda, people killed each other over of the shape of their noses! Does this even make sense to anyone?

Racism, prejudice, or generalization by color, race, religion, body shape or gender, is just plain stupid.

Yet so called "religious" people continue this insanity. All people are reluctant to change. Especially, if what you are trying to change, is making them money.

Today there seems to be so much ignorance about the Islamic religion. Therefore, I will share some facts I learned. One section is about the founder of Islam, and the other section is about Sharia law.

Often confused with other Mohammed's, Mohammed (AD 570? 632) founded the Islamic religion after a vision with the Angel Gabriel. At first he was ridiculed by his own people, but later he was accepted by some as their prophet. When the people of Mecca began to feel threaten by him and their way of life. He fled north with his followers to Medina. There, he gained a great following and became head of the community. He was friendly towards Jews and Christians because **he believed his beliefs completed the sacred teaching of Abraham, Moses and Jesus.** Mohammed had his followers face Jerusalem for daily prayers. And like the Jews, Friday was also set aside for prayer in observing the Sabbath. The Jews and Christians however, wanted control of the community and broke alliance with Mohammed and conspired to have him betrayed. He was justifiably angered and drove the Jews and the Christians out, and established a purely Muslim society. From this day forward his followers were instructed to turn toward Mecca.

His followers are called Muslims.

When he began to preach in the 600's, Arabia was lawless. There were many fierce tribes fighting bloody wars: No one was safe. There was extreme poverty and suffering among the poor. Mohammed taught there is only one God; and required his followers to make "Islam" which means "submission" to God by praying and kneeling down to God five times a day. This is how the religion got its name.

Mohammed told his followers to abstain from alcohol; to stop the practice of killing unwanted baby girls; He also limited polygamy; and single handed changed the lives of millions people for the better. Remember this was done in the 600's.

Muslims respect Mohammed, but contrary to popular belief, they don't worship him. He was one of the most influential men of all time. (Reference: The World Book Encyclopedia, Volume 13, Copyright 1973.)

After reading the Quran, it dawned on me what Sharia Law actually is. With what I already knew, I concluded the following:

Sharia Law

The first few chapters of the <u>King James Bible</u> are part of the <u>Quran</u> (also <u>Koran</u>, and <u>Qur'an</u>), the Muslim bible. At one point the <u>Quran</u> splits off.

The Old Testament is what is now called Sharia Law. They are often referred to as Mosaic laws because they were written by Moses.

These old outdated laws by some misguided loyalty to Moses or god, some people have refused to let go.

Mohammed believed his beliefs completed the sacred teaching of Abraham, Moses and Jesus. (Refer to the box above.)

In the lawless wilderness away from Egypt, Moses had to have complete control, therefore set himself up as a god, "... put a miter on his head ..." Leviticus 8:9. Throughout the chapters he repeats, "I am the Lord your God." God said do this and that. In Leviticus chapters 11-15 he was able to set up several laws against disease, condemned sacrificing babies, and was able to get the meat which "was sweet to the Lord". In Chapter 17 he banishes people who won't share their kill with the "Lord". Anyone who questioned "god" was put to death. Leviticus 24:11-17. His guilt caused Moses his great sin which would not allow him to cross to the Promised Land.

I wouldn't judge Moses too harshly, after all, he had 603,055 people who were constantly nagging him: According to Numbers 1:46, this is the amount of people in the census two years after they escaped from Egypt. Can you imagine 40 years of nagging? Yes I suppose some of you can.

Moses and Mohammed faced the same basic problems. They both had to deal with an extreme sense of lawlessness. They both had to take extreme and drastic measures to take care of very serious situations: Disease, addictions, killing babies, ignorance, poverty and suffering.

My hope is now, many Sharia laws will make more sense.

Oftentimes the problem(s) which result from the different religions is with frustrated people, not with the original intentions of any one religion. When Jesus started his ministry, his beliefs were thought of as radical. They disrupted the norm and Jesus was crucified. We all go through periods in our lives when we generalize. The problem comes when we start using it as a weapon to hurt others who are truly innocent. Many don't bother to reason it all out. Unfortunately some of today's religious sects, still refuse to let go of some of their harmful beliefs

An example is the abortion issue. Many people are strongly convicted. People should care how laws affect the poor and disenfranchised. Remember: "There for the grace of God go I." These same laws will be applied to your grandchildren.

Most politicians and religious leaders expound on abortions because it is making them money and/or winning elections! To some it is about their financial survival. The more people they convince, (whichever way the tide is moving,) the more elections they win.

Another prime example is the slave trade in the 1800's. It was rationalized as making the world a better place.

The "heathens" and "savages" were better off, etc. Oftentimes all I can do is shake my head and turn it over to God.

Religion should be a personal thing:

"When you pray enter into your closet...shut the door, pray...in secret; and God...will reward you openly."
— Matthew 6:6

Why is it so important for other people to think the same thing in exactly the same way? I know change is hard for people in general. I will go into my theory about why later on in the book.

Unfortunately, we have to deal with so many of these same problems today, as when Moses and Mohammed were running things. But today we try to adhere to more humane ways to deal with "the evil that men do."

More recently, there have been people like Gandhi and Mother Theresa who put God first, and make the world a better place with their teachings. Teachings which live on for generations after them.

So much of what we learned about God has to be reexamined.

If any preacher claims to have all the answers. He does not! Only the Spirit inside of me has the answers which are right for me at any particular space in time. A teacher's job is to simply guide me to that end. And always remember it has nothing to do with the flesh. It never ceases to amaze me what some people will fall for.

For one thing, fear cannot be used as a motivator to bring us closer to God. If some preacher or self-proposed prophet is using fear or conditional love: Run!

"Avoid it, don't get near it, and keep away from evil."
— Proverbs 4:15

And to expand on this idea, if you or anyone is trying to harm you by any means, financial or otherwise: Remember Ecclesiastes 6:12 "It is not about the flesh...." God doesn't need anything from you. Why would it, God is perfect!

The one thing I found that is contradictory to all which I have been generally taught about the bible and God: We don't have to do anything for God to love us. God loves us unconditionally. This makes perfect sense in regard to what genuine love is. I know personally I love my children and they do not have to earn my love.

"What man would give his son a stone, when he asks for bread?" — Matthew 7:9

"The gifts of God are without regard to what we do."
— Romans 11:29

"God's gift can't be purchased with money." "
— Acts. 8:20

"The Father loves His son." — John 5:20

"Cast your cares upon God: He loves you."
— I Peter 5:7
"Let it be, God is with you." — II Samuel 10:7

My father-in-law once told me he was taught a German song in Church. When I asked him to translate it for me, he sheepishly told me a part of it translated: "I am the worm of the earth." This is another contradiction of what is generally being taught about the bible. I can only suppose this was done for the purpose of teaching humility. The Osage American Indian tribe has a similar custom. When you do something great, it is up to the cousins to verbally put you down so you won't become egotistical about it.

However, if we believe the bible, then the very first premise is we are made in the image of God. If we are made in the image of God, then we are Spirit, because God is also Spirit. All things being equal then these verses make sense:

"I was made higher than the heavens."
— Hebrews 7:26

"God has made everything beautiful."
— Ecclesiastes 3:11

Of course after we were made in the image of God, we have the fall of Adam, so the children became images of the earthly father. Remember Adam has not yet awakened. It changed from Spirit to spirit. This is why we have to remember what we really are.

"You are more than a body." — Matthew 6:25

"The Spirit itself is witness that you are a child of God."
— Romans 8:16

"We are all children of the light."
— I Thessalonians 5:5

"Whatever God does, He does forever."
— Ecclesiastes 3:14

"The Spirit of life from God entered into you."
— Luke 11:11

"God did not give me a Spirit of fear."
— II Timothy 1:7

"You are of God: Greater is He that is in you, than he that is in the world." I John – 4:4

When I ask guidance from God, I realized long time ago I first had to figure out if the advice was any good. Was it really my Spirit, or was it my spirit which was only fooling me?

I once asked a truck stop preacher if Satan could disguise itself as Jesus. I did not know it at the time, but it was a trick question: If the preacher said, "No." Then Satan did not have much power and therefore we could not be frightened into worshiping God. If he said, "Yes," we might be worshiping Satan. I never got a straight answer from him. However, the answer is "Yes," But as anyone who has ever been a survivor of domestic abuse can verify: If anyone is posing as good, his true character will eventually be exposed. Before it gets close, learn to recognize its true character.

Emotional love

One of the biggest deceptions the ego uses is emotional love.

"Give me an understanding heart to discern between good and evil." — II Kings 3:9

Have you ever fallen in love? It can be very addictive. We get an initial high, before reality hits us. I have often seen people make the same mistakes I used to make. I wanted so much for people to love me, and take care of me. However, when they tried to show me how much they loved me, I would not believe them or it was never enough. I wanted them to show their love to me in the same way I expressed it to them. It did not take me long to realize their love was never going to be what I wanted, nor was it ever going to be enough to satisfy me.

> 1. I didn't know what I wanted in the first place
> 2. I didn't know what love was, and
> 3. I didn't know I had to set boundaries.
> (Duh, even God had the Ten Commandments.)

All I knew is when loved happened, it felt good and I wanted more. I wanted people to love me unconditionally. Something they simply were not capable of doing. I learned the hard way, if I am not careful I can become addicted to the feeling which comes with the experience. When I read Euripides, I thought, *"Now you tell me."* I loved without reason and so profoundly I lost all sensibility.

> "When love is in excess, it brings a man neither honor nor worthiness." —Euripides

It was only after much heartache and abuse I found out what love was.

In the 60's there was a very popular movie called <u>Love Story</u>. A friend used to drive me crazy with a line which came out of the movie: "Love is never having to say you're sorry". It wasn't until years later I finally realized what it was trying to say: Love is never having to apologize for who you are. It has nothing to do with saying you are sorry. If you hurt someone or make an honest mistake, then you should say you're sorry.

Not only did I learn I didn't have to apologize for who I was, I learned love also meant I needed to take care of myself. We need to learn to take care of ourselves so the people we actually love, and really care for us, don't have to worry about us. If a person doesn't take care of himself, it is probably an addiction to the mind set of feeling unloved and hoping someone will come to his rescue. He does not want the responsibility and wants someone else to care for him.

Even with extreme handicaps many people are capable of caring for themselves. One amputee who had climbed a dangerous mountain put it this way, "I don't ever consider myself disabled unless I am looking for a good parking place."

Extreme physical handicaps aside, many crave, expect, and even demand someone else take care of them long term. They have no idea how much control they give away.

Find some way to take back control of your life. I would strongly suggest you only use the power you actually have, not the power you wish you had. Stay away from fantasies and fanatics who live in them; they are twice removed from reality. There are so many people in mental hospitals; in jail; or on drugs because they have not learned this valuable lesson.

You often hear in the news how a person took the object of their affection to the extreme and how it ended in a homicide. You cannot force someone to love you!

People can make the same mistakes when they love God as they do when loving others. When you fall in love with God, it truly is a high. I think because we feel like:

"God loves each one of us, as if there were only one of us." —Saint Augustine.

People with good intentions can also lose their common sense when it comes to loving God. Oftentimes they are so overwhelmed with love it becomes an addiction like any of the other addictions. This gives birth to fanatics and to otherwise good people who hurt others and fight for control of their souls. Tragically some are encouraged to mutilate their bodies.

Usually the fight for control is motivated by greed

or by a firm conviction that others should come to the same conclusions in the same way that they did. They don't take into account that everyone is different and that each one of us is at a different level of learning. This is why the Spirit deals with us in regard to the amount of faith each individual has, not on the faith he wished he had.

I was fortunate enough to learn this because I come from very large family (17). I realized while many of my brothers, sisters and parents were experiencing basically the same thing, they would often remember the same thing so differently. We are all different and unique individuals and are very capable of learning in our own unique way. In much the same way, this is why there are so many religions.

I love to see the hundreds of people that attend Joyce Meyer concerts. I love to see the hundreds of people giving audience to the Pope. I love to see hundreds of Muslims in their mosques bowing in prayer. And, it also makes me happy when I see Jews praying at the wall.

I often think, *"Someone is listening to you God"*.

"All flesh will see the salvation of God." — Luke 3:6

The Hindu Bible (The Vedas) says: There are many paths to the same summit.

I believe there is only one God, but so many ways to worship and love Him. **To worship simply means to love, honor and respect** something. There is nothing weird or bad about worshiping God unless you take it to extremes. So much can be taken to the extreme. For example: Desire.

It was taken to the extreme by the early puritans. Desire was most often associated with anything having to do with the flesh.

It is interesting that the word desire literally

means "from God". 'De' is translated "from," and 'sire' is translated from Latin word meaning "Father (in Heaven)".

During the Victorian era, extreme taboos against desires manifested itself in all kinds of mental disorders. They tried hard to keep away from temptation. I think this made the object more tempting. Especially in an immature person.

"When I was a child I thought as a child, but when I grew I put away childish things." — I Corinthians 13:11

As we mature, we learn to question authority. We learn to question: Why is this bad? How is this bad? When is this bad? And for whom is it bad? We also learn to question our desires. And hopefully we can mature enough to be able to think twice and project the consequences of our actions and reactions into the future — before we act on them. As we mature, our survival instincts and common sense help us to question, and curb our desires into healthy expressions.

The story of Adam and Eve in the garden tells us that obedience is important. Disobedience to God, according to the bible was our first "sin". Obedience is good, disobedience is bad, and therefore we are constantly warned to curb our desires.

I believe that our desires are an underlying need for love. If we feel love we obey blindly. We seem contend and feel we have everything we want. Even hunger gives way to love. If we feel unloved, and lack the self-discipline, we rebel. We disobey without asking questions.

Can a God that created us and that loves us also lead us into temptation? No! God does not! God is about the Spirit in us, not the flesh. Remember: We are trying to wake up to what we are. Maybe we unwittingly put ourselves into difficult situations that will help us to that end. I don't know. Maybe we feel guilty and think we have to punish ourselves. I don't know!

Why would Jesus ask God, "Lead us not into temptation"? He was teaching people how to pray, so maybe he was saying it for the benefit of the people he was teaching. Maybe he knew what he would go through, and wanted God's help.

It takes courage to ask for help.

Does God encourage? The answer is, "Yes," but we are only conscious of it if we ask consciously! This is because He gave us freewill. In other words, whether we realize it or not, we are constantly asking. We are asking with our thoughts. Our thoughts are ultimately up to us.

The Comforter (Holy Spirit), Jesus talked about will put ideas in our minds; to the level we can understand them. (Remember? It's according to each individual's faith.)

The rule of thumb is that: If it's about unconditional love, then it is about God. God is the only one that can give us unconditional love.[13] If you are not looking for love here, you are looking in the wrong place.

Does God want us to question or to blindly obey?

Nothing that is good would want us to blindly obey. God cannot force us to love Him because He gave us freewill. Therefore, the answer is "No", God does not want us to blindly obey.

For me: **The bible's teachings have to be consistent.** We have to learn to recognize love. You can find love in some of the most unsuspecting places. The trouble with us is that we often have a hard time separating conditional love from unconditional love.

Take my cat Samuel (not meant as a joke): Unlike dogs, cats are very independent, wild animals, and hard

---

[13] Although God can use anything as teachers: People, animals, and especially children.

to train. It took two years for Samuel to trust me.

Cats, in my humble opinion, are mostly for observation. They are certainly fascinating to watch.

I get such a kick out of Samuel when he throws a rubber band in the air and runs all over house trying to catch it. In the morning I will find a number of rubber bands in his food bowl: Such a triumphant gesture!

Personally I think, like all animals, Samuel makes a great psychiatrist. It's obvious what he thinks. When I tell him my problems, all he does is yawn.

I will give Samuel some credit: He is a great help when it comes to getting rid of mice and other small pests.

The thing I love most about Samuel is when I am lying there watching television he snuggles up to me. When he was smaller he would lay his head on my chest; wrap his arms around me; and start snoring. He looked like a miniature bear rug. I didn't dare move for fear I would lose a precious moment.

I know Samuel loves me unconditionally. When I drive up, he runs to greet me, and bounces like a little lamb. The neighbors have commented that Samuel acts more like a dog then a cat. He follows me everywhere and comes when I call him. You can't force this kind of behavior. The funny part about Samuel is that I never really cared much for cats. I inherited Samuel from my son. Shortly after we rescued him from the Humane Society, I tried to call him "Sammy". My son was adamant, "His name is Samuel: It's a nice Jewish name". From that day forward, Samuel became my "Jewish cat".

I keep the scale by the refrigerator and weigh every morning. This morning I had to laugh at Samuel: After I weighed myself I went to retrieve my cup of morning tea from the microwave, I happened to look down and saw Samuel sitting on the scale with his head to one side, staring at me. It almost seemed as he was asking, "How much do 'I' weight?" (He weighs 12.2

ounces).

I had to learn about cats to know that I could not change Samuel's basic instincts. He will kill mice. And contrary to popular opinion: A cat is not playing with the mouse when he bats it back and forth. They do this to make sure it is no longer capable of biting them. Who knew?

Over the years I have learned to communicate with this strange and wonderful creature. When I am putting on my makeup and don't want to be bothered, (Cat-us interrupt-us) I learned that if I face him and close my eyes, he understands and he walks away. When he is hungry and I am sleeping, he will, ever so gently, touch my face to wake me up. Often I confuse, him wanting my affection, for love. He is simply trying to remind me that I forgot to feed him. I feed him then he goes back to whatever he was doing.

Over the years it has become obvious that Samuel's love for me is genuine and for the most part it is unconditional. If I am not careful this whole book will be about Samuel. I think this genuinely qualifies me as an official "Cat lady".

Animals are not the only place there is unconditional love. I remember the way, my then husband, looked at his son for the first time after he was born. If you want to experience unconditional love: Have a child. And even though some people are incapable of bonding with them, the opportunity is certainly there.

Love isn't really love unless it is freely given and freely received. It comes without conditions. Like I recently told someone, you can love anyone and don't have to be on top of them all the time. Love transcends time and space whether they are dead or living.

When my daughter was learning to talk, I was so fascinated with this little tiny person. She could walk, talk, and think on her own. I had not realized how intrusive my love had been until the morning she woke up from a nightmare. She told me that this giant eye was looking at her through a magnifying glass.

My unconditional love for her, caused me to stop my hurtful behavior as soon as I realized what was happening.

The older I get, the more people I lose contact with. Not only in death, but also in the different paths friends and family have taken. However, this does not mean I am not grateful for the beautiful times we have spent together. I cherish the time they spent with me, however short. I try to remember that I have to love the life I still have and the friends still ahead of me.

In extreme cases, this "love energy" goes to extremes. Instead of just enjoying it in that particular time and space, we try to control it so we can keep it forever. Much like a picture. They are nice to keep as a reminder but I finally had to realize that it will never again be the same. Nevertheless, I understand how it can be addictive to the point where it becomes dangerous to ourselves and others.

Not feeding any addiction will cause the body/mind to exhibit withdrawal symptoms.

So often times we are hurt by the fact that the other person wants nothing to do with us. We can take it so personally that our ego can't handle it. We can go into a state of depression or hopelessness, or worse, strike out at them.

I remember one time a lady that I liked started acting strangely every time I saw her. I finally asked her, "Have I done something to offend you?"

"I was at the grocery store last week and you looked right at me and you didn't say anything to me."

"I would never do that to you on purpose. I really like you. Sometimes, I concentrate so hard on things or have so much on my mind, I can be looking right at you and not realize it."

I read somewhere that Abraham Lincoln did the

same. His wife scolded him when he didn't hear his son crying after a fall.

If anything like this happens to you, don't take it personally. Speak up. If this friend would have faked our friendship, we both would have lost a wonderful opportunity to clear the air.

In time we mature. Whether it comes in spurts, or very, very slowly, eventually we learn to get comfortable with love by embracing and giving it back unconditionally.

When you truly love someone, you want them happy. And if they truly loved you they would want the same for you. However, boundaries need to be set. You have to know what you want. Our goal should always be to get closer to the Spirit within, with or without another person. Emotional love can help us get a glimpse of what real love is. Everyone we meet is a teacher to that end.

To question is to progress, to live, to mature, to come alive with energy, and to have enthusiasm for life. This is love of self: Where all love begins.

I cannot talk about love without talking about self-respect or self-love. This is where forgiveness comes in. When a person holds a grudge against another person: The person is only hurting himself. You cannot control the emotions of another person. The other person can walk away smiling, while you are left with a great deal of pain. Another way of putting it is: You drink the poison expecting the other person to die. How dumb is that?

When we are angry at the other person who is causing us so much pain, who are we really angry at? Without realizing it we are angry at ourselves because of the pain we are experiencing; we are angry with ourselves for letting them hurt us; and angry with ourselves for having gotten into the relationship in the first place. But without realizing it, the choice had more to do with what we needed to learn.   It was a subconscious choice.

The bibles teach us that God is within, so who or what are we really fighting against? Right! We are fighting ourselves!   And you will never win this fight because there are two equal opposing mental forces fighting at the same time. It's a stalemate. The Law of Cause and Effect states: For every action there is an equal and opposite reaction. There are so many ways to say the same thing. A Christian might say, "You reap what you sow." A Hindu might call it "Karma." A truck driver might say, "What goes around comes around." But I like how my ex-husband (also a truck driver) put it because it has a nice ring to it, he'd say, "Pay backs are hell!"

What I needed to learn was that I was really fighting myself. I was pitting two mental forces against each other with the same amount of force: The law of cause and effect, just like the law of gravity, affects us all. It is like playing tick tack toe with oneself; there will never be a winner. The more vicious, and passionate the fight, the more destructive it is.   How dumb is that?

"In meekness instruct those that oppose themselves."
— II Timothy 2:25

I strongly believe that people are trying to make sense of their world, and that they are simply trying to find a better way to live. I believe that we do this unconsciously. The soul is trying to wake up. We do this by attracting lessons that we need to learn so we can grow. I see so many that get lost through self-loathing; unhealthy relationships; or have wrong ideas about whom or what they are.

Remember that we have to come to terms with the past, so we can move forward.

"Rejoice in all your years and remember also the days of

darkness." — Ecclesiastes 11:8

All traumas need to be dealt with; whether it is financial loss, as in a theft or physical disaster; a physical loss, as in an amputation of a body part; or in a devastating emotional loss, as in a rape or incest; or as in the loss of a child or other loved one. A betrayal of any kind, big or small, can be less obvious but equally as painful and hard to deal with.

1. This pain has to be dealt with or it will bury itself and will fester.
2. This pain may cause you to get ill: Physically or mentally.
3. Recognize that everyone is different in dealing with pain.
4. You might be in a very vulnerable position.
5. When an injustice or trauma happens, go easy on yourself.
6. With most situations, wait before you make matters worse.
7. Try to stay away from drugs that will only mask the pain.
8. Get real and don't go into a fantasy world.
9. Understand that what you really want is some sense of justice.
10. There is a smart way to get justice and there is a dumb way to get justice,
11. Choose the right kind of justice, or you will make matters worse.
12. Always turn to Spirit of God within for guidance, and if necessary, get help from someone you trust.

"Don't be afraid: Remember God. Fight for what is yours." — Nehemiah 4:14

I believe there are five kinds of justice:

1. An eye for an eye.

This type of justice is found in Exodus 21:24, "...wound for wound, stripe for stripe." Basically this is saying, do to others what they did to you. Usually people wanting this type of justice come from communities or households that used fear as a control. If fear is done as the only means of control: It does not work. And more than likely, it causes trauma which leads to further injustice. Though this is an outdated form, it still exists.

Done in excess by the one having the most power, the recipient might get a condition called learned helplessness. The basic premise of the 'learned helplessness theory' is that an individual senses he is unable to act and control his life: "Nothing I do makes a difference". This brings on a sense of helplessness which leads to depression. (Hiroto & Seligman 1975) The individual gives up hope and becomes depressed or gets Stockholm syndrome, where a victim identifies with the abuser, who in turn goes on to abuse others.

I did not find Stockholm syndrome in any of my many psychology books or reference books: Diagnostic and Statistical Manual (DSM-IV), psychology dictionary, or other dictionaries. However, I do hear it referred to from time to time especially on television. It is my understanding that the term had it beginnings in Stockholm after it was observed that after being held captive, some prisoners identified with the abuser and learned to inflict pain on others. I have also heard it called the Patti Hearst Syndrome.

Depending on the perceptions, and chemical makeup of the individuals, this type of justice can breed several conditions of mental illness.

"The old law of sparing the rod" falls under this category. The often misquoted verse is:

"He that spares his rod hates his son: but he that loves him punishes him early." — Proverbs 12:24

Any punishment done in excess without allowing the child a sense of freedom to discover who he is can result or exasperate mental illness. The punishment should fit the crime. The child is supposed to trust the very people that are hurting him: A conundrum for the small child that does not fully understand why he is being punished. This is why punishment should be done early when the child is still able to associate the exact crime with the exact punishment. ("...punish him early." Proverbs 12:24.)

I would strongly advise that you listen to what children are really trying to tell you. Punishment does not necessarily mean for you to hit the child. If you read Proverbs 12:24 as a metaphor: The rod might mean justice and hate might be translated as fear.

Here is my take: "He that spares justice for his son is afraid of him..."

It can also mean a time out, but don't forget to set the timer. If you don't it will make matters worse the next time.

Think before you use any kind of punishment. After I would punish one of my kids, I would think to myself: *"They'll get even. I don't know how or when, but they **will** get even."*

Any punishment done in excess is illegal in the United States and could land you in jail with a very long "time out".

The bible says in Exodus 21:22: "...As the judges determine." In other words let the courts take care of it. That's why vigilante justice is illegal.

In Matthew we find: "...if the right eye offends you, pluck it out..." but to understand what it is really saying we need to read the whole passage (or chapter):

"...if the right hand offends you, cut it off. For it is profitable for you that one of your members should perish and not that their whole body should be cast into hell." — Matthew 5:30

This is saying that it is better to get rid of something (or someone) so it can keep the rest safe. Putting someone in jail is a prime example.

We can replace hand for anything that keeps us from our overall well-being. This can be anything physical, financial, or emotional. For example, if my bad habits keep me from enjoying life and being closer to Spirit, I need to get rid of them.

2. Something bad happens.

In primitive cultures, there was "a mental curse" that was placed on the offender. You paid a price (usually with pigs) to a sorcerer, shaman, or witch doctor who would guarantee results.

There is a sense of satisfaction seeing your offender go to jail or at the very least, suffer some other calamity; a divorce, or even an accident, etc. Thus he got his "come-up-pence", or his just deserts.

This is the same as "an eye for an eye..," except it is done mentally. Sometimes just seeing the one that has done the injustice suffer is enough to help us let it go, put it all behind and begin the healing process.

Unfortunately, there are times the person that has wronged us seems to be rewarded or continues to profit. And then there are also times when the person turns his life around, get sober, or finds God.

If you continue to feel anger with the injustice, and get even angrier when the other people seems to be profiting, then you have to look within.

3. Letting it go

Most people fall into this category. This one is the combination of #1 and #2 above. However, it is for the majority of us, who don't like confrontation.

As much as we can, we need to hold people accountable. However, oftentimes we tend to rationalize the injustice, sometimes to the determinant of society, and ourselves.   We don't want to get involved. Many times we suffer silently or think "sour grapes."[14]

When an injustice happens to me, so often I look the other way and chock it up to "The school of hard knocks" (In which I think I'm close to getting a doctorate degree); or I think "sour grapes." These attitudes can fester into vindictiveness. I am learning that these are all forms of learned helplessness.

With this type of justice I do some soul searching because it takes heavy doses of courage and wisdom. Painstakingly, I have to learn to pick my fights. Oftentimes I have had to understand that there will never be justice. At times I will have to postpone the injustice until I have dealt with more immediate high priority problems and simply move on one minute, one hour, or if I get really good, one day at a time.

If you are a little more mature and maybe a little more financially well off, depending on the offense, you can more easily put the situation down as a learning experience; vow that it will never happen to you again; and then move on. But you need to be careful that you don't start generalizing to anyone with the same physical characteristics or become distrustful of everyone in

---

[14]There is an Aesop fable about a fox that sees some delicious grapes he very much wants. But they are just above his reach. As hard as he tries, he is unable to reach them. He finally realizes the futility in trying. In order to make himself feel better, he convinces himself he really didn't want the grapes and they were probably sour anyway. In this way he is able to put the grapes out of his mind

general.

4. Identifying with the offender.

With this type of justice a person gets to the place where he can identify with the offender. The victim sees the offender as also being a victim. A victim empathizes with the criminal's struggles and his frustrations and empathizes over all the injustices done to him. If carried to the extreme or if a person does not fully understand what is really going on, it can be detrimental to society and to the victim. The abuser will be protected and will be kept from being held accountable for their crime(s).

I see this in domestic abuse relationships and on a massive scale with terrorist sympathizers. A very strong bond is held in place with loyalty to that person or persons. The victim of the crime plays the role of protector.

On a healthier level, it is a way for the abuser to get a glimpse of change. The abuser might be able to see other possibilities of living other than the way he is currently living. He can get help to clean up his act. And more importantly it is a way to forgive the injustices done to him and move on.

But one has to be smart enough, strong enough, and careful enough not to get caught up or sucked into the offender's vortex.

We all need to learn and know when enough is enough.

Very often the offenders are master manipulators and have refined this existence for many years. People are resistant to change. I would have saved myself so much heartache if I would have learned this sooner. I often think that sometimes we are just not ready to learn the lessons that we need to learn. It will help to simply be aware of them.

At the very least we need to remember that it is about life not death; love not fear; and freewill not forced will.

5. Giving it to God

The fifth and final way to get justice is by "letting it go, and letting God". But how can we do this, if we feel we have not yet received the justice, we feel we deserve?

First off all, before I turn anything over to God, I first need to get a clear idea of what I think God is. This is earth not heaven. There are laws that we all have to answer to. So we need to get real. If we are doing this to impress others on how forgiving we can be, it is ego you are turning it over to, not God. This is why this type of justice takes a great deal of brutal honesty, and can be fraught with self-righteousness and dilutions.

The real forgiveness is so everyone will benefit. There will be no doubt and no fear. There are many people who think they know God, and don't deal with their traumas properly.

Most often their dilutions come from a source of fear. However, if done with the right understanding, and if we really know God, it can be the most rewarding. We will have the peace that passes all understanding. In the end we might be honestly grateful to the person who has done us the wrong and for teaching us valuable lessons about what we are. Then we let them go. Not only do we forgive but we also forget the pain. We become grateful and think it was really God's plan for us to learn what we needed to learn to become a better person.

If I let go and let God even just a little bit. The pain will lessen. In the end we begin to realize that we are all trying to figure things out and find the best way we can to lessen our suffering. It is a wonderful world. So often we need to merely change our perception of its reality.

"Birds sing after a storm. Why shouldn't people feel as free to delight in whatever sunlight remains to them?"
– Rose Kennedy

"The gem cannot be polished without friction, nor man perfected without trials." — Confucius

"The true nobility is in being superior to your previous self." — An old Hindu Proverb

"Let it be ... for God is with you." I Samuel 10:7

Truck Stop Chatter

We all go through hard times. And it is in those times we need the most encouragement. So often, it is impossible to get that encouragement from family or friends. Often our thoughts are all we have.

There are times when I would think of something funny that happened and I would laugh out loud. A couple of times it was so funny I couldn't even tell anyone what I was laughing about because I was laughing so hard.

Verses, poems, jokes or anything else that helps us through those bad times are worth remembering. They might seem irrelevant at the time but they are the building blocks to the future.

I memorized parts of William E. Henley's poem Invictus. I often thought about the poem that was written by Henley more than one hundred years ago. I was an over the road truck driver and there are times when I needed an "unconquerable soul".

As semi-truck driver, one is the commander and chief of high priced equipment: Large trucks are sometimes referred to as "ships". When I drove through

101

Kansas I would look out at the wheat fields as the wind caressed the wheat. The wheat fields looked like an ocean with gentle rolling waves. It was at these times I would recall Henley's poem.

The poem is about being the "captain of my soul". Or as I like to put it: Responsible for myself.

Someone once described truck driving as hours of tedium boredom with seconds of horrific terror. There were times...But not all of it was boredom. There were also so many wonderful memories.

I remember the eagles and bears in New Hampshire and Maine. I remember the curlicues of steam emitted from lakes at five thirty in the morning in Ohio.

One time, during the early morning hours while driving on I80 in Pennsylvania, I saw a huge deer with an enormous rack. I will never forget this incredible sight. The sun was filtering through the green trees and the lush green meadow that particular morning. This majestic giant stood with his head outstretched overlooking his family: Two does and four fawns as they grazed on the side of the mountain.

America is such a beautiful country.

I remember the mountains laced with snow in Colorado and the unbelievable sunsets in New Mexico and Arizona. From the skylines in New York to the prairies in Nebraska: America is so very beautiful. There is not enough paper...

I am most grateful to all the drivers like "Mikey" (James Mikey) that are wonderful decent people that will forever hold a special place in my heart. I will forever wonder what happened to him, his beloved family; most especially his newborn (at that time) Elizabeth, and to the rest of his eleven children. These wonderful memories and the verses that I memorized help me to stay in touch with my values that gave direction to my life. They help remind me to be strong and rely on my source. I need to stay awake to see all the beauty that surrounds me. And remind myself that anything can happen.

I drove the first semi at the age of seventeen. (Yes, it was illegal.) I would continually go back to truck driving after attempts at several other things.

On my very first run after truck driving school, I went to California. On that first trip I started a conversation with a driver named Charlie who was making his last run. He would retire the next day and told us that he was "...goin' fishin'".

This poem was inspired by that first day as an over the road truck driver, in which unknowingly, I was to spend thirty years of my life.

I wrote this poem in 2010:

The Long Haul

Rolling into Kansas after a long haul
Thinking back all those years, 30 in all
Charlie told me on my first week's run
"I'm goin' fishin', gonna have me some fun."

And we laughed Charlie and me.

"10.4 Charlie," I hollered back then.
"This is the Pink Panther, good Luck to you my friend."
I'm sure he'd laugh at all I've been through.
The fires, hurricanes, tornadoes, and the LA earthquake, just to mention a few.
And we'd laugh Charlie and me.

I've dealt with bad weather, bad roads and bad cops.
Traffic, log books and all them mountain tops.
Cabbage Patch, The Grape Vine, Cajon and the black hills
      of Tennessee,
"Heck, Charlie, it tweren't nothing for a gear jangler like

me."

And we'd really laugh Charlie and me.

Bad directions, dispatchers not answering the phone,
Freezing my fingers and crying, "I just want to go home!"
The pins that won't pull, and those scary weight stations,
And Charlie, "I won't even mention those DOT [15] regulations"

And we'd laugh Charlie and me.

Low bridges, tight schedules, impatient jerks, not to mention bad drivers and all of them sexual perverts.
So many years ago you were just a tired old voice on the CB[16],
But Charlie "Oh how you made such an impression on me."

And we'd smile Charlie and me.

Having to face all those countless fears
Then silently wiping away all those bitter tears.
He wished me good luck, and then Charlie was gone.
"I'd rather be fishing, but my time is not yet done."

Then there was silence between Charlie and me.

When I look at my past, I remember all the wonderful times I had in all those heated, passionate arguments, discussions and shared conversations. I am grateful for all the truck drivers and people across the country that shared their time with me. I loved it,

---

[15]Department of Transportation.
[16] A citizen-band radio is a radio for shorter distances and is different than the Ham radio.

especially when the driver's lounge was packed. I learned so much about myself.

I would try to get everyone involved in the discussions. I think this need began as a young girl. I used to love large family gatherings. Everyone would get excited, and rattle off their opinions and ideas and I loved the excitement of the conversations. I would sometimes want to participate, but I had an extremely bad stuttering problem growing up.

In these heated conversations: When I felt the slightest bit of tension, I would defuse the conversations. I think I developed this skill from the frustration I felt when my very large family would argue, I wanted so much for them to share in the conversations that took place in a healthy manner, and always imagined what I would say to them if I could control the situation.

People if given a chance, can remain civil.

Sometimes someone would say, "This is America, we don't talk about religion or politics." My response would be: "This is America, and that is exactly why we should talk about religion and politics." Or depending on the situation and my mood I might say: "My people fought in two world wars so I could have the privilege of freedom of speech."

I have two flags in memorial frames in my library: One with 50 stars and the other with only 48 stars. They are a constant reminder of the sacrifices family members and others have endured so I could have the privileges I have today. However, if they really didn't want to talk I tried to be respectful of their wishes.

I remember walking into a restaurant and seeing some older couples occupying two corner booths. And since it was Sunday I suspected they had just come from church. There was a loud conversation about homosexuals among the drivers at the counter. At the time, their right to marry was a source of much discourse. I wondered what the older people thought, and occasionally would see them shake their heads in agreement. Impulsively, I decided to ask the one driver, whom I thought was the most blinded by his believes, if he believed in the Constitution of the United States of America.

My theory was that the most stubborn link, would give me the best challenge.

He answered that he did in fact believe in the constitution but added that he was a Christian and proceeded to quote Romans. I looked up Romans later and I could never find the verses that he quoted. In Romans verses 1:27-32, I think Paul was talking about lust or addictions to the flesh in general, because he also writes about the misuse of women by man. Lust and love are very different. In Romans 2:1 he is warning us to "Let God be the judge, otherwise, we condemn ourselves." 2:11 "God is not a respecter of persons." God judges the heart and Spirit of the man. By the time he gets to Romans 12:10 he reminds us to "Be kind and affectionate to one another with brotherly love."

Since I had not yet reviewed Romans, I stuck to what I knew. I reminded the man that quoted Romans, that homosexuality is not addressed in the Ten Commandments. I also reminded him that we live in America where churches as a rule don't pay taxes because there was a separation between the Churches and the States. There are so many belief systems in America and that is why the Constitution is the law, not the bible. Contrary to popular belief, the founders of the Constitution, although rooted in Christianity, were Deists.

Deists, believe God created the Universe and then left it up to us, and basically "abandoned us". This is contrary to the general Christian belief in a personal God that will never abandon us.

The reason for the separation of the Church and State is so that certain religions can't impose their laws on nonbelievers. For example Sharia law (discussed earlier).

I reminded him that if anyone loses their rights, he will also lose his. One example is what happened in Germany. People started losing their rights very slowly.

Germany was bankrupt and needed money. The first thing they did was to start eliminating their own handicapped people who were draining their finances.

After the war started, the practice of eliminating the handicapped was taking a heavy toll on the service men's moral. The Generals argued, "Why fight, take the chance on losing a limb, and then return home to have the government eliminate you." Then laws were passed to start eliminating others, thus finding money to continue financing an expensive war. This is how people generally start losing their rights. The money for wars has to come from somewhere.   I told the driver that governments first attack the poor and defenseless. They are the canary in the mine. And if the canary dies we need to pay attention. Another example is what happened in the Salem witch trials. The poor were the first to be accused. The trials did not stop until the governor's wife was implicated. The same thing happened in France. All the signs were ignored and finally the king's head rolled.

"Better a poor and wise child, than an old foolish king."
— Ecclesiastes 4:13

You can't ignore the canary for very long, because we are all connected. One infected part will affect the rest.

In the end of these sometimes very passionate discussions, I found friends and gained their respect. A few times those same people would defend me against others that had not been there from the beginning of the conversations.

I feel that I am able to relate to many types of

people. Maybe it is because I came from a very large family, or maybe it is because I have found certain commonalities in all religions.

Most people, whether they are aware of it or not, believe in the same things. Sometimes it is simply a matter of semantics. For example: You can tell people to believe in God, universal consciousness, or string theory, it's all the same thing; or you can tell people to pray, cross their fingers, or think positive thoughts: Same thing. Every thought, whether we like it or not, is a prayer.

So what are your daily thoughts? What are you constantly praying for? Will the thing that you fear the most, befall you? (Job 3:25) Even the word 'pray' in legalese means to 'petition'.

There will always be some people that disagreed, but in the end walk away, agreeing to disagree. In my life time, only two people come to mind that walked away angry, and cussing at me. I remember one that was so upset at my beliefs; for a brief moment in time, I feared for my life.

I was at a Flying J, one of several truck stop chains across the United States, when a driver put his fist in my face, and threatened to hit me. God put it in my heart to use this as a teaching moment, so I moved closer and I looked straight into his eyes. "Make my day," I said calmly, "I will own you. You will lose your job, your wife and kids, and you will be up to your ears in debt, so make my day." Luckily it was enough to make him think. It was a teaching moment alright, "*I'm never going to do that again.*" I thought as I saw him walk away. I would like to think that in America it is still possible to express oneself without fear of physical threat.

I remember everyone laughing at my reactions one day in the driver's lounge: I heard on the news that a man shot another man because he owed him $10.00. I got caught up in the moment, stood up and yelled at the television, "I WOULD HAVE GIVEN YOU THE $10.00."

One time I had a serious conversation with a driver about birth control. He said he didn't believe in it. I asked him how many years he had been married?

He proudly told me, "I have been married ten years and have two boys ages ten and nine".

"So, you are telling me that you had sex only two times in ten years?" The room burst with laughing.

I remember one day when the driver's lounge was packed with about 25 to 30 drivers. We were having a heated conversation about abortion. The conversation would heat up and then cool down again. While in the heat of the conversation, I said, "Okay guys, I'll tell you what, the very next guy that comes in will decide it all." Everyone quieted down. We only had to wait a few seconds for the unsuspecting driver. A nice looking, tall, lanky, thin, black man with graying hair stepped in the room. Everyone turned to look up at him. He hesitated then slowly looked around the room. I suspect he first wondered what the heck he had walked into.

I was the first one to speak.

I asked him, "Hey mister, the guys and I were having a disagreement and we want you to settle it once and for all. Do you believe in abortion?"

He looked around the room once more, and then with an apologetic look said, "I'm sorry guys. I'm the wrong guy to ask. I have eighteen kids."

The whole room cracked up laughing. And the beautiful part about it is that everyone was satisfied.

I still hold strong opinions on the way people should live. However, it seems that the older I get, I hear myself talking about it less and less. I guess it is what motivated me to write beyond part II of this book. I learned, as a rule, most people are set in their ways.

People take several lifetimes to change and end their unnecessary suffering. Some, it seems are still working on pain they suffered several lifetimes ago.

The truck stop stories are a reminder of how strongly I held different opinions about everything.

There are three stories I would like to share. Each one taught me reasons why I felt I could no longer tell people how to live their lives. The first one is about Mahatma Gandhi, the second one is about a man people called Wild Bill, and the third one is an old parable from Asia called "The Farmer's Son".

Gandhi

One day a grandmother with her grandson in tow, goes to Mahatma Gandhi, and tells him:

"Mahatma Gandhi, tell my grandson to stop eating sugar".

Mahatma Gandhi looks at her, then the young child, and then tells her, "Come back in three weeks."

In three weeks the grandmother once again, comes back with her grandson, finds Gandhi and tells him. "Mahatma Gandhi, tell my grandson to stop eating sugar."

Mahatma Gandhi looks at the boy and says, "Stop eating sugar."

The grandmother looking confused and expecting more, asks Mahatma Gandhi, "Why didn't you tell him three weeks ago.

He tells her, "Three weeks ago, I had not yet stopped eating sugar."

***

The moral to this story is that I can't go around telling people what to do with their lives when I have not yet learned myself.

This brings me to the second story:

Wild Bill

"Wild Bill" was one of the inmates of the concentration camp, but obviously he hadn't been there long: His posture was erect, his eyes bright, his energy indefatigable.

Since he was fluent in English, French, German, and Russian, as well as Polish, he became a kind of unofficial camp translator.

Though "Wild Bill" worked fifteen and sixteen hours a day, he showed no signs of weariness. While the rest of us were drooping with fatigue, he seemed to gain strength.

When "Wild Bill's" own papers came before us one day, I was astonished to learn that he had been in Wuppertal since 1939! For six years he had lived on the same starvation diet, slept in the same airless and disease-ridden barracks as everyone else, but without the least physical or mental deterioration.

"Wild Bill" was our greatest asset, reasoning with the different groups, counseling forgiveness.

"It's not easy for some of them to forgive," I commented to him one day, "So many of them have lost members of their families."

He began slowly. The first words I had heard him speak about himself. "We lived in the Jewish section of Warsaw, my wife, our two daughters, and our three little boys. When the Germans reached our street they lined everyone against a wall and opened up with machine guns. I begged to be allowed to die with my family, but because I spoke German they put me in a work group. I had to decide right then," He continued, "Whether to let myself hate the soldiers who had done this. It was an easy decision, really. I was a lawyer. In my practice I had seen too often what hate could do to people's minds and bodies. Hate had just killed the six people who mattered most to me in the world. I decided right then, that I would spend the rest of my life — whether it was a few days or many years — loving every person I came in contact with."

This was the power that had kept a man well in the face of every privation.

***

There are several morals to this story: If you want to be healthy learn to love and forgive, but mostly to me, it is about how I should strive to be.

The third story is an Asian parable:

The Farmer's Son

One day in late summer, an old farmer was working in his field with his old sick horse. The farmer felt compassion for the horse and desired to lift it burden. He left his horse loose to go to the mountains and live out the rest of its life. Soon after, neighbors from the nearby village visited, offered their condolences, "What a shame, your only horse is gone. How unfortunate you are! You must be very sad. How will you live, work the land and prosper?"

The farmer replied: "Who knows? We shall see."

Two days later the old horse came back now rejuvenated after eating the wild grasses in the mountainsides. He came back with twelve new younger and healthy horses which followed the old horse into the corral. Word got out in the village of the old farmer's good fortune and it wasn't long before people stopped by to congratulate the farmer on his good luck.

"How fortunate you are!" They exclaimed, "You must be very happy!"

Again the farmer said, "Who knows? We shall see."

At daybreak on the next morning, the farmer's only son set off to attempt to train the new wild horses,

112

but the farmer's son was thrown to the ground and broke his leg. One by one the villagers arrived during the day to bemoan the farmer's latest misfortune. "Oh what a tragedy, your son won't be able to help you on your farm with a broken leg. You'll have to do all the work yourself. How will you survive? You must be very sad," They said.

The farmer answered. "Who knows? We shall see."

Several days later a war broke out. The Emperor's men arrived in the village demanding that young men come with them to be conscripted into the Emperor's army. As it happened the farmer's son was deemed unfit because of his broken leg. "What very good fortune you have!!" The villagers exclaimed as their own young sons were marched away. "You must be very happy."

"Who knows? We shall see!" replied the old farmer.

The old farmer's son's leg healed but was left with a slight limp. "Oh what bad luck," His neighbors said.

"Who knows? We shall see!" replied the old farmer.

As it turned out the other young village boys had died in the war and the old farmer and his son were the only able bodied men capable of working the village lands.

The old farmer became wealthy and was very generous to the villagers. They said. "Oh how fortunate we are, you must be very happy,"

To which the old farmer said, "Who knows? We shall see!"

***

The moral to this story is that no one really knows whether what happens throughout our life is good or bad. What seems bad at the time might be the one thing that can change life for the better.

Through the ages there have been many examples of the same thing, for example: In the town of Enterprise, Coffee Co., Alabama, they erected a monument to the boll weevil. Yet the boll weevil had ruined their cotton crops and totaled their town economically. The town endured great personal hardship to raise enough money to start again. So why would the town commemorate a bug that had caused them so much hardship? Because the boll weevil had ruined their crops, they were forced to diversify their crops. They prospered far beyond what they had in all the years before. They were so grateful that they erected a monument to the bug that had ruined their crops.

The great physicist Steven Hawking wrote a book that was made into a movie: A Brief History of Time.

Apparently, while at the university, Hawking loved dancing, and beer parties a bit too much. One morning, after one of those parties and shortly before his 21st birthday he fell down a stairway, lost his memory briefly, but recovered.

The doctors diagnosed Steven Hawking with Amyotrophic Lateral Sclerosis (ALS) or motor neural disease. They gave him two and a half years to live. The doctors told him that in the end of his life only his heart, lungs, and brain would function. He vowed that if reprieved, there were lots of worthwhile things he would do. He married, and was even fortunate to conceive a daughter.

Hawking admitted that if it had not been for ALS, he would not have been able to focus on solving some of the problems of why we or the universe exists.

It seems to me that Steven Hawking did not say there was no God, but was trying to prove that there was limits on when he created the universe.

I found it interesting that the scientists are coming to the same conclusions that are in the bible: Revelation 1:8.

A Jesuit Priest, Teilard de Chardin in the Phenomenon of Man (1955), in my opinion is basically saying the same thing. I think that the priest however, is saying it in metaphysical terms. He said that what appears to be chaos settles down and reaches an omega point where a new mind set or **consciousness** is born, and then the process repeats itself. I imagined it as several circles "standing" on top of each other. The points where they touch are the omega points. Each circle symbolizes consciousness and the omega point is an end to one conscious and beginning of another, a new birth. Basically expanding, coming together and then expanding into chaos before coming together in a new form.

And just to clarify: Consciousness is the state or condition of being conscious: Thus to be conscious is to be aware of one's own existence, and capable of more complex responses to the environment.

Conscience is to be at different levels of understanding: I have a clear conscience or I have a guilty conscience.

I think Hawking is saying the same thing that Teilard de Chardin had developed with his theory of the expanding universe, but in physical terms.

As for me, maybe the expanding universe is one of God's lung cells, and the expansions are of God simply taking a breath. What do I know? However, much like the theory of evolution, I like Teilard's idea that as humans, our consciousness is growing and evolving.

After all, we are children of a LIVING GOD.

"You are with the Spirit of God: The living God."
— II Corinthians 3:3

"You will be called a child of the living God."
— Romans 9:26

115

The Human Body

"And God blessed them (Adam and Eve)...Be fruitful, and multiply and replenish the earth and subdue it: and have dominion over...every living thing..." — Genesis 1:28

Procreation

I mentioned that in this world we are all born with an ego. And that the ego is trying to survive. It goes without saying that in this world is all about survival.

We procreate to insure the survival of the species. The fewer the resources the more people reproduce[17]. The more abundant the resources, the population tends to stabilize or slow down. As the population increases, it will produce another cycle.

Nature constantly tries to find ways to resolve the problem of resources. Predators, or disease in cases of heavy populations, and moving and bargaining, and technologies in others. There are many examples, it is enough to know that if the lower food chain goes extinct, the higher up on the food chain will also be affected. Like it or not it is all connected.

I see it like a giant amoeba[18] one arm getting longer and then getting smaller and so it goes, finding resources where it can.

Instincts

When we are born we are born with certain

---

[17] The study of sexology.

[18]These are one cell microorganisms. Also "amebas" which get their name from the Greek word amoibe, meaning "change," because their shapes are constantly changing.

116

instincts to help us survive. Our five senses and others such as sucking, and crying are there to help with our odds of survival.

Then there are automatic responses, such as adrenaline rushes which can trigger the flight or fight response. They can cause us to run, or paralyze us or numb us when we can't. We don't question where it is really a bear getting close, or if it is just a curtain blowing in the breeze. Our first instinct is for the body to increase its adrenaline levels. This is a precaution in case we have to make a run for it.

I know when I have to deal with a trying situation, it seems like it will last forever. But any condition is temporary.

"...these things must come to pass..."
— Matthew 24:6

The pain, can be physical or mental such as guilt. To little or too much can cause insensitivity or trauma.

Either way, all these instincts, much like our intuitions, or "gut" feelings, are there to help us survive.

When we are born, we bond with a caretaker. No one can live for long without some kind of love and care.

As we grow, if it is not with our loving parents, hopefully it is with good substitutes. This gets us by until we learn to think on our own. At some point we will realize that everyone is in the same boat, and that we are all have similar problems and are trying to figure things out just like us.

Growing is where our DNA, ancestral DNA, instincts, family, friends, TV, the internet, and other forms of communications come in. Our senses ultimately decide if what we are exposed to has a ring of truth. And we stumble through life. If we make a mistake, we keep trying until we get it right or prematurely die in the process.

Patterns

Balance, like predictability is vital for all life forms to exist. At any rate, recognizing these patterns should make our lives more predictable thus increase our odds for survival. This awareness will help us understand others and ourselves better.

Slowly through trial and error, I have started seeing patterns in what I filter or see. I start to see patterns in what I react to or how I react to them. I can change the pattern or keep it the same. They will show up in my actions, words, or deeds.

"By their fruits you will know them." — Matthew 7:20

When I look at God, I start recognizing patterns all around me. My eyes open up to new discoveries. From the beautifully engineered body to the world around me. From religion to physics, patterns are everywhere.

One pattern that has always fascinated me was the Fibonacci sequence and the Fibonacci spiral. Every time I put my hair up in a French braid,[19] I think of it. This pattern is found in seashells or even snails. The ratio between lines was discovered by Leonardo Fibonacci around the 1200's: If I add 1+1, I get 2; if I add the last numbers 1 and 2, I get 3; if I add the last numbers 2 and 3, I get five and so on. The sequence then becomes: 1, 1,2,3,5,8,13... This guy Fibonacci had way too much time on his hands. The sequence is found most anywhere and pertains to God's creations. It was supposedly used by Leonardo Da Vinci in all his painting including "The Last Supper". It is said that unconsciously it is how we define

---

[19] A French twist or bun that is in the form of a winding staircase. Popular in the 1950's

beauty. We look consciously or unconsciously for a relationship between the lines in our faces or bodies.

Pythagoras (586-506 BC) was another guy that saw God in patterns, in nature, and in numbers.

The Masons or Freemasons is the largest and oldest fraternal philanthropic organization in the world. Their symbol was what rousted my curiosity. It is square (right angled ruler), a compass for drawing circles, and a G in the middle. Every once in a while I will see the symbol on License plates.

The Masons see God as the "Great Architect." And apparently they embraced Pythagoras.

Pythagoras is attributed to being the first one to say, "Eureka". He yelled out "Eureka" when he became excited that he had finally discovered the answer to a problem that had baffled scientists for years. Originally the Pythagoras problem was called "The 47th problem of Euclid."

He discovered that in every right angle triangle, the square of the hypotenuse (the line opposite to the one that forms a right angle with it) is equal to the sum of the squares to the other side. For example: If I take the square root of an angle in which one side is 6 inches and the other 8 inches and add them up, I get the distance of the 3rd side. The equation looks something like this:

$$36" + 64" = 100$$
$$6" \times 6" = 36"$$
$$8" \times 8" = 64"$$

What is interesting about this problem is that with it we can find the distances from anywhere to anywhere and throughout the galaxy. Isn't that awesome? For centuries the problem had baffled men: Then "Eureka!"

There is no greater satisfaction then when I am

trying to teach somebody something, and they get their "Eureka" moment. It is also called the "aha"moment". It is the moment when the mind finally gets it. It is that moment when I know that I know. I own it, and I know that no one can take it away from me. It is not tangible and no one can steal it.

Laws

"Laws are good if used lawfully." — I Titus 1:8

When patterns are consistent and or when we want to get the same results each time, they (lawmakers, scientists and others), set them up as laws.

I mentioned earlier that we only really need one Commandment. The other nine commandments are there for our protection.

If we hope to survive, we have to respect the rights of others. If we don't respect the rights of others, then we want them to respect ours. We create laws to that end. We strive to enforce these law to protect ourselves. Laws such as the Ten Commandments are created and enforced for our protection.

I try to remember: If someone loses his rights they're coming after me next.

Civil disobedience does not mean anarchy. It means you try to create change through nonviolent methods. While we live in a society, like it or not, you will have to obey its laws. For instance, the abortion issue has been going on in America since the early 1900's. (The little Blue Book: Aspects of Birth Control, written in 1910 by Adolphus Knopf). Granted, some changes take longer than others.

I have touched on some of the laws of nature throughout the book I want to expand my thoughts about these laws in this section.

For example, the body and the mind have to

adhere to certain laws: The law of gravity for instance. I don't have to be a rocket scientist to figure out that as we age we shrink. If I don't like this law, I could exercise and hope science and technology will prevail. Until then, I have to live with it.

I once had an argument about climate change years back. I finally told the driver, that there was only one formula he had to remember:

"More people, more shit,[20] more heat."[21]

"Do not hurt the earth, sea, or trees." — Revelation 7:3

Another law is the law of attraction.

This is where we always seem to go back to what is familiar and the reason why it is so difficult for people to change. I think this is where Adam meets Eve. Similarities attract for a reason. One might argue that Adam and Eve had gender differences. They were, however, the same species. It's about survival. To me the law of attraction and its opposite (repulsion) have more to do with love and fear.

Similarities create love. Differences that can't be overcome create fear. Similarities have more predictability. Differences at first sight, not so much.

There are many reasons why we fear what is different:

1. We want to see similarities so we can know what is expected of us. If things are different we get confused or feel uncomfortable. We are out of our element.

2. We want to fight to protect our beliefs, and principles

---

[20] Fertilizer, junk, technologies, or trash.
[21] When things breakdown, it causes chemical changes that create heat.

even if they have become outdated. We feel threatened by anything that will change them.

3. We resist change because it feels unpredictable and this threatens our survival.

This law exists in all animal life. Knowing things ahead of time certainly helps us to survive. The more we see similarities between ourselves and others, the better the predictability and the better our chances for survival.

Years ago one of my professors said that an average man can throw a stone 300 feet. How that was determined is a mystery to me. And even why I would remember the "300 feet". However, I also remember him saying that it was no coincidence that a smile or a perceived threat in the form of a facial expression, can also be recognized at the same distance. I don't remember what point he was trying to make. My guess is that we should smile more often so we can increase our chances for survival. By smiling, we are signaling or sending out a social message, "See, *I am smiling, therefore I am not a threat.*" or on the other hand, "*I'm an idiot, keep away from me.*" You can interpret the smile anyway you want.

I think at the time I heard this lesson, I was detracted by my thoughts of hoping the person with the menacing look had 20 20 vision.

Eye glasses aside, perceived differences are fear based, therefore a threat to another person's survival.

This learned predictability protects us with the ability to read future abuse by reading facial cues. This is the same as a weather forecast that warns us of a tornado. The mind will filter through our experiences, once we perceive objects or situations as threats.

Children are less fearful because they have no previous experiences as references.

"Become as little children..." — Matthew 18:3

Life needs balance in order to survive. Too much of a good thing or too much of a bad thing can kill us. For instance, if I start killing everything that is different from myself, several things could result: Extreme isolation can also kill me; I might use up valuable resources (people) that could aid in my survival; or this might cause others be so fearful of me that I become a threat and people start to come after me.

"The eye cannot say to the hand I have no need of you." — I Corinthians 12:21

When I googled 'the law of kind,' all I could find was 'the law of kindness.' Maybe I expanded the law of attraction in a moment of inspiration. However, they are similar. I started noticing a pattern. Everything produces after its own kind: Humans produce humans, cats produce cats, dogs produce dogs, and birds produce birds. And it keeps producing after its own kind and keeps going unless you manipulate it, stop it, or generally change it by some physical means. An example would be when a donkey is mated with a horse to produce a sterile mule. This works in the physical as well as in the mental realm. When I read Mark 4:25, I didn't think it was fair. However when I made the connection the following verses made sense:

"To him that has: To him it will be given." — Mark 4:25

"What you treasure, there will your heart be also." — Mt. 6:21

Hate produces hate, love produces love, and greed produces greed, etc., unless it is stopped by: a revelation, an inspiration, a trauma, or a catastrophe. I will continue to create love or hate in my life. It will always be my choice to repent or continue the same course. A friend once said, "A drunken horse thief that stops drinking liquor, remains a horse thief." Maybe that's where the old saying comes from: Two wrongs don't make a right.

Respect for others also works in economics.

John Nash expanded on John Adams original law of economics. John Adam's law stated that society benefited, when "an individual's ambition helps everyone if it basically serves the common good."

For years this was the common misconception.

John Nash argued and proved scientifically in his law of governing dynamics that everyone doing for himself and **also for the group,** improved on John Adam's law of economics. This keeps everyone from blocking each other.

This law won John Nash a Noble prize in 1994. What I believe John Nash was saying was that if I consider and respect others, it's better for everybody.

My friend Joe Blair put it this way, "If my wife is happy and my kids are happy, then I'm happy."

In the meantime we are frustrated children all in the same boat and we are all trying to figure why we are here on planet earth. We all long for God's magic love. It seems we search everywhere except inside of ourselves.

In order to get away from my survival mode mentality, I have to know some of the pitfalls.

"So that evil does not overtake you, learn it devices."
— II Corinthians 2:11

"Give me an understanding heart to discern between good and evil." — II Kings 3:9

Drugs

People are constantly being bombarded with advertisements about the body.

Consumers pay billions to sell us things that promise to make us look good, feel good, and claim to be healthy for us. Most people don't even question if what they see in advertisements is just wishful thinking.

I think some companies go too far. We are bombarded with so many advertisements that I am surprised any advertiser can still make money. But maybe what P. T. Barnum is attributed to saying is true: "There is a sucker born every minute."

Advertisers will tell us that in order for us to be financially, emotionally and physically secure, we need to buy their products. They use fear, much like our parents did, in order to illustrate that the fear is real and we should pay attention to them.

The most distressing ads are the ones that target children. If you pay close attention they are riddled with very bad values such as stealing, cheating, or violence. It never ceases to amaze me what consumers will fall for. I think consumers, out of sheer desperation, will try just about anything. If you pay close attention, the company's own ads will also reveal its true character. And while you are at it, pay close attention to the "small print."

I was in a truck stop lounge watching television one night. During one of the commercials, I told everyone there to pay close attention to what one part of the commercial said. I thought everyone would laugh when they heard it. I was expecting laughter, when suddenly, one lady gave an audible gasp and said, "Oh my God! I was thinking of getting some of that!"

The commercial was announcing some of the negative side effects of their product: Sexual and gambling addictions. It was then that I realized that people don't pay attention to the "small print."

I am grateful that in the United States the pharmaceutical companies, at the very least, have to disclose these sometimes lethal side effects.

I crack up every time I see the advertisements on the television. They are so teeny tiny that you need a microscope to read them. Recently, I saw an ad that was for a symptom that a drug caused by the previous symptom, that had caused the previous symptom. All I could do was shake my head in disbelief.

One would think a person would become suspicious. Especially when, on one station, the advertisers are looking for people for a class action law suit that had bad reactions or died to the same drug they are selling on another channel.

Medicines are for short term use. You don't take medicines to feel good, you take them so you can get better. The medicines are a God sent. However their use is to give the body a chance to repair itself. Too much of a good thing can cause more harm. If you don't believe me, just ask anyone that is in rehab for drug addiction. Also, you might consider that stress and/or pain is a good thing because it is trying to tell you something? I know from personal experience that my pain sometimes has to become so unbearable before I do something about it. The bottom line is that my body is trying to communicate something to me.

I once had a tooth pulled and the doctor prescribed a pain pill (Lora-tab) to reduce the pain. The pain immediately went away. In fact it worked so well I became frightened that I would get addicted. I crushed them up and threw them away so I wouldn't get tempted. Every time I hear of housewives getting addicted to pain pills I think about it. Don't get me wrong, if the pain had been worse I probably would have kept them. But only until the pain got better. The point I am trying to make here is that you have to use common sense. Only you, can know you. Having worked at Loma Linda

Medical Center for a short time, I have seen firsthand the amazing things medicine can do. I don't want to minimize the great work that medicines or that doctors can do. I am only suggesting that before we put anything into our bodies: Get all the facts!

Stress

I try to live within my means not only in money, but also time, and energy. I try to question what is actually making me sick.

I reduce the stress to my body by being brutally honest and stop trying to be like everyone else. This is not easy. The bible specifically tells us not to compare ourselves to others.

"...Comparing ourselves among ourselves, is not wise."
—II Corinthians 10:12

As often as possible, I try to remove myself from any situation that is causing me pain.

After I retired from truck driving, I remember noticing that on a normal trip to the grocery store how stressed out I was.

"*Calm down. No one is going to hurt you.*" I kept saying to myself.

I laughed out loud; remembering all the near misses in bad weather.

For the first time I noticed my hands and how tightly they held the steering wheel. Even when I knew that I was not going to be late, or that I was in no immediate physical danger, my body would tighten up.

This physical reaction was not just with driving, I noticed when I was talking on the phone or talking with people, and well, with just everything. Even when I was doing something I liked, I was afraid I should be doing something else. I was noticing this more and more.

Oh my how old habits die hard!

This is known as neurotic anxiety. It can be caused by something we think is going to happen (objective anxiety) or something that is actually happening (realistic anxiety). I have to remind myself that it took years to develop these reactions to this objective anxiety; I was not going to get rid of these reactions in just one day. I decided not to make myself feel worse by feeling guilty when I caught myself getting tense.

The most enjoyable thing about retirement is that it is the time for true adult education (self-discovery), beyond the stars not just the village lights. To live in the moment and to be able to examine it.

I know that if I make a mistake, and everyone makes one, I can correct it. If I am writing something with a pencil and make a mistake, I can take an eraser and rub it out. Although traces might be left behind, for the most part, errors can be generally overlooked. If I make a mistake when I am creating something, it might cost a little more but it too can be corrected. And my health is worth so much more than the tiny pennies I can save worrying about it.

Correcting mistakes, also applies to my body. It will begin repairing tissue. This is one of my favorite verses on the subject:

"I (God) took your sin: made it as dust, and then cast it into a brook." — Deuteronomy 9:21

Even though, trace amounts are there, the troublesome part is no longer around.

Health Insurance

I know of people that are stressed out because they can't afford to pay the hundreds of dollars they pay each month on health insurance. You'd think that people would wise up and find a way to reduce the stress by learning to live within their means. What did people do years ago before there was health insurance? At the very least don't make yourself sick because of it. And please vote on health reform! Insurance companies are like teenagers, they are not going to give up billions just because we want them to.

If nothing else, less insurance means less access to drugs that are often experimental. It also means we have to take more responsibility for our overall health.

Old Age

There are so many things to blame my problems on. These problems can in turn, affect my body. Old age is a big one.

I remember one day, I was waiting in line behind a lady and her husband, at Walmart. I was in an especially happy mood.

The woman's husband noticed my bubbly excitement, "My but you seem happy today." He commented.

"Yes, today is my birthday."

"Well happy birthday," He said.

After I thanked him, his wife said, "You won't be so happy when you get my age."

"How old are you?" I asked, wondering how old I had to get before things went downhill.

"I'm forty years old." She emphasized 40 years as if she had been in a war for that long.

"Well uh," I said, with relief, "I'm fifty five."

I probably insulted her, but maybe it was something that she needed to hear. After that day, I started noticing more, "walking zombies."

I know when I hear about a person that is 100 years old that finished a foot race, I get encouraged. Hulda Crooks at 91 climbed Mount Fuji beating the old record holder who was 90. I keep a file on these amazing people. Myrtle Youngberg, lived to be 101 and was an active judge in her mid-80's. She was admitted to the Kansas Bar in 1916, four years before women won the right to vote! I heard in the news yesterday that a women 102 went skydiving. There's hope for me yet!

"...Remove sorrow from your heart...childhood and youth are vanity." — Ecclesiastes 11:10

In wealthier countries, a great deal of value is placed on remaining youthful, especially when it pertains to physical appearances. Age does not necessarily mean you are ready for a retirement home. At the very least, if you manage to stay reasonable healthy, you can become a valuable babysitter. Have something to do every day and put God (others) first and the body won't be such a burden.

A Word to the Wise

We need to listen to what our body is saying.

To be responsible to one's self and to have a healthy respect for your body is a far better and painless way to live. This is a hard lesson to learn. Even Saint Francis of Assisi in later years regretted the unnecessary damage he did to his body. The Reluctant Saint by Donald Spoto is the most comprehensive and detailed that I have read. The Life of Saint Francis of Assisi *by Reynolds, E.E.,* is one that I cherish. It is one of a series of books on the saints, written by several authors, but all published by Saint Mary's Press in Winona, Minnesota. All ten were beautifully illustrated by my very talented friend, Elaine Kohner.

I take care of my body as much as I can by watching and listening to it and going to the source, my Spirit.

People will listen to the sounds their cars make, yet will not listen to what their bodies are telling them. Treat your body with as much respect as you would an antique Corvette.

I remember my car. It was around 1971 when I purchased "George". George was a 1963 Chevy Impala with electric windows and seats. I loved it because the seats could recline all the way back and make a bed.

George was stolen a total of five times. I think this was because it would start without a key.

The first time George got stolen, my daughter walked in and asked, "Where's George mom?"

While the officer kept writing out the report, Julie kept expressing her sad concern about "George". Finally, it seemed that the policeman could not contain himself and asked, "Whose George?"

After I bought George, my little girl asked me, "What's his name mamma?"

"Julie it's a car."

"But it has to have a name. It's our friend."

A short time afterwards we went on a trip to Texas. As we crossed the border, I got excited. I had wanted to make the trip for such a long time. Now here we were. I had made it back to the state where I was born. I think the conversation with my daughter was in the back of mind, because as we crossed the Texas border, without thinking about it, I slapped the dash board and yelled out, "Way to go, George!"

That's how George got its name. I must have subconsciously read the tag "Body by George Fischer" on the floor board. George Fisher, ironically, was the name of a horse jockey and dear friend.

I later realized that by naming the car I would pay more attention to what it was trying to tell me and make repairs in a timelier manner.

George later became the hand me down car to my brother Ramon's kids. George lived out his remaining years at the family farm. From time to time his name is fondly mentioned.

When a part of my body is bothering me, I try to treat it like I would a car. If I do not know what's going on with my body, I ask God (the mechanic) to reveal its source.

Not everything is going to go perfect. I still have a lot to learn and neither is each day going to be a spectacular miracle. I now take so much pleasure in such little things. I have personally experienced God's "magic" and miraculous healing. But I also know, from many years of trial and error, that how I handle a problem can determine unnecessary pain. If I remove the immediate stress, the body unlike a car will find creative ways to survive. The forgetting or repeating the same mistake will be totally up to me.

I once heard that different parts of the body will repair themselves. Especially the liver and the lungs. Yet, I also marvel at what Steven Hawking accomplished with just his heart, lungs and brain.

I am reminded of a book called The Violinist's Thumb by Sam Kean. This book has so many remarkable stories. I would strongly urge everyone to read this book. It is an example of God's amazing handiwork.

According to this book and what I gleaned from the internet, Mr. Yamaguchi was the only double victim recognized from the Hiroshima and Nagasaki atomic bombs. He somehow miraculously survived the bomb dropped in Hiroshima, managed to get to his wife in Nagasaki where he also survived that bomb. Mr. Tsutomu Yamaguchi died in 2010, he was 93. I think something similar happened to our former President Jimmy Carter. He saved millions of lives by exposing himself to radiation while in the Navy.

The point I am trying to make here, is how our body can miraculously repair itself. Even our DNA finds a way of recopying itself.

It seemed like most of my life, I was fighting

everything. I was afraid of what people would think, I was afraid of being lazy, I was afraid I wasn't doing enough. All this fear and I was not conscious of it, but it took a toll on my body. After I retired I had more time to reflect, and once I realized it, I could start doing something about it. This time the fight was different: I started listening very closely to my body, but closer to my Spirit. Deuteronomy 30:19 says the same thing. We choose between life and death. Our thoughts about what we were taught; experience; and perceive, will determine our overall health. Our thoughts need to be reexamined.

The Temple

In I Corinthians we are told that the body is the temple of the Spirit within:

"Don't you know that your body is the temple of the Holy Spirit which is in you, which you have of God, and you are not your own?" — I Corinthians 6:19

I think we always forget the last part: "...you are not your own." Have you ever rented anything and brought it back damaged? Wow, it would have been cheaper if you had bought it!

The bible continually tells us (adnauseam) that we are not a body but a Spirit. I think the mistake that we make is in trying to eliminate the Spirit at the expense of the body, and vice versa.

For example Buddha, at the beginning of his awakening, had to be rescued by his friends. He ignored his body completely, and almost died. Saint Francis of Assisi, according to The Reluctant Saint was very hard on his body.

My argument here is that maybe we are trying to separate ourselves from God. This is much the same as when we try to separate ourselves from others: The body and the Spirit are one. It's all connected.

"You are also built as a house for God through His Spirit."
— Ephesians 2:22

"The body without Spirit is dead." — James 2:26

Love God with all your heart and you take care of all of it: The body, the soul, and the mind. Maybe this is why it is repeated several times.

"Love God with all your heart and soul."
— Deuteronomy 11:13

"Love God with all your heart, soul, and strength."
— Mark 12:30

Bhakta yoga teaches that people tend to become what they love. Christianity teaches the same with their love of their Savior Jesus. Some religions want to teach you to adore God. Others strive to have you become one with God. Yet it is not easy to love God above all.

This world clamors for our affection. Our family, work, friends, hobbies and our everyday existence require our body's attention. So where do we draw the line, between God and the world? We don't. We come to the realization of God very gradually. Like the habits you try to gain every day with the card system I introduced. Little by little you start building the "muscles". Like the athlete competing for the Olympics. At first we start out competing against others, but in the end we come to realize we is competing against our individual selves. At first we want to be loved by others, but in the end we come to realize that Love never left.

One day we will all come to know that:

- God is everywhere yet I worship Him here. (Wherever 'here' is.)
- God is without form yet I worship Him in these forms. (Whatever form 'it' is.)
- God needs no praise yet I will continue to praise Him. (Why? Because I love Him.)

Very slowly we will come to understand that the Spirit is to be experienced and this experience will become a habit and then hopefully it will become a way of life.

The mistake as to what's important in this world is a common and understandable mistake, after all:

"Vanity of vanities; all is vanity." Ecclesiastes 1:2

There is nothing wrong with taking care of the body. Eat right; exercise; take precautions to be safe; be careful with toxins etc. We have all heard this fine advice all our lives from our parents, teachers, and friends. I try to live by this advice as much as possible. The problem is I get so carried away with my body that I forget the Spirit.

Oftentimes it is just plain common sense: Which is what the bible has been saying for centuries.

"May you be ever seeing never perceiving." — Mark 4:12

Sometimes things would change merely by changing our perception or our attitude: The mind (brain) affects the body. Read Norman Cousin's book, Anatomy of an Illness. The only thing that was able to cure him of an incurable illness was laughing.

You never hear of a doctor prescribing: Laugh and sing a song at least once a day. Feeling we have to control everyone and everything; not enough respect for others; or not listening to our own thoughts will take a toll on the body. By simply being kinder and seeing things from the other person's point of view, will most certainly improve our lives.

So many people over the centuries have been saying the same things. In fact I think there is so much repetition that people would laugh out loud when they become aware. I think you would be pleasantly surprised that the bibles have been saying the same thing for centuries. And if we stop to listen, maybe just maybe, our overall health would improve. The bibles can certainly serve as a valuable tool.

These are just a few of the things the bibles have been saying for centuries. Love and respect others: If not for the sake of others, we have to do it for ourselves. It's called survival! It is about taking care of the body.

The Mind

What exactly is the mind? We certainly talk an awful lot about it. "I've lost my mind;" "They are out of their minds;" or "It has a mind of its own, etc." The dictionary[22] tells us that the mind is:

1. The human consciousness that originates in the brain...
2. The totality of conscious and unconscious processes...that directs the mental...behavior of a sentient organism.

The dictionary tells us that a sentient organism is:

1. Having some perception; conscious.
2. (The sentient organism) is the mind.

These definitions did not come easily. Man has been in search of what mind is for a long time.

---

[22] I used The American Heritage Dictionary of the English Language (1969).

Dictionary definitions are not very useful. In the definition above the mind is the sentient organism which is mind. Basically it is saying that the mind is the mind.

Immanuel Kant found that he could not even invent a precise word for the matrix. Scientists and philosophers have tried to identify man's ability to be conscious of self, our place in the planet and in time.

Aristotle argued that the mind existed independently of the body. Rene Descartes in 1629 realized that it was up to him: I think (the mind), therefore I am (the body).

God put it this way:

"I AM THAT I AM... (tell them) that I AM has sent me."
— Exodus 3:14

I think this is a way of giving us freewill to make our own decisions: I am weak; I am strong; I am beautiful, I am ugly; I am happy, I am sad...we decide. I think that the mind is like God because it is comprised of many parts (us) doing so many things at the same time. I like to think of it as a sorting area between the body and the ego. The area between the conscious and unconscious decisions. In the same way that the majority of the people will ultimately decide how things are governed.

The housing for the Spirit is the body. If the body is not working right, the mind which makes many of the decisions, can get crazy. For example: In the study of abnormal psychology, there are many examples of how reality can go amok. Besides my text books, in the book, The Man Who Mistook His Wife for a Hat, by Oliver Sacks, there are several examples of clinical cases in which perception can sometimes vary from the normal. This helps me when I came across people that I feel are incapable of being reasonable.

Some people "Just don't get it!"

I no longer beat myself over the head with it.

That's just the way it is. I go my way, hoping, that in this lifetime they will outgrow their "condition".

I smile when I remember that I once dealt with the similar "condition". Well-meaning people tried to advise me, yet, I wasn't ready either.

Over the years people tried to get through to me to what, to them, seemed so obvious. Some were more than willing to tell me what was wrong with my life and that I was doing it to myself. I did not believe them: Mostly because I was in so much pain. But sometimes the advice was from a person whose life, I felt, was in a worse mess than my own. As long as they don't do anything to physically harm me or others, I turn it over to Spirit.

The mind serves as a translator for what we see. But sometimes one's mind also has ulterior motives. It is very important that a person translate or accurately perceive what is happening. A good translator is one that you trust will give you actuate information.

I make this point with this story: There was once a bandit from Mexico. The bandit kept crossing the border and robbing banks in the United States and after each bank robbery he would return to Mexico. This went on for years. Finally the United States decided they had had enough. They found out that he was in a "cantina" (beer joint) just across the Mexican border. They were able to cross into Mexico and capture him.

"Tell us where you buried the gold, or we will hang you," They threatened.

He timidly said, "No speakit th' English,"

They asked for a translator, to which the bartender volunteered. The translator told him why he was being held. The bandit thinking the gold might save his life, said, "I buried it out back. Dig 10 paces east from the old tree."

The translator then said, "He said you might as

well hang him, he will never tell you."

If the translator is faulty, the reality will also get distorted.

Some are born with wiring that can be seen as a handicap, yet others cause damage to themselves. it would behoove us not to do anything that would intentionally cause the mind any physical harm. When I realized marijuana was causing short term memory loss, I stopped taking it and started listening to my body.

Perception comes primarily from our senses, our minds then translates the vast amount of information.

I have to smile when I remember my daughter when at the age of about four: She said, "Oh mamma, you have such pretty feet."

It made me look down at my feet. I said, "Julie they aren't that pretty."

"Oh, mamma, they have such pretty colors: blue, yellow, red, and purple..."

I was doing okay until she started with the colors. This is before I realized she was commenting on the small varicose veins on my ankle.

Perception is everything!

Not everyone sees the flaws in our body, or looks at us in the same way as we do. Remember these worn out sayings: "Love is blind" and "Beauty is in the eye of the Beholder." As far as I'm concerned, beauty can be two "ugly" people falling in love. There is a difference however, between being "ugly" and personal hygiene. In psychology 101 we learn that bad personal hygiene is an indication of mental illness. I think we have to be careful with any value judgments. Everything comes in degrees. And not everything is what it appears.

Since beauty is in the eye of the beholder I think it is more important on how we act on our thoughts.

"By their fruits you will know them." — Matthew 7:20

Ultimately, we are all children of God: Whether we believe it or not, it is totally up to us.

I see so many people doing drugs, legal and illegal. People hurt their bodies by over exercising or under exercising. They over eat or under eat. Some are obsessively concerned with their numbers, cholesterol and such. I know from personal experience that what is best is often such a battle. I now realize it is none of my business what people do with their bodies. Besides everybody's body is different. It is best they find out for themselves. They know when something is wrong, and they also know when it is time to do something about it.

I try to mind my own business and listen to my Spirit, and my body. As you can well imagine, I have enough problems listening to myself. I do try to listen to what everyone is telling me and try to measure it. When a person needs a teacher, one will appear. Only time will tell when I am ready to hear:

"Heed what you hear and measure it". — Mark 4:24

"I that have ears will listen to the Spirit."
— Revelation 2:29

"Do what is in your heart for God is with you."
— II Samuel 7:3

"Search the heart and you will know the mind of the Spirit." — Romans 8:27

the mind is such a wonderful engineering marvel. It is constantly creating, searching, finding a better way to survive. It is both curious and creative. It can be mature and deal with pain properly or stick to what it knows and acquire more pain and create blind spots in order to deal with the pain. But it always moves forward and always strives to mature.

What is maturity? I think that it is being fully conscious or awake. That's the end goal, however maturity happens in degrees. Most people agree on these characteristics:

1. A mature person is guided by long range goals not immediate desires. They are able, without frustration, to accept authority, and know the limits.

2. A mature person accepts people as they are; not judging them for what he thinks they ought to be. They love and don't expect anything return.

3. A mature person grows out of frustrations and hardships. He does not need to create a fantasy world, and accepts the challenges of everyday life.

What do you desire? What are your concerns? What does your mind concentrate on? But more importantly, are your thoughts disciplined? Remember how this all started: Philippians 4:8 "Whatever things are good... think on these things."

So often we take our eyes off what we really want. In this modern world we often want to 'attend to' too many things at once. This is sometimes called, "Spreading ourselves too thin" or, "Having too many irons in the fire."

When we try to do too many things at once, we have less energy to concentrate on one thing. Another term commonly used for such a person is a "scattered-brain." We need to stay focused.

"Be thoughtful of where you go, and set your course."
— Proverbs 4:26

I always felt that that was what this bible verse

was trying to teach:

"The light of the body is the eye: therefore when your eye is single, your whole body also is full of light."
—Luke 11:34

I see it as a laser beam concentrated on a single purpose. Unfortunately, we often want to be everything to everybody and be everywhere at the same time. We need to be responsible for ourselves and not compare ourselves to others.

"Why behold the mote in your brother's eye, but consider not the beam that is in your own eye?"
— Matthew 7:3

We need to learn to live within our means in respect to money, time and energy. There is 24 hour in a day for everyone, yet we all have different energy levels as well as strengths and talents.

Just like the cells in our body: I need to be aware of my limits. (A heart cell is in the heart, the lung cell is in the lung, etc.)

Unfortunately, when we fail the expectations of other people we often feel guilty. I call them the "should do" tapes. I realized this in a conversation I was having with one of my sisters. While she was talking, I was counting. Around the number seventeen, she finally got irritated enough to ask me, "Why are counting?"

I am counting all the times you said, "You should do this. You should do that. Don't do this. And don't do that." I'm sure that she did it out of her concern for me.

She meant well.

We all do this without realizing it. These mental tapes could have originated from any situation, but our mind chose to hold on to them.

The mind is the culprit.

Sometimes people do not know that the information is good for some situations and bad for others so we generalize good advice and try to apply it to too many areas. Remember:

—The more you understand an idea the harder it will be to generalize it.
—The more generalized the idea is, the harder it will be to understand that it is situation specific: Good in one thing and bad in another.

Often our biggest fight in the mind is against guilt. I know guilt can hold so many people spiritually captive. Guilt is something that you have not yet erased because you still feel responsible for the wrong that has occurred.

Someone once told me that he felt guilty about everything, and that sometimes he even felt guilty about being alive. This is a huge amount of responsibility to bear. I think there are many people walking around that are held down with the heavy burden of guilt.

Even Mother Theresa was tormented with guilt feelings. She wrote to a friend expressing her anguish and guilt, thinking she could have done more. This was nicely explained in the movie The Letters. Somehow, I think all of us; never feel like we are quite good enough. As long as we are in a physical body, fully coming to terms with life physically and mentally will oftentimes be difficult. Take baby steps.

I always thought the following verse came from the bible. I often paraphrase, so this is probably why I was unable to find it. I have used it so much over the years. Whose knows maybe I originated it?

"Do the best you can and then stand."

I try to listen to my heart and respond accordingly.

"I do the very best I can, I mean to keep going. If the end brings me out all right, then what is said against me won't matter. If I'm wrong, ten angels swearing I was right won't make a difference." — Abraham Lincoln

To me the following verse means almost the same thing: The past is done. Don't worry about it.

"Which of you by taking thought can add one cubit unto his stature?" — Matthew 6:27

It is a good idea, however, to be aware of what is happening in our minds.

In other words, I try to put my mind to the best possible use.

The hammer cannot only pound in nails, but its claw can pull them out. Then if you get better you can place a board under the claw to get torque or leverage.

When you buy a computer find out what it can do besides playing cards otherwise it's an expensive deck of cards.

The bottom line is that it is good idea to be aware of what the mind is used for, know how to use it properly and don't leave it where will rust.

One of the main functions of the mind is to act as a filter for the overload of information. Perception is selection, and for the most part this filtering is good.

Perception is done consciously, and other times it is done unconsciously. Some filtering are habits, some filtering is based on what we prefer. When we are in doubt or get confused, we go back to what is familiar. We want things to be predictable. There is less confusion there. This is why it is hard to break addictions.[23]

This is also a reason why it is hard for people to change their opinions on things. These patterns continue until a sudden shift occurs, for whatever reason, a trauma etc., and we are forced to choose another course.

I will go into more of my beliefs on this, in the section I called <u>The Evil Men Do</u>. In the meantime I want to stay with how to use the mind best.

There are two important days in my life: The day I was born and the day I find out why. To find out why I was born, many small trips in my Spiritual journey are necessary. I will also need some good, well-kept tools (i.e. the mind) for my journey.

The mind will certainly help to make it easier to navigate through life's pitfalls, keep my life less complicated, more manageable, and hopefully more enjoyable.

Tools for Life's Journey

In my spiritual journey, I learned that my mind will need: A good map; I will need to stay focused; and I will need motivation or drive to keep going.

A good map:
Maps help with predictability; therefore they are handy survival tools.

Maps in whatever form they take are used mostly for the purpose of finding or giving information about a person, place, or thing.

For example, a diagram is used to map out the

---

[23] In this case I am referring to the cerebral cortex (the gray matter on the outer layer of the brain responsible for higher nervous functions) I like to call it the translator. A good translator attempts to translate word for word, but also understands that it is mainly about what the person is actually trying to say that matters.

areas of the human body. This is much the same way an atlas or globes are maps used to locate a particular place, or even to locate star systems.   Books are special types of maps. Books can tell us how things work, how we should live, but mostly they relate a person's experience and what worked or didn't work for them.   It was basically the same for most of us. We all had to learn how to walk, talk, and conform in order to get along with others.

The best map we can have in the beginning of our lives, is the map that teaches us right from wrong.

There are all kinds of maps, but all maps come from experience.

Whether we like it or not, we have all been challenged with the ups and downs of life. It makes us interesting. These experiences or what I like to call maps, become templates for future mapping, later some maps become out dated.

We started out with some sort of parent, or surrogate. We learned to navigate the world around us from these primary caregivers. Our world continues to expand and include people in our immediate vicinity.

I think of these as "maps" we can hear, feel and touch. If you live in an electronic world, you have the advantage of movies and plays. Besides movies we also learn from mentors and teachers. I like to think of these as GPS coordinates because they are mostly visual. You know that arrow in the universe that says, "You are here." Our mind is there to tell us which direction is best. When I know the directions are wrong. I don't go there. I also don't pick up a map of China, when I want to go to Ireland.

My point is: If the road is not there, and you have a gut feeling that it is not, but someone tells you it is. Maybe it isn't?

For example, I remember one time, it cost me

$150.00: I was driving a forklift at the time and was loading a truck. The door was not all the way up.

My boss kept yelling at me to go. I kept yelling that it would not clear. He kept insisting I go. I kept yelling that it would not clear.

Finally I reasoned that his view was different than mine, and since he was the boss, I went.

I heard a loud "crunch", then heard him say, "I guess you bought a door."

What I should have done, is gotten off the forklift and said, "You do it." In the long run, it was a valuable lesson.

Some of us were fortunate enough to have access to people we will never see. I am referring to the hundreds of people who write books. One bible teaches us "The Golden Rule", or basically to treat others as we want to be treated. Another bible teaches us "To do what we have to do..." While yet another bible teaches us to "...be still to know God." They all seem to want us to learn self-discipline; to be responsible for ourselves; and to live with respect for God and others.

The United States Constitution, is a living document, a guide/map to treat people "...with justice for all." It tells us that no matter what our religion, or status in the community: We have a right to fair and equal treatment.

Encyclopedias show us all the beauty in our planet; the different species of animals and insects, and vast amounts of accumulated knowledge. Unfortunately, if we are not careful, we can easily get lost or sidetracked. If you want to go somewhere it helps if you remain focused.

Stay focused:

In order to stay focused we need a good mind. Ironically, I think staying focused becomes easier as we get older.[24] I guess because now my life depends on it. I lost my keys several times when I was young. Bad memory has nothing to do with the aging process. Forgetfulness is not due to old age. I had to climb through windows several times when I was young. Frankly, I think forgetfulness has more to do with stress than anything else. I do know, that oftentimes, when I am stressed I don't pay as much attention to what I am doing. When I was younger I could do 3 or 4 things at the same time. Although, I wonder if doing too many things at the same time, was ever a good idea. Something will always suffer. Maybe I'm just getting wiser? (*She said with a wide grin on her face.*)

I know that if I pay more attention to what I am doing I can enjoy things more. The pun is: I am so poor, I have to "pay" attention.

I used to always write things down so I could remember them. Schedules, lists, and even routines help us to stay on track. Yet we continue to blame old age.

I remember my sister Maggie and I were driving to my sister Mary's house. I causally mentioned a sign that was specifically for truck drivers, "No trucks allowed." She thoughtfully said, "In all the years I have driven through here, I have never noticed that sign."

"If you had to pay a huge fine, I bet you'd notice it." ($500.00 for a fine, if the driver is caught!) We are more apt to pay attention and stay focused on the things we feel are important to our survival. Since I was a truck

---

[24] Dementia can also afflict the young. I was fortunate to have ancestors still in their right minds that lived well in to their late 90's. One great great grandfather on my Mother's side (Luis Ruiz) was said to have lived to be 115.

driver I would naturally notice it. The sign, in this case, was about my financial survival.

Buddha once said: When you sit, sit. When you stand, stand. In other words; to be focused is to be aware or to pay attention. The card system I mentioned on page 51 helps me to stay focused. When I go to fix something that is bothering me, I have to remind myself to stay on track. It is so easy to lose focus when I start digging through things to get the right tools. Making lists or having a card system helps me stay focused. If I am running low on toothpaste and I don't run to the kitchen and add it to my grocery list, I know I will forget it later.

Speaking about my card system. I found these two cards the other day. Maybe this is a prime example of how easy it is to get sidetracked:

Card 1

```
Things to live by:
If it's broke fix it,
If it's obsolete get rid of it.
If it helps in the future store it.
If it's any good take care of it,
If you know what it's for, use it.
```

Card 2

```
Things to Remember:
Don't shoot raccoons that are too close to the
          propane tank.
Don't look for a gas leak with a match.
Don't mix bleach with cleansers.
          (The fumes can kill you.)
Don't take an aspirin with a carbonated drink.
```

> (It takes one teeny tiny bubble to kill you.)
> Take paper cuts seriously.
> (Bacteria could result in an amputation.)
> Life is easy if you think it's hard.
> Life is hard if you think it's easy.
> Anything is easy if you know how.

Motivation:

We all need drive or life to keep going.

My daughter was the complete opposite of my son.

Julie would wake up at 5:00 in the morning; go to work at Dairy Queen; go to school; and still manage to be a top student. David, on the other hand, was hard to wake up in the mornings.

There are various ways to motivate. And there are several reasons why it is sometimes necessary.

In order to keep going my circumstances have to get right and organized. If they are not right, I will be under constant <survival mode>. I want to learn to get comfortable with the <desire mode>. In order to get from point A to point B, I have to prioritize.

Let's say I am still in my pajamas; sitting down eating my breakfast; reading the morning paper; and waiting on a cup of tea. The tea pot is whistling so I get up to retrieve the tea, but then I notice that the house is on fire.

There are three motivators in my story:

I am motivated to do something I love: Read.

I am motivated to get something to drink: Tea.

I am motivated to survive: The house on fire.

The adrenaline will give my body the will or desire to move and drive me forward. The bottom line is, that life is about survival, the second step seems to be making survival as comfortable as possible.

I was constantly trying to think of clever and creative ways to motivate both of my kids until they could learn to do it on their own.

For example, in order to get David to eat his spinach, I once paid four of the neighborhood kids a quarter a piece to come over while David was sitting in his highchair and pour out phrases like:

"Wow, David you sure are lucky, I love spinach."

"Yeah, David, I wish my mother would cook me some spinach."

Needless to say, my dollar was well spent.

Waking David up for school was another matter. "David, come quick. There's a bunny rabbit in the yard."

This worked a few times before he realized what I was doing.

Running out of ideas, one day I asked at the dinner table how each family member managed to get motivated.

"I count to three."

"I shake my body to get the blood pumping"

"I first have to see it in my mind."

Finally, my daughter said, "I just do it."

And there the conversation ended with a Nike ad.

I remember how a little boy of three motivated himself. And in doing so, scared the heck out of us.

All of us started noticing that without any extra urging, David suddenly started to go in for his nightly baths. But his behavior did not stop there. Anything we told him to do, he would not argue, and calmly obeyed.

Needless-to-say, his sister, his dad and I became very concerned. We started discussing among ourselves what could be the reason for his sudden change in behavior.

"Maybe he thinks we are going to die?" Our concerns and speculations continued as his unusual behavior persisted.

Then one day, at the dinner table, David calmly

asks, "When is Christmas?"

"Well," I said, "Tomorrow is Christmas Eve, so Christmas is in two days."

Suddenly disgusted, he yelled out, "I'm tired of being good! I'm tired of being good!"

I guess what I am trying to say here, is that we all have to figure out what we really want, and be willing to sacrifice for it. This is not easy. My son illustrated a good example.

Some people have to put away childish things: Old patterns; old routines that turn into ruts; old ways of thinking; and old habits.

At times I purposely use fear or guilt to motivate myself to get right with myself. I figure since my mind tricks me. I can trick it. I don't like to use this type of motivation but I am aware that I use it.

Try both ways:

1. In the morning, tell yourself God loves you and ask God to help you.

2. In the morning tell yourself that if you don't do this or that, something bad will happen.

Which way works best for you?

Although I have touched on staying focused and staying motivated throughout the book: The main thing I want to remind myself about here, is that, I move when I make it important to myself to move.

The bible repeatedly tells us what we are. Over and over it reminds us that we are Spirit.

Every body builder can tell you the same thing: It is in the mind. We wouldn't even be able to get up in the morning if it was not because the idea to get up first comes into our mind.

Years ago when my son was about three years old, I happened to look at him while I was washing dishes. He aroused my curiosity: I saw him very intently watching his hands and feet. As he was sitting on the couch, he would raise his arm and foot at the same time, first the right side and then his left, he kept alternating them. He was very intent and focused. It looked like he was imitating a puppet.

So I asked him, "David, what are you doing?" Expecting him to confirm what I already knew.

To my delightful surprise, he turned to me with a wide grin, and said, "Mamma, I can move and I don't have no strings on me."

"*Wow*" I thought, "*He is realizing "self"*. Then I said, "Remember that David, forty year old men don't know that."

"A wise child makes a glad parent." — Proverbs 10:1

Ultimately it is this Spirit inside of us that will motivate us to move, or to motivate us to rest when we need to.

This is why I elaborated on Steven Hawking. He had only, a heart, his lungs and brain, and look at what he accomplished.

I believe that all people have reasons for their behavior and for what motivates them. Love is a good motivator. However:

- Some well-meaning people confuse hate for love.
- Some people, in what I like to call a virtual reality training camp, are beginners, or in the process of beginning to recover from traumas.
- Some are more advanced in parts of their recovery process.

Don't let belief systems fool you. Everyone has their own particular lessons, and/or tools, by which to "find God", and will eventually move to where they need to be.

God will never leave us. He is there all the time.

I don't know about you, but it makes me feel

good to realize that I will never be alone, and will always have someone who loves me unconditionally no matter what trials I have to go through.

"God is with you in weakness and fear."
— I Corinthians 2:3

"Everyone is born of God." — I John 2:29

I now know that what religion someone is, is no longer a reason for fear. Every religion can be misused. And every religion has a skeleton(s) in the closet.

I use someone's religion for identifying and respecting their culture. No belief system is of any value if it is not practiced, questioned or studied. And everyone worships God in their own unique way.   Religions are not about fear. By their very definition: Each is about love. If they profess or teach fear they have been misinterpreted. And it is so unfortunate because they are all so beautiful.

The Evil That Men Do

My definition of evil is anything that causes unnecessary destruction or harm to myself or others. The bible's advice:

"Don't fellowship with the unfruitful work of darkness."
— Ephesians 5:11

"Give not that which is holy to the dogs, neither cast ye your pearls before swine, lest they trample them under their feet, and turn again and rend you."
— Matthew 7:6

Unfortunately it is not as simple as it seems because it runs from the obvious to the least obvious;

from the sociopaths to the morally corrupt; or from the degrees of intention to premeditation. Generally it is consistent with breaking laws. Remember we are dealing with **the deceptions of our own ego** which goes by various names.

I think that there is a series of names given to evil. I rank them like this: The first is "spirit" (with the small s). This is the least harmful. It is the ones innocent children acquire. It is not Spirit, (with the large S) because it brings with it, garbage from past lives.

The second one is "ego". It chooses what career, profession, or way of life in this lifetime. It places us in a position that helps resolve problems or character defects caused by our past and in the present time. Since life is growth, it can't go back just forward. Unfortunately for some people, it can take an eternity to figure out, when and how we wake up, is totally up to us.

The third is the Trickster or imp. This is the one Paul talks about in Romans 7:19. Although it is the one that we need to be most aware, we tend to give it more control than it has. It tricks and cunningly confuses us, by using our weaknesses, and our sense of right and wrong.

The fourth is the devil, or demon. It is depicted as being outside of ourselves. This is our alter ego on which we can blame our misdeeds on, so we don't have to feel responsible. Unfortunately, we can also blame the demon in others, to keep us from the work we have yet to do in ourselves.

The fifth is Satan. With this type of evil, we can not only use as an alter ego, but we remove him further from ourselves. It can become an object of religious worship and it is often used as a weapon to aggravate others that are fearful.

And then there is Beelzebub, a more outdated form of Satan. It was worshiped by many ignorant and fearful people. In biblical days it was a full blown religion requiring human sacrifice.

The name that "evil" is given depends on how afraid of yourself you are. Or how much you are into your nightmare here on earth. If Spirit (God) is perfect love, and God is in everything, then evil has to do with man not God. Remember: I believe that we are in the process of waking up from a nightmare. We deal with the spirit not Spirit.   And since God let man have free will, man can do whatever man wants. Evil often appears to "win." However, by its own greedy, and addictive definition, eventually it will destroy itself.

"They that plow iniquity, and sow wickedness, reap the same." — Job 4:8

Matthew 5:39 warns us not to resist evil. I believe Jesus was warning us not be get carried away with it; to let it pass by us; or not to dwell on it. If we resist it we acknowledge that it exists to a larger degree and give it even more power. For example if I say, "Don't think of pink Elephants."

"Warn and teach all men wisdom." ⸺ Colossians 1:28

Man is continually warned that he will be held accountable with the law of cause and effect: For every action there is an equal and opposite reaction.

Although some have tried to disproof the fact: I argue that there is no such thing as pure evil. I give you three main arguments:

1. Satan was a fallen angel. Angels are below God.

2. God has always been the main honcho, boss, jéfe, or main man.

3. As humans we will never be equal to God because one

person can never be equal to all humanity.

Therefore there can never be anything completely opposite; that has more power; or is equal to God. I do however; believe that some people have tried to prove that there is such a thing as pure evil. The TV series, Criminal Minds will attest to this. These people, however scary, (*maybe because of it*) are like cancer, that will be eventually be eradicated from society.

"...if the right hand offends you, cut it off. For it is profitable for you that one of your members should perish and not that thy whole body should be cast into hell." — Matthew 5:30

In the book of Job, God tells Satan that he can do anything he wants to Job, except kill him. Again this shows that God is in control. He never leaves his son(s) to the mercy of Satan (Fear). Whether I am the victim or perpetrator, the verse in Job (3:25) suggests that we have the power to decide for our Spirit (God), or for our spirit (Ego). Humans, especially ones that are fearful because of ignorance, like the ones that crucified Jesus, tend to blame others for their fear. What causes that fear is what I want to discuss in this section.

"Evil" can be culturally or communally determined. The majority of people in a small community can say it is against the law to do one thing or another. There are several examples: Dress codes, smoking or spiting on the sidewalk. I think Romans 14:2, 3 addresses being a vegetarian when Paul talks about herbs:

"...Let **not** him that eats (herbs), despise him that **eats not** (herbs)." — Romans 14:2, 3

Insensitivity

People that can't feel any physical or emotional pain are a danger to themselves and others.

They can cut, burn, or in other ways harm themselves or others. Some are incapable of putting themselves in another person's place; unable to read social cues; or lack empathy that can cause them to be insensitive to another person's pain. Pain is the body's way to signal the brain that it has had enough.

The pain is there to tell us to change course. It also tells us, "Find a way out of this or I, (the Spirit or mind) will!" Sometimes a single thought is all it takes to change direction. God will do the rest. Maybe this is why criminals subconsciously want to be caught.

In extreme cases, our minds will resort to shock[25], or an out of body experience.[26] And this can happen even before you reach for the drugs.

I try to be careful about my mental, and emotional pain. I often pretend it didn't happen or pretend I really don't care of how hurt I am. I also begin to recognize when I need to get real.

Sometimes we don't realize we are causing it. For example: Once a lady pointed out how sarcastic I was.

She asked me, "Can you say anything without being sarcastic?"

"Of course I can." But then the strangest thing happened: When I tried, to my complete surprise, I couldn't do it.

"You need a basket to you can carry a tune."

"You're so skinny, if you stick out your tongue you look like a zipper."

---

[25] Where parts of the body will shut down, or become paralyzed. Like a car that won't move until you fix the problem.

[26] Extreme dis-associative states created by the mind to escape situation too hard to endure mentally.

We have all heard these jokes: "You are so stupid, ugly, old, poor... etc."

Even though these were directed at me and I thought they were funny. I had to realize that to another person these same "jokes" could be hurtful. There is a time a place for everything.

I was lucky to have found someone that noticed this social insensitivity in me and took the time to point it out.

I am grateful for my dear friend 'Pilo' Flores. One day he gently reminded me that what I had said was hurtful to the other person. I remember thinking how wonderful it felt that he was not afraid to tell me. Now that's a true friend!

I learned how to pay complements but more importantly, I learned how to accept them. You would be surprised how many people are unable to accept a complement graciously. I had to learn to just say, "Thank you," then keep the rest of the negative comments to myself.

In this modern age, with so much stress, we are experts at deadening emotional pain. Sometimes there is a massive amount of information that in order to cope we have to shut down parts of our perception. These can become blind spots.

Physical impulses can be misdirected. You can perceive false associations or make excuses for people or situations.

"He loves me, and sometimes get frustrated."

"But, lady! He beat you up and you ended up in the hospital!"

When a person is 'in your face' lying, I try to warn them that the person is a diabolical, egotistical, narcissistic maniac. But they simply can't see it. They created a blind spot. All I can do is shake my head in disbelief, and leave the rest to God.

These excuses are especially tempting to a mind-set hypersensitive to pain. Whether it is childhood trauma, or torture, sometimes it is absolutely necessary to shut down. But understand, these types of situations should only be temporary. We need to come back to reality and deal with our problems before the consequences have grave results (pun intended). If you don't want to do turn the criminal in because you forgive him: Then do it to protect others, or so the person can get help.

I remember watching a television program years ago. Two soldiers were being interviewed about being captured and tortured by the enemy. One was describing how he heard his bones crack as he was being strung up. Suddenly, without provocation, one turns to the other and asks, "I didn't feel anything, did you?" Both realized they had felt no physical pain at the time.

I once asked a severely burned victim, what she had felt during the ordeal. Her nightgown had caught fire while cooking breakfast. She ran outside, where a neighbor rushed out and put out the flames. Evelyn, told me she could smell and hear the frames burning her skin, and even hear herself screaming, but she could not feel anything at the time.

With extreme pain, or embarrassment, the body finds many creative ways to deal with it.

"God is faithful and will keep you from evil."
– II Thessalonians 3:3

Unfortunately, experiences like this are often generalized to other parts of our life.

Whether the pain is self-inflicted or not, God will not leave us. Eventually, if we let it, the Spirit will help each of us deal with all our blind spots.

Mental torment is the body's way of telling us to stop and try something else. I try seeing pain as a good thing. My body is trying to tell me something and the only way I can relieve this pain, is to try to find the source of the pain. If I do not pay attention, my body keeps trying harder, or tries other avenues.

I try not to make the mistake of blaming my situation on someone or something else. I know blaming will only work for a short time. Eventually the truth will come out. This is a waste of time and will only cause delay in reducing the unnecessary pain. And trust me when I say the pain remains until we learn its real source.

Yes there are injustices, yes; they did such and such to me. Yes this happened, and I will probably never really know why it happened to me.

What I do about the situation(s) is totally up to me from now on. I don't need to let all of it go. I just need to be aware of what is really happening in the moment. This is my responsibility. I don't need to let whatever someone did to me or whatever happened to me get me into more trouble.

"Hurt me once, shame on you.
Hurt me twice, shame on me."
— Ancient Chinese saying

I laughed my head off, when I heard a former president try to remember it. He didn't quite get it right:

"There's and old saying in Tennessee. I know it's in Texas, probably in Tennessee, that says: Fool me once, shame on—shame on you. Fool me, you can't be fooled again." — President George W. Bush

Addictions

We can be addicted to anything. I don't really know if a person who is superstitious is addicted. But I do know sometimes he can't get his thinking into control. So I think he can get addicted to how he thinks about certain things. At any rate, I try to be vigilant or introspective of my thoughts which no longer make sense. I find the superstitions surrounding Friday the 13th interesting. Some hotels don't allow a room or even a floor with the number 13. I guess there were just too many superstitious people when hotels were built.

Interestingly enough, the number 13 signifies Jesus: Twelve disciples plus one. I can see why Friday would be a thing to fear, since Jesus was crucified on a Friday. Friday was also the day most executions took place. However, in this era, we commonly hear, TGIF or "Thank God it's Friday!" I think customs are hard to get rid of because people like to keep things as they are. People are resistant to change whether it makes sense or not.

There is an old story I read as a young girl. I found that same story in one of my English Literature text books. It is called The Lottery, written by Shirley Jackson (1919-1965). [27]

I think Jackson's story, tries to exaggerate the point nicely: Most people don't want to be bothered with what is going on. They don't want to question why things are done a certain way.

In Shirley Jackson's story everyone put their names in a box every year for a drawing. Year after year the "unlucky" winner was stoned to death. It was just the way things were done.

I think Jonathan Swift in The Modest Proposal was also trying to exaggerate a point. He was so appalled by the treatment of children. He decided to shock everyone by suggesting children would be a valuable food source.

Exaggerated fear which is projected into the

---

[27]Literature an Introduction to Reading and writing, The Fifth Edition: Edgar V. Roberts, Henry E. Jacobs 1998 by Prentice-Hall Page 233.

future appears to be a good catalyst for change. This is what preachers, teachers and parents have done for years. We outgrow most of these fears.

Preachers, teachers and parents alike are often seen as liars. We either understand why they lied or we change our concepts: Santa Claus becomes the Spirit of Christmas, or a thing for little children.

Sometimes what we really want, can become fuzzy. We exaggerate our fears and project them into the future and hurt the people we love.

Without realizing it, this happened to me.

It was a Saturday, Julie had been playing in her room and there were toys thrown all over her room.

"Julie, pick up your toys and clean up while I make dinner."

"No."

Since it was the first time she had ever stood up to me, I half way admired her. I also thought it was cute this little tiny creature would dare stand up to me. I was a giant compared to her.

"Julie, I mean it honey. Pick up your toys."

"No."

I thought I would give her a little time to think about it, so I went to start the dinner.

I came back; the room was still a mess. Her answer was the same.

Finally I had had enough. I pulled out my belt. At the time it was something I thought a good parent would do. I threatened her. She was still defiant. Finally I gave her the spanking I felt she richly deserved. I left and came back. *"Who was stronger, a five year old little girl or a full grown woman?"* It was no longer cute.

After two hours, I had compromised; it had all come down to just one toy! "Pick it up!" I yelled. Each time she yelled back, "No!" This continued for two more hours. I would go to the kitchen then I would come back. With every step I prayed she would change her mind.

At the point my hand shook, is when I knew I had to find another way. "*This was a little girl, my little girl. How could I do this?*" I thought, "*God please help me.*"

Shaking, I flung the belt from my hand, and walked outside. "*I couldn't let her see me cry. I had to be stronger than a five year old. I wanted to be strong, but more importantly I wanted to be a good parent. I had never met anyone this stubborn. Where did she get it from?*" I sat on the grass and leaned up against the side of the house. And through my puffy eyes I saw the sun through the trees and it reminded me of when I was a little girl. "God please help me!" Then I heard, '*What do you want?*' I want her to grow up with good habits, and a clean house she can be proud of.*"

The "Voice" returned, "*Tell her.*"

I went to the bathroom and washed my face. I dried it and looked hard into the mirror. "*What did I really want? What was the fight really about? Somehow it all had gotten mixed up in my head.*" I walked into her room. It was still a mess; the toys were scattered everywhere. I called to her to come to me. She was reluctant.

"It's okay; I'm not going to hit you. Sit on my lap I want to tell you something. Do you know why I want you to pick up your toys? Julie, I don't want people to tell me how dirty you are. I want you to be clean and grow up healthy. I'll tell you what, I love you so much. You don't have to pick up the toys. Let's forget the toys. Wash up and I will finish dinner, and we'll do something fun. Don't worry about the toys. I will pick them up later." I went into the kitchen to finish up, I walked back in the room. Every single toy was picked up and put back. Oh the awesome power of love!   I reexamined an old system and changed my thinking about what a good parent should be. I started listening to her, and learned the art of negotiation. We   get caught up in our own egos, we sometimes need to step back a take a second look at an old problem. I see it in addictions where the need keeps increasing and will never be able to get satisfaction we crave. People can build up tolerance toward the fear, and become participants in the fear. Eventually they also get fed up; reach their limits; and finally do something about it. It will ultimately be up to each individual person. In whatever form, if left unchecked, it can go to the extremes. I think people in jail can attest to this. However do keep in mind:

"It is always good to be zealously affected in a good thing." — Galatians 4:18

I once asked to speak to a group of children who were addicted to alcohol. I specifically remember a twelve year old sitting in the back corner slumped in a fetal position, sucking his thumb. A suffering child always seems to tug at my heart strings the hardest.

I watched while the other speakers spoke: Don't do it; Stop it; it is bad for you. (The should do tapes.) The boy continued sucking his thumb. I tried to listen as if I was him; I felt his pain, I mistrusted the people who were there to protect me, and I continued to listen to each speaker. As I looked around, it struck me that they had heard this all before. I wanted so much to engage this little boy.

"If you had to choose between heaven and hell," I asked, "What would you choose?"

With a little urging came the replies, "Heaven." The boy in the corner stopped sucking his thumb and adjusted his chair as he sat up a little straighter. ("*Mission accomplished*," I thought.)

"How about you," I asked a boy in the front row?

"Heaven" he said timidly.

"You would think so, but actually, everyone would pick what they are most comfortable with. It's called "taking the line of least resistance..." The question now becomes, "What are you comfortable with, heaven or hell? And how bad do things have to get before you decide to do something about it?"

Racism

When we are fearful of what is different, our survival instincts kick in. The more differences we see, the more fearful we become. Anything which is different from ourselves, i.e. culture, race, etc., becomes a threat.

We look for people who share similarities or with whom we are comfortable with, because the transition for the change will be easier.

Instinctively we want what is predictable. We fight change because we want things to stay the same, because the unpredictable causes fear.

Fear is about control and predictability. The less control, the more fearful we become.

Unfortunately, the predictable has a downside because nothing can stay the same forever. Somethings can turn rotten or old, right before our very eyes. With somethings, we have no control. This can be extremely difficult for some people, yet they adapt. And if what Darwin said is true than, our chances for survival increase.

There will always be an adjustment period for everything: When we move, go to a new restaurant or club, marriage, divorce, babies, change friends, etc. It helps us to adjust:

- If we understand what is going on.
- If we have former experiences we can compare them to, or to which we are familiar.
- If we have developed a certain degree of love and confidence for ourselves, whatever the situation.
- If we are given enough time to adjust.

Predictability protects us in much the same way a weather forecasts warns us of a tornado.

What is different has an element of the unknown, thereby unpredictable.

Some people attack what is different. To them the threat is real. This often happens without getting all the information or making assumptions on bad information.

I am reminded of the panic H. G. Wells (1866-1946) caused, when he interrupted a radio broadcast and announced Martians had landed. People missed the part of the broadcast where he announced that it was only a story: The War of the Worlds (1898).

Like H. G. Wells ignorance about how people would react, racism is an exaggerated projection of fear into the future. In this case, the people thought the Martians had invaded earth, felt extreme fear, and assumed their lives were in danger.

Recently I saw an interview in the news; a mixed race journalist was interviewing a racist, running for office.

Journalist: "So you are saying Whites are more intelligent?"

Racist: "Yes, by 20%."

Journalist: "I'm part black and I went to Harvard."

Racist: "Well, the part of you that is white is smart.

At one time during the interview, I wished she would have said, "Well if the part of me that is white is smart, then all the races should mix, (miscegenation) so everyone will be smart." This is something akin to what the comedian George Carlin once said: There would be no racism if everyone mixed and became the same color. (*I cleaned it up a little.*)

Or to put it another way:

"Let's remember that it takes both the white and black

keys of the piano to play <u>The Star-Spangled Banner</u>.
—Anonymous

In reality, IQ (Intelligence Quotient.) is a bit more complicated. If you doubt it, go read or see the movie <u>Hidden Figures</u>. It's a true story about three exceptionally intellect women, who happened to be black. History will show how valuable they were to the NASA (National Aeronautics Space Administration) program in the 1960's.

These women and countless of other people, provide evidence that "Whites" [28] do not have a monopoly on "smarts".

In the second millennium BC, Aryans who were tall, fair and blue eyed and straight hair went to India.[29]

They divided themselves into 4 groups:

1. The first group were called seers. They were the thinkers. They searched to understand the intuitive grasp of the mind.

2. The second group was the administrators which I like to call politicians. They were born with the valuable human talent of orchestrating and governing human affairs.

3. The third group was the producers. These people

---

[28]In the middle ages people divided the races into only three groups: Negroid (Black), Mongoloid (Yellow) and Caucasoid (White). This created a limited picture. The word "Caucasian" is problematic even today, especially when one is taking a census (Hispanics are also Caucasian). This was also very problematic when they found the Aborigine. Reference: <u>The World Book Encyclopedia,</u> Volume 16, Copyright 1973.)

[29]Besides the <u>World Book Encyclopedia</u>, races, religions and Indian history, I obtained some information from <u>The World's Religions</u>, by Huston Smith page 55.

possessed the natural trait to create. These were the artisans and farmers.

4. The fourth group were the followers. These were the servants and unskilled laborers. The ones who seem to work best under supervision or can 'play' well with others.

Can you see that one person can be all of these? I try to balance the four groups in myself. I want to seek truth, govern my circumstances wisely, create, and work well with others.

Unfortunately, to the determent of society, the groups in India got perverted into others sub casts which became the untouchables. While many tried to remove these perversions, they could not. Today in India there are about 3,000 of these sub casts.

Trying to insure maximum fair play and creativity exists in all societies. People, for various reasons which I list under fear, pervert abilities and attack individual races especially the most vulnerable.

It ceases to amaze me, how blind some people can be. Recently I kept repeating the same thing over and over again to someone, they kept insisting I said something completely different. I recognized it as a "blind spot." I don't think they would "hear" it, if I wrote it down or made it into a video.

This is the way some people are. We have all met them. But it is okay. Sometimes we have to find creative ways to go around them. I simply have to remember:

"Don't argue with persons with corrupt minds.
— I Titus 6:5

"Be not deceived: Evil communications corrupt good manners." — I Corinthians 15:33

If you can't escape it, do what Wild Bill did, don't let it change you. In my opinion what Franklin D. Roosevelt once said rings true today as it did then:
"If civilization is to survive, we must cultivate the science of human relationships—the ability of all peoples, of all kinds, to live together, in the same world at peace."

A friend once told me the same thing in a different way: We can learn a lot from crayons, some are sharp, some are pretty and some are dull. Some have weird names and all are different colors, but they all have to live in the same box.

Assumptions

Prejudice, or racism is making false assumptions into the future. We judge people often prematurely by many things.

"Judge not that ye be not judged" — Matthew 7:1

When it comes to the distribution of jobs, a racist assumes outsiders are taking their jobs. Yet, the problem is not the undocumented immigrants but the fear they are running from, and/or the companies which hire them. However, we can also even blame the politicians, and law makers. Yet if we are truthful, it comes to a full circle and back to us.
We need to get actively involved.
I know of some people who don't take their responsibility of voting seriously. Millions of dollars are spent by politicians just to get that one vote! Your vote! It does not matter who you vote for: VOTE! The reason is important. It is much like the importance of a census. The more people that vote the better the outcome. It is like herding cats, the more cats going in one direction the better the result.

I know my neighbor will always cancel my vote. He votes for the opposite party. Am I canceling his vote or is he canceling mine? What would happen if one of us did not vote? When we choose to do nothing, fear and corruption will get worse.

So many immigrants want to go back home. No one wants to be where they are not wanted. But if they go back home, many risk being killed. What would you do? These people should serve as a warning to stop corruption and misuses in our own government.

As far as jobs go, the companies that hire undocumented immigrants want cheap labor. They want to be able to stay in business. Why would a company be any different than myself: I also shop for bargains.

I also know it is easier to pick a fight against undocumented workers, than it is to win a fight with a big company. But again we need to get to the source of the problem and not attack the symptoms.

Immigrants are more likely to endure so many injustices, hazards, or conditions below OSHA (Occupational, Health and Safety Administration) standards. These conditions can go undetected and make is unsafe for all of us. However, the problem with cheap labor and bad working conditions, is not solely a problem with immigrants. An example is the plant in Tennessee years back when several workers burned to death because of conditions. Americans are also afraid to lose their jobs. If you witness corruption, or unsafe practices, please have the courage to speak up. We also need to hold the politicians responsible so they can, in turn, keep fear (greed, desperation, and frustration) in check.

Find out how each politician voted. This is something they can't lie about. More importantly: Find out why. Sometimes we don't get all the information. Then vote accordingly. So ultimately, the responsibility comes back to us.

Fear can take the form of Jealousy which can

escalate to anger. Thinking foreigners are making more money, or playing the blame game can cause a great deal of destruction to others. Therefore:

"When the spirit of jealousy comes on you, search for God." — Number 5:30

I think there are as many excuses for Americans not being able to find work, as there are people. Ultimately, it is up to each individual to find the source of the fear which they often carry with them.

There are many reasons why people can't get jobs:
- Some are simply afraid to go on a job interview.
- Others are afraid of a simple drug test.
- Some lack confidence
- Others are afraid of rejection.

There was a joke among the truck drivers of a big burly male who went to take a UI (Urine analysis), where you pee in a cup, and then the urine is tested for drugs.

After the test results came in, the doctor tells him, "I have some good news and some bad news. The good news is, your urine sample showed no drugs. The bad news is, you're pregnant."

I was applying for a driving job once and the lady before me came out to the waiting room elated. "I passed it, I passed it," She said, hardly able to contain her joy. I thought, "*Wow, the test must be really hard. I hope I can pass it.*"

As she sat there waiting for her boyfriend, my curiosity, mixed with much anxiety, finally got the best of me, so I asked her, "What was the test like?"

She gave me a curious look then answered, "I had to pee in a cup." All I could do was chuckle and shake my head."

What are you afraid of? How afraid are you? You don't have to convince others. Only you know.

The following two stories, I was going to place with the other three previous stories on page 80 but decided to put them here, mostly because they are assumptions we sometimes make about people.

Have You Ever Danced?

An old prospector shuffled into town leading an old tired mule.

The old man headed straight for the only saloon to clear his parched throat.

He walked up and tied his old mule to the hitch rail. As he stood there brushing some of the dust from his face and clothes, a young gunslinger stepped out of the saloon with a gun in one hand and a bottle of whiskey in the other.

The young gunslinger looked at the old man and laughed, saying, "Hey old man, have you ever danced?"

The old man looked up at the gunslinger and said, "No, I never did dance... Never really wanted to."

A crowd had gathered as the gunslinger grinned and said, "Well, you old fool, you're gonna dance now. And started shooting at the old man's feet.

The old prospector – not wanting to get a toe blown off started hopping around like a flea on a hot skillet. Everybody was laughing, fit to be tied.

When his last bullet had been fired, the young gunslinger, still laughing, holstered his gun and turned around to go back into the saloon.

The old man turned to his pack mule, pulled out a double-barreled shotgun, and cocked both hammers.

The loud clicks carried clearly through the desert air. The crowd stopped laughing immediately. The young gunslinger heard the sound too, and he turned around very slowly.

The crowd watched as the young man stared at the old timer and the large gaping hole of those twin barrels.

The barrels of the shot gun never wavered in the old man's hand, as he quietly said, "Son have you ever licked a mule's butt?"

The gunslinger swallowed hard and said, "No sir... but I've always wanted to."

***

The lessons in this story are: Never be arrogant; don't waste ammunition; whiskey makes you think you are smarter than you are; and always, make sure you know who has the power. But the most important lesson of all: Don't mess with old men. They didn't get old by being stupid.

What Causes Arthritis?

A man who smelled like a distillery flopped on a subway seat next to a priest. The man's tie was stained, his face was plastered with red lipstick, and a half empty bottle of gin was sticking out of his torn coat pocket. He opened his newspaper and began reading. After a few minutes, the disheveled guy turned to the priest and asked.

Say, father, "What causes arthritis?"

Mister, it's caused by loose living, being with cheap, wicked women, too much alcohol and contempt for your fellow man."

"Well I'll be." the drunk muttered, and returned to his paper.

The priest, thinking about what he had said, nudged the man and apologized.

"I'm very sorry. I didn't mean to come on so strong. How long have you had arthritis?"

"I don't have it father. I was just reading here that the Pope does."

***

The main point here is on erroneous assumptions

we sometimes make. Sometimes we need more information before we speak. And I might add, you cannot believe all you read.

When I was seventeen, I worked at the USS Ordinance Lab in Norco, California. One day in the lunch room, the people I worked with, were making fun of this guy that was sitting at the table across the room. He appeared to always be in deep thought. One particular time he was twirling his hair around his finger. The more he did it, the more they made fun of him. I felt for sure he would hear. I was so embarrassed by the situation, but since I was the newbie, I was afraid to speak up. I was somewhat comforted that this man was oblivious to everything around him. I asked them who he was. To my great surprise, he was an extremely valuable scientist to the lab. I could not understand why the people I worked with acted in such a childish manner. They laughed and made fun of him, yet he was the genius. It never made sense.

This will be a nice introduction to my next subject.

Bullying

Years ago my daughter was being bullied in school.

I woke up in the middle of the night and heard my daughter walking around in her room. The second night I heard it again. So I decided to talk to her. "What's going on Julie?"

"Mamma, it's my problem, and you said I have to learn how to figure things out on my own."

I told her, "Okay, take care of it".

The next night, Saturday, it happened again. I found her pacing back and forth in the middle of the night.

That morning, when she objected to my interference, I said, "Not this time Julie. This is a grown up problem. I have to step in before it ends up costing me, so tell me what is going on."

Reluctantly, she began to explain that on Monday after school, some black girls were going to beat her up.

"Why?" I asked.

"Mamma, they said David is my baby and that I was lying when I said he was my brother." (There is a 13 year difference between them.)

"I told her, "That's right Julie, David is your baby, and don't you remember you got pregnant and went away and had him?"

"Mamma, how can you say that? You know the truth!"

"That's right Julie and so do you, and nothing you can tell anybody will make a difference. Now what is the girl's name?"

Reluctantly she told me her name. I called her mother and asked if we could come over to talk. She sounded nice but I had to admit, I did not know how it was going to go. As far as knew, her husband could have been a redneck with a gun.

As it turned out, she was a lovely black woman. She was also a single mother trying to raise two kids.

We sat around her dining room table, Julie told her side, and then the other girl told her side. Unfortunately they had two opposing versions. It was a stalemate. Fortunately the little brother who stood by the door way, suddenly yelled out to his sister, "You're lying. I was there." I heard myself heave a sigh of relief.

After their feelings were heard, and the problem resolved, we left. A few days later, I asked her who was on the phone. As it turned out they both became friends.

I think the messages in Matthew 5:39 are very clear: **Truth needs no defense.**

We hear so much these days about bullying. It has been around for hundreds of years. The strong picking on the weak, for as many reasons as there are people. The problem is not with bullying but how to deal with it. We have to learn to pick our fights intelligently.

"Resist no evil: but whosoever shall smite thee on thy right cheek, turn to him the other also."
— Matthew 5:39

When my daughter was in kindergarten, she kept complaining about a bully. First I told her "Tell the teacher." Then I told her to "Move away from him." Finally on the third day I told her to hit him and run like hell." What I should have done is what I ended up doing years later and find out what was really going on.

But what about when kids don't tell you what is going on?

We use to have practice fire drills in our family, just in case of a fire. Maybe this is a good place to start. Discuss things before they happen or before the actual subject has to be discussed.

Discuss subjects from both sides. Sometimes we are harder on ourselves than others would be. Keep this in mind when talking to a child. "What would you do if...?" This might be a good way to start. Know your kids and do it from where you think it is appropriate. If you are wrong, your kids will be more willing to forgive you if they think you are being honest with them. Keep conversations private or get professional help from people who can be sued if they don't.

There are so many things which can be discussed, besides the bully and the bullied. There is: Sexual assaults or harassment; gender identity; anger; suicidal thoughts etc., or even feelings in general. Don't discuss anything with your kids if you are an inflexible, insensitive jerk. Get help for them and you both.

Always remember: You are the adult/parent. Children are not to be used as a dumping ground for your confessions. If you do, then you are an idiot. Get help immediately.

The Spirit

I believe the God within us wants us to respect the engineering marvels He created, us. He wants us to love all of His creations with common sense and some measure of discipline. In the meantime we will remain asleep only thinking we are awake. We will all eventually, wake up.

Though I can look for inspiration from teachers, verses and poems in the past, I need to start with the only person I can change **now**. I need to be responsible for my thoughts and actions **now**. I need to appreciate what is happening **now** and live in the present.

"The past is now. God wants what is now."
— Ecclesiastes 3:15

I memorize things I read: Verses which would inspire me during the hard times; make me laugh; or that I like. It was a quick way to reinforce positive thoughts in the present.

However, I also believe sometimes the past has to be dealt with so we can move forward.

"The further backward you can look the further forward you will see. –Winston Churchill

Before we get to our final destination, we need to wake up to where our "home" is. It will help to learn why we are here. I believe I am here on earth to become a better person, and like Jesus, and others, I am here to help others. I want to share my experiences. I want to build a bridge for them so in some small way, I can lessen their suffering and give my life a purpose.

I found a poem in a book by Dorothea Kopplin,

called Something to Live By. I have always loved this poem. It written by Will A. Dromgoole. I hope you can get a chance read it. The poem is called Building the Bridge. The pilgrim builds the bridge for others, unlike the pilgrim, I know I will pass this way several times.

Although, I have already written about the body and the mind I want to expand on them in this section. Like it or not, it is all the same. They are so intertwined it is often hard to tease one from the other. This is probably why I tend to repeat myself. Many verses pertain to the body, the mind and the Spirit.

Anytime I think I might have spoiled my kids because I loved them too much. I think about how God "spoiled His children" by giving them freewill. God was into "tough love" before people thought up that particular phrase. The story in the bible about the Protocol Son eludes to this. He gave the two of them their inheritance and each did what each wanted. They had to learn the lesson: There are certain laws or boundaries that we all have to adhere to.

As early as genesis we are told we can have what we can imagine.

"Nothing will be kept from you: Just imagine it."
— Genesis 11:6

"What you treasure, there will your heart be also."
— Matthew 6:21

With this project, I found myself a happier person. I found verses which for centuries were saying what our psychology, and new age books are saying. There are books which explain a practice called visualization: The Secret of the Ages" by Robert Collier, (1948); a small pamphlet printed by Unity Church; and the book and CD called, The Secret.

I know it as treasure mapping. It is a process that

can get us what we desire.

Hinduism has its basis in desires: Just like the rest of the bibles, it teaches we can have what we want! The problem, is to know what we want. If you want success, money, or power, go for it. There is nothing wrong with wanting. But seek it intelligently and do it **while obeying moral laws.** I think people forget this part.

Hindus' guiding principle is not to turn from desire until desire turns from us. The path of desire is littered with "toys". It further states that it is sad for a child not to have a toy, but even sadder for adults who have out grown their toys.

A person does not have to try anything he already knows will hurt him. No matter how much fun the toy appears to be. I can learn from the burns on others: I don't have to place my hand in the fire to find out the fire will burn it. The choice is totally up to me.

Put God first! And any toy we want can be ours. Or another way of saying it:

"Put God first then do what you want." Saint Augustine

Remember John Nash's law of governing dynamics? The ultimate goal should be to benefit the group. The body is a group in and of itself. I am a group of cells. From the micro to the macro, it is all the same principle. Keep this in mind with treasure mapping.

The process of visualization or treasure mapping is to take a picture of something you like and place it in a scrapbook, and look at it religiously every day and thank God it has been manifested in your life. See it, feel it, and know that it is already there. Then let it go, knowing it will come.

"Continue in prayer, and watch in the same with thanksgiving." — Colossians 4:2

I tried this with amazing results, for example: I cut out a picture of a man measuring a small girl and placing a mark on a door frame measuring her height. Five years later, I was married, and we bought a house.

One day my daughter was standing on the door frame while my husband was making a mark on it. I could not believe my eyes: The antique chair in the picture was miraculously much like the actual one next to my daughter standing against the door frame. I didn't even ask for the chair! When I cut out the picture to put on the scrap book, I was asking for a husband and a father for my little girl. The man and girl in the picture also looked like my husband and my daughter.

Golfers and other athletes use this same technique. In the book, WAIT by Frank Partnoy, I read that the few micro seconds in which a professional's mind has to react can make a big difference in his game. He earned those micro seconds by hard work and practice.

The resistance we often experience comes from us (the ego) which tells us we are losers and don't deserve anything good. Years of bad habits can be hard to erase. And although we are not conscious of it: We are sometimes canceling what we think. This canceling is caused by what we surround ourselves. We need to be aware of the movies we watch; the people with which we surround ourselves; and to what we are habitually attracted. These things will influence our thoughts. It is exactly the same process as if we consciously ask for it.

"Whatever things are good... think on these things."
—Philippians 4:8

The idea of treasure mapping is to keep something is your mind long enough and it will manifest itself. This is not as simple as it seems. **Some things are hidden in the subconscious.** So often we are not conscious of what is causing the havoc in our lives.

The following is a personal experience I had. It is good example of what might be buried in the subconscious:

It was first related to me by my sister, and then verified by my mother. The incident occurred when I was about two to four months old. This event would change the course of who was going to raise me, and fostered subconscious feelings of abandonment. In the book My Mother's Diary, (Lulu.com.), I wrote:

(Fifty years later when I read my mother's diary)...a revelation: the moment of absolute clarity, when I knew, that I knew, why I was crying. After finally breaking through the pain and facing it, it dawned on me what had happened to me so very long ago...At the age of about two months old my parents left...intended to be gone for only a short time, (and according to her account, left me in the care of my oldest sister)...the car broke down. Out of desperation, (according to my sister's version)...still feeding (her new born) daughter... decided to breast feed me...By the time my mother got back, I was quite content. My mother however, realized she no longer had to be bound to me...turned me over to her (my sister's) care. My sister became my wet nurse and surrogate mother.

The pain of "losing" my mother and unconsciously being emotionally rejected by my older sister, had been hiding in my subconscious.

When I found the pain and confronted it, my life changed. Putting God first became less of a struggle. In the immortal words of Ward Cleaver, the "father" in Leave it to Beaver (A 1950's TV show.), "What's the sense of going through something bad if you don't learn from it?"

Keeping a thought in your mind takes practice. I have even tried to write a complete sentence over and over attempting to change my mind set. Although it helps, I know my ego will continue to put up resistance:

Especially since I have a strong stubborn will. I also have a tendency to try too hard. I relax and keep at it; eventually I start seeing results.

"Blessed are the meek (patient): for they will inherit the earth." — Matthew 5:5

If God knows only the Spirit of man, then asking is not about words or pictures cut out from a magazine, but the spirit.

"God knows not man, but his spirit."
— II Corinthians 2:11

"The things which are seen were not made of things which do appear." — Hebrews 11:3

You might be asking yourself: "I keep asking God for a million dollars, and if what you say is true, then why can't I get a million dollars?"

The short answer is, "I don't know. Why can't you?"

I know why I can't get a million dollars. Sometimes I'm just like everyone else and fantasize about what I would do with a million or even 20 million. Fundamentally, I know money comes with responsibility. Like a diabetic in a candy store. My dear friend Larry received $80,000.00 from an inheritance, and eight months later, he was worse off than if he had never received it. There are times when I think I would get, lazy, scared and paranoid. People as a rule can't handle changes especially sudden ones.

Money can't buy what I, or what everyone else really wants: Peace of mind.

Besides, I have everything I want, and when I want something, I ask God. I often test the theory of visualization. I did it a lot more when I was younger. I'm at the age now when I want to get rid of things.

One time I wanted a piano. I owned a cleaning service at the time. After clearing a place*[30] in the living room for a piano, a lady called. She said she had heard of my reasonable rates, and would I mind coming over to see the job and give her an estimate? She showed me the second story windows which were causing her so much misery.

I gave her my quote and then she asked when I could start.

As I turned to leave, she apologetically added, "I don't have any money right now, but I am trying to sell this old piano." Then she added, "As soon as I sell it, I can hire you."

As soon as she said that, I thought to myself, *"Thank you God for my piano!"* It was a simple trade.

'You have not because you ask not." — James 4:2

"God knows what you need, before you ask."
— Matthew 6:8

The years go by, things change, and reluctantly, I had to leave the piano behind. One day I decided I wanted another Piano. I thanked God for my new piano, knowing I would get another one sooner or later. Low and behold, a month later, a boyfriend gives me a beautiful, blonde, console piano for my birthday. Even though I love to play it, I find excuses not to. It's taken nine years to completely play ♪"The Impossible Dream".♪) I did this by memorizing most of the seven pages of this song.

Nevertheless, I am thankful and so grateful to my friend because it is there whenever I want it. But never do I forget where it really came from.

---

[30] A visualization technique by which you act as you expect it.

"Go in peace, and may God give you what you ask."
— Samuel 7:17

"Ask what God can give you." — I Kings 3:5

"Ask and you will receive." — I John 3:22

"You have not because you ask not." — James 4:2

"Whatever you ask it will be given." — Mark 6:23

"Ask: It will be given, Seek: You will find. Knock: It will open." — Matthew 7:7,8

"God being good can give you more of what you ask."
— Matthew 7:11

And a slightly different take:

"Whosoever shall say … and not doubt … and believe …
he shall have whatsoever he says." — Mark 11:23

Just yesterday, I was coming home from the grocery store; and as usual, I watch my budget, there were a few things I wished I could have bought. I unlocked the gate to bring the groceries in, when I looked up and see my neighbor with a big sack coming towards me.

Inside the sack was a large piece of watermelon, grapes and a large container of strawberries: Just exactly what I wished for.

She had no idea what a miracle she had performed.

I told her, "Cảm ơn, bạn tôi đẹp."[*31]

If I was younger, and 'living on the edge' as some

---

[31]Vietnamese for: "Thank you, my beautiful friend".

people call it: I would have bought everything I craved. I have since learned, because of going from 'feast to famine', the law of cause and effect comes into play. With all this asking and wanting, I also have to apply some brutal honesty, by living within my means. This applies to all people: the rich and poor alike. Just ask the ones who got caught and ended in jail.

That's what the wisdom in the bible is about. The laws governing love, faith, and understanding.

"According to your faith be it unto you."— Matthew 9:29

***

Something strange just happened, and since it seems pertinent, I thought I would share it with you:

My cat Samuel whom I dearly love, was trying to get my attention. He accidentally (I hope) pushed the computer mouse off the desk into the floor. I could not get it to work, so reluctantly, I decided to shut down the computer and assumed I would have to do a lot retyping. I was happy nothing was deleted. However, when I recovered the program I found twenty one pages of this:

"God knows not man, but his spirit." — *II Co. 2:11""God knows not man, but his spirit."* — *II Co. 2:11""God knows not man, but his spirit."* — *II Co. 2:11" Anyway, I think you get the picture. I deleted the rest of the twenty one pages.*

Maybe God is trying to tell me/us something: Twenty one pages which emphasized the message about what God uses as a gauge for judging us? I was elated I would not to have to have to buy a new mouse, but even more relieved about not having to retype all I had previously typed. I fed Samuel and things are back to normal. Anyway, I thought I would leave this in. Then I thought about something else.

***

Samuel trying to get my attention reminded me of two stories about my son. He was about three at the time, and like Samuel, was trying to get my attention.

The first time, the following conversation took place when I was, as usual, deeply engrossed in something.

My son said, "Mamma." I kept ignoring him but all the time thinking, "Hurry up and get done so I can find out what he wants."

He said, "Mamma." Once again my son was trying to get my attention and once again I kept thinking, "Hurry up and get done so I can find out what he wants."

Then all of a sudden I heard him yell, "HEY, SWEETHEART!"

This absolutely got my attention.

***

Another time, I again was deeply engrossed in something. This time I told him to wait a minute.

I almost lost it when I heard him say, "Ah, can I wait five minutes instead!"

I remembered thinking, "Man, I really messed this kid up. He thinks one minute is longer than five minutes."

Kids, our greatest teachers!

***

What are your thoughts like? What are you manifesting in your life. Remember the law of kind: Consciously or unconsciously we will keep creating whatever he have in our minds. It's our choice.

This comes into play with visualization: In fact this is why visualization works: Everything produces after its own kind. This is why Philippians 4:8 is so important:

"Whatsoever things are true, honest, just, pure, lovely, of good report, if there is any virtue, or praise, think on these things." — Philippians 4:8.

If visualization is not working for you, I became aware of certain guideline and want to share them with you. These rules helped me get better results with my daily thoughts in general.

Rules for Treasure Mapping

1. You can only ask for yourself. If you pray for another person you cannot ask for anything specific. If you are praying for someone to recover from an illness, be non-specific. Pray for what is best for the person, or pray, "This or something better." (You don't know what is good for you, let alone someone else.

2. You cannot ask for anything will cause undue burden on someone else. (The example I use is: If you want a new camper, your husband should not have to get an extra job, just so you can get what you want.)

3. You cannot set a time limit on it. (Sometimes things are better in their own time.)

4. What you want has to benefit everyone. (It has to come out of love not fear.)

5. There can be no doubt. (You know that you know and that what you want comes out of love.)

To some people I would warn: Be careful that what you wish for doesn't land you in jail or worse. An example is when you want someone to love you and you start stalking them. (Read the rules again.) This is from your ego. Stop it.

Which begs the question, if you can have anything you want, why choose what can hurt you? My guess is ignorance.

At one time in my life, I was renting a house in Hugoton Kansas, and there was a house five houses away with which I fell in love. It was what I would call a "New England" type house, in a blue on blue color. I later found out, the color was called 'fog blue'. It had a beautiful old shade tree in the front and it also had 3 bedrooms we so badly needed at the time.

One day a 'For Sale' sign went up. I wanted so much to buy the house but I also knew I could not afford to buy it. Nevertheless, one day God put it in my heart to stop and talk with the lady who was trying to sell it.

Every day, I would pass the house, and every day, I would say, the same thing: "This God, or something better. Thank you God."

The months went by, and winter came. I would think the same thoughts as I drove by the house I so much wanted to own. Then one day there was a knock on the door. The lady asked me how much I was paying rent. I couldn't believe my ears; she said I could move in, live one month free, and pay the same amount as startup money or I think she called it earnest money. The loan payments would be the same as I was paying on rent! It cost me absolutely nothing extra!! I could not believe my eyes when I signed the papers to my new house. I kept thinking over and over. "*Thank you God*"

Apparently, Evelyn had to move to another state, she was afraid to leave the house abandoned during the winter months, and felt like I could be trusted. And there was no way in God's green earth I was ever going to disappoint this wonderful lady. I think if I would have forced the issue, I would have probably gone bankrupt or this might not have been as good a deal as it turned out.

What a difference knowing how all this works? With the proper tools, (right knowledge, right mind) we can begin to fix whatever messes we are creating and reduce the suffering, if not for the world, at the very least, for ourselves.

What if we don't know the truth about what we are and get lost in this world? What if we try to live up to the world's or people's expectations instead of God's? What if we operate totally by our egos and don't necessarily hurt others?

This brings me to the inevitable: Everybody dies. The bible speaks of death, I know of only two: Physical death and spiritual death.

Physical death

First I want to say all of life teaches us that it is all about survival. Something inside of us wants to survive. But why? If life is sometimes so bad, then why do we insist on keeping on, and keeping on?

I talked about the ego wanting to survive, but I believe it is the Spirit which also wants to live. But why?

If we know we will die; especially if we believe we can come back or reincarnate; or go to a place like "heaven", then why do we struggle against incredible odds? I believe it might be because we want to get as much into this life span as we can. I believe the older we get, the better chance there is to learn what our existence is really about. Compulsively, we want to figure out what we are, why we exist, and how to end our suffering. We all want answers with which we can be satisfied.

"(To) know the truth, (so) the truth will set (us) free."
— John 8:32

When I think of one story I read years ago, I crack up laughing. Here is what I remember of the story:

A king heard about a man who was 126 years old but was still quite healthy. The man lived in the mountains near his castle. The king wanted to know the secret of this man's longevity, so he asked his soldiers to bring him down from the mountain. The king wanted so much wanted for the man to reveal his secret for his long life. He had his cooks prepare the most delicious delicacies. While the man ate the delicious meal, he died. I hope the King got the message:

WATCH WHAT YOU EAT!

There is hundreds of ways we can die.

According to the book, titled Ending Aging, by Aubrey de Grey, we could reverse human aging in our lifetime. Until they can discover a way to eliminate aging, we can't cross aging from the list of ways to die.

With time running out, our next priority is to extend the time. This we attempt to do by developing healthy habits. And then if we can't cheat death, our third priority for our ego, becomes leaving something behind, to say, "Remember me, I was here".

In Moses' time, great pyramids were constructed, by order of the king, so he could be memorialized after his death.

Similarly, a great amount of energy and emphasis was placed on the body. The belief was the dead lived on into the afterlife, and their bodies had to be preserved for use there.

Mummification was perfected to preserve the body after death. The body would then be able serve a person after it was projected into the next world. If a king got sick, one could find an anxious queen, who along with their slaves was buried alive with the king.

The belief was they should die with the king and care for him in the afterlife.

I find these beliefs disturbingly flawed.

How could the body get out for use in the proceeding life? Hopefully they let the king in on it. If the queen knew, I am certain she would have made a run for it. And since the slaves and his wife's bodies were not mummified, how would they be able to be projected into the next world with the king?

Maybe I missed a footnote.

Nevertheless, when the king died, he could make the afterlife more comfortable by taking everything he loved in this world into the next one. Apparently the old saying of "You can't take it with you" did not apply.

"We brought nothing into this world: It is certain we can carry nothing out." — I Timothy 6:7

While we live in this world, there will always be the fear of death.

I think most of us fear death because:
1. It appears to separate us from loved ones.
2. It can come sudden and catch us unaware.
3. It can be perceived as painful.
4. We don't know what happens after we die.

It is natural to fear the unknown and the unpredictable. Like our instinctual fear of falling, we fear anything in which we have little or no control. And, the body's instinct is to survive.

Death also seems so permanent. Indeed, when we lose a loved one, the only thing left is a memory. Thus by finally accepting the fact death is inevitable it is easier to turn to God for comfort. Some bible verses give rise to hope.

"All that are in their graves will hear His voice."
— John 5:28

I woke up this morning singing ♪'you are my sunshine...'♪ It was bittersweet remembering my German shepherd dog, 'Sunshine'. I had to remind myself that the time I had with her was a blessing. But I also have to come to terms with the painful loss.

If we turn to God for comfort, why believe in a

cruel God? As it stands, this is what most religions teach. That is, that God is a vengeful God. Is it any wonder why there are so many atheists, or so many people who have lost hope?

Like it or not, eventually, we all have to find some way to come to terms with death. It does not matter whether it is a beloved child, a love one, or even our own death. And this is also whether you are an atheist, or anything else. Ask God to help you through the trying times. Get help, read what others did, but do something. Don't wallow in your grief forever.

"Don't give evil a foot hold." — Ephesians 4:27

I believe in a loving God: A God who gives my life purpose, value, and hope. I know from personal experience what it is to live without God, and what it is to live with God. To live with God is so much easier.

One day I was driving with a friend and our two girls: Julie and Corrine. Both girls were seated in the back seat and we happened to be passing a cemetery.

"O-o-o-o", I heard Corrine say, "I don't want my mother to die."

"Oh, that's okay," Julie said calmly to Corrine, "It's okay if my mother dies."

Needless-to-say, my friend and I stopped talking. My friend and I looked at each other with a look you would not believe. But my daughter continued. *"There was no way I going to interrupt this conversation."*

"When my mother dies, by that time, I will be old and have kids, and then I'll die, and then my kids will be old..."

I think I gave an audible sigh of relief, *"Wow!"* I remember thinking, *"The circle of life, and my five year old daughter understands it."*

"A wise child makes a glad parent." — Proverbs 10:1

I like to think God says basically the same thing, it is okay if you die; a part of you will always live on.

I woke up this morning asking God what I should write about as far as death, and the story of the prodigal son came to mind. Even though it deals more with jealousy or Spiritual death, I thought I would start here, and then compare it to what other books say about death. I found the story of the prodigal son in Luke 15:11-32:

A certain man had two sons. He divided his fortune among them. The younger son took his money and left. He wasted his fortune on riotous living. He fell into hard times, and then came back to his father. Hungry and homeless, he begs for help, and at the very least, to make him his hired servant. His father delighted to have his son back, held a great celebration in his honor.

The interesting part about this well-known story is the older son:

***

25Now his elder son was in the field: and as he came and drew near to the house, he heard music and dancing.
26And he called one of the servants and asked what these things meant.
27And he said to him, your brother has come; and your father has killed the fatted calf, because he has received him safe and sound.
28And he was angry, and would not go in: therefore came his father out, and entreated him.
29And he answering, said to his father, "Lo, these many years do I serve you, neither transgressed I at any time your commandments: and yet you never even given me as much as a small goat that I might make merry with my friends. (*Never mind that he could have bought it himself.*)
30But as soon as this son comes, who has devoured your money with harlots; you have killed for him the fatted

194

calf.[32]

[31]And he said unto him, Son, you are ever with me, and all that I have is yours.

[32]It was right that we should make merry, and be glad: for this your brother was dead, and is alive again; and was lost, and is found.

This parable teaches us so much. However, when I thought of it this morning it was in relation to death. In order to explain, I first need to briefly touch on one text which was turned into three bibles. According to some accounts, these bibles were written more than 2000 years before Christ. The texts are called the Vedas. The first books of the texts are hymns, instructions regarding rites and ceremonies, and rules of conduct. The second texts are called the Upanishads (108 of them). The third texts are the most known portion. These became the Hindu bible the Bhagavad-Gita. This is the most translated of the Vedas.

This is my oversimplified shortened version of the Vedas:

There were seven brothers who fell in love with seven sisters who were from the same kingdom. However in order to marry them, they agreed to become slaves for seven years. (*This is somewhat similar to Abraham's story.*) But after seven years, excuses were made to keep the women. The family kept changing "the goal posts". The seven brothers go through various trials: This portion of the Vedas is called the Upanishads.

Finally the brothers get to the point where they had enough and a huge battle ensues: This part of the Vedas is where the Bhagavad-Gita begins.

In the beginning of the Bhagavad-Gita, Arjuna

---

[32]A fatted calf is one that is raised on whole grains, and killed only on very special occasions.

the King, is talking to his God, Krishna, overlooking what is soon to become a battlefield. Arjuna tells Krishna he cannot go through with the war, because the people he will be fighting are his friends and even members of his own family. Krishna tells Arjuna if he does not fight he will be considered a coward and will be dishonored, and if he fights many will die. Krishna's advice to Arjuna is:

"Do what you have to do, whenever you have to do it."
— (*My very oversimplified translation.*)

I think maybe Krishna is saying that we are sometimes faced with the inevitable. There are things we simply can't walk away from.

Maybe on some level it is what Shakespeare advised in Macbeth:

"If it were done when 'tis done, then 'twere well, it were done quickly." — William Shakespeare

The King James Bible in Ecclesiastes 3:1-8 puts it this way:

"$_1$To everything there is a season, and a time to every purpose under the heaven: $_2$A time to be born, and a time to die...$_3$A time to kill, and a time to heal...$_8$a time of war, and a time of peace.

The part that is more aligned with what I am trying to get at, is in the Upanishads. The Upanishads are about the trials of seven of the brothers.

Nachiketa is the youngest of the seven brothers. Vajasrabasa, makes a sacrifice of some cattle, but his son, Nachiketa thinks it is not a very good sacrifice. Nachiketa repeatedly pesters his father.

"Father, I too belong to you: to whom do you give me?"

This is repeated several times.

"Father, I too belong to you: to whom do you give me?"

Finally, his irritated father says, "You I give to death."

The father immediately realizes his grave error.

However, Nachiketa tells his father not to go back on his word for fear bad things will befall them. (*This has some similarities to Abraham offering Isaac as a sacrifice.*)

Nachiketa then goes to the King of Death. The King of Death, however, is not at home and is gone for three days. When The King of Death returns, his servant tells him someone has come for three consecutive days to see him. The King of Death is so impressed and offers Nachiketa three boons (wishes) one for each day:

1. The first wish is that God not worry about him.
2. The second wish is for God to love him and give him peace.
3. And with the third wish, Nachiketa wants to know the sacrifice which leads to heaven.

The King of Death is again so impressed he offers him a fourth wish.

4. Nachiketa tells him he wants to know how to overcome death.

To which the King offers him long life etc., anything but that: But Nachiketa won't hear of it, and insists on getting his wish.

And again, my very oversimplification of the text: It goes on to explain reincarnation, and ultimately, how to keep from dying. I guess the reason it reminded me of the prodigal son, was like the eldest son, we had the ability to cheat death all along.

"Son, you are ever with me, and all that I have is yours."
— Luke 15:31

There are several references of promises to immortality in the bible, for example, Matthew 19:30 or Luke 18:18: John 3:16 is probably the most quoted:

"For God so loved the world that he gave his only begotten Son, that whosoever believes in him should not perish, but have everlasting life." — John 3:16

The Christians made it their own; compare it to how I read it:

"...whosoever believes in Him (God) should not perish..."
— John 3:16

The Christians have a better reference in 3:36, however, if you were paying attention, it's all the same and the message is very consistent, put God first. This is what all religions are about.

I remember a friend of mine once asked me how I would interpret what Jesus said:

"I am the way the truth and the light, no man comes unto the Father, but by me. — John 14:6

I told her, "Mindy, **you are** the way the truth and the light, because if I love everyone in the world but exclude you, then I missed the mark: I didn't put God first."

"A man that says I love God, and hates his brother, is a liar." — I John 4:20

"If I do it to the least of my brothers, I have done it to God." — Matthew 25:40.

If I put God first, I will not perish, and I will have everlasting life.

In my belief system, everlasting life has to do with reincarnation.

"We are of yesterday, and know nothing, because our days on earth are but a shadow." — Job 8:9

I want to expand on this, or what I think the bible is referring to as immortally.

The 23rd Psalm has always been a favorite of mine. It gives me a beautiful image of God as a shepherd. Like the book of Job where it says God will not abandon us. The 23rd Psalm says, He won't abandon us even in death.

"Yea though I walk through the valley of the shadow of death I will fear no evil for thou art with me."

It reads, "...through the valley of the shadow..." We go through the valley of death, we don't stay there, and it is the shadow of death. Shadows are not the actual object.

I once asked a minister what references there were in the bible to reincarnation. He told me it was a common belief in Jesus' time: Probably because of the Egyptian influence. However, the minister also told me there could be at least three verses which could be argued as references to reincarnation. There might be more than three, but I remembered two:

"1And as Jesus passed by, he saw a man which was blind from his birth. 2 And his disciples asked him, saying, 'Master, who did sin, this man, or his parents, that he was born blind?'" — John 9:1

The reason for the belief in reincarnation in this

verse: The only way the man could have sinned was if he had reincarnated. This man had been born blind.

"₁₃ (Jesus) asked his disciples, saying, 'Whom do men say that I, the Son of man am?'" "₁₄And they said, 'Some say that you are John the Baptist: some, Elias; and others, Jeremiah, or one of the prophets.'"— Mathew 16:13-14:

The reason for the belief in reincarnation in this verse: The disciples were naming people that had died. This suggested that Jesus had been reincarnated.

There are other verses that suggest reincarnation or the resurrection of the dead for example: I Corinthians 15:12-31. These are references to Christ's resurrection. With this in mind, in John 14:12, Jesus said everyone would be able to do the same.

"The works that I do, shall you do also, and greater works than these shall you do."—John 14:12

There are many books on reincarnation.

I feel some people get too carried away with reincarnation. They get involved too much with past life experiences. I think you have to use past lives regression only if it helps you deal with traumas in this life time.

Don't get stuck in the past. There is a reason for our forgetfulness. I think the bible also address reincarnation with this verse:

"The thing that hath been, it is that which shall be; and that which is done, is that which shall be done: and there is no new thing under the sun." —Ecclesiastes 1:9

I remember one day, in a Chemistry class at Cuesta Community College. I got excited when the professor was telling us that even the smallest emission of light will go on to the atmosphere to create new star systems. He called it: The law of conservation of energy.*[33] If nothing can be created or destroyed, then this is in total agreement with the bible.

In other words, everything is recycled. I was on the fence about reincarnation, then the professor's words made sense. Why would we die permanently and never come back. It's like finishing kindergarten, just as we begin to learn, then being told by a parent: "You got just one chance kid. Don't blow it! And by the way, no matter how hard you try, you are going to fail and you will not be able to repeat the class ever again."

In my belief system, this is something a loving God would not do. Yet this is exactly how some religions try to scare people into loving God. They teach about hell, death, and eternal damnation. It does not make sense, yet some people actually buy it. We need to wake up but let's do it gently?

Not to love is the real hell. I believe we remain there until we finally 'get it' whether we believe in God or not, or no matter how many times we reincarnate.

Personally, I like the idea that this world we live in is a virtual reality training ground. But this does not necessarily mean that we have to reincarnate in order for us to learn all we need to learn. All the learning we need, can be done in heaven or on earth. No one knows for sure and no one can really give us any proof one way or the other. It is all based on faith.

After reading many books on OBE's (Out of body experiences), I want to believe Betty J. Eadie's account of her near death experience (NDE) in Embraced by the Light. In To Heaven and back, and many others too numerous to mention, they talk about seeing a light. The

---

[33] This law is also known as the first law of thermodynamics: Pure energy can neither be created nor destroyed in any physical or chemical change.

bible says the same thing:

"They that sat in darkness saw great light, and those in the shadow of death the light sprung up."
— Matthew 4:16

I am not the only one who has seen things which can't be explained. I also know **truth needs no defense.**

If heaven is our home as some people believe, then by reason: Are we never allowed to leave and come back? After all, didn't God give us freewill?

The movie Groundhog Day starting Bill Murray nicely illustrates what I am trying to say. The movie encapsulates several life times in one day. He keeps waking up to the same thing day after day.

Even if you don't believe in reincarnation: It makes sense that this is eternity no matter how many times we come back or not. There is nowhere for me to run but to look within and take responsibility, here and now, for my own mind, and its thoughts, And even if I didn't believe in God, I want to learn how to make my life better so I can lessen my suffering while I live here on earth.

In my opinion, the movie Groundhog Day, is what the bible has been saying all along. The character, Bill Murray's plays, in the end, "gets it" and start turning his life around.

When I tell you that you take your hell with you, I know this from a personal experience. You don't have to die. Even in life we take our hell with us. Every time I removed myself from a bad situation, things seemed to always go back to what I knew. Even some of the "new" people had the same bad habits I was "running from". I was always the common denominator.

It does not matter where you are: Misery breeds misery. But since the mind is not trained we need to stay where we are and start there. We have created a worthy goal for ourselves: To get healthy. This in itself is something to live for.

An example of what I am trying to say, i.e., that dying won't change anything, I want to tell you of something I heard from a friend.

Years ago, my then husband and I were invited to a party. The party was at a farm house of a close friend. Friends kept coming all day until it ran into the night; many were close friends and a few had grown up together. There must have been at least a hundred people there. Cars were going in and out. Cars were parked everywhere in the field and alongside of the dirt road. I became good friends with Carol (Not her real name). About a week later she invited us back to the farm for a small get together.

Since this was not the only weird thing which ever happened to me, her story seemed possible. Especially knowing what I knew about the people at the party.

Apparently, a girl at the party had gone to pee by one of the parked cars, a car hit her, and was killed. Three days later. Carol was in the bathroom, looking in the mirror standing over the sink casually combing her hair. From the corner of her eye, Carol saw something which caused her to look down. There was the girl all slummed over on the floor against the wall. Carol said she could not believe her eyes, and related the following:

"I asked (calling her name), 'What are you doing here? You're dead.' "

"The girl then said, 'Oh is that what happened.' Then she disappeared."

When the girl died she had probably been high on drugs, and her Spirit became disoriented after she died.

"In my Father's house there are many mansions."
— John 14:2

The many mansions can be interpreted as different levels of: consciousness; understanding; or physical dimensions.

The fact remains, no one knows what really happens after we die. We can only speculate and take it on faith. Some people have more faith and have had different experiences on this subject. Therefore, not everyone shares the same beliefs.

How can we expect someone to see the beauty in death while they are burying their loved one? But yet some people with good intentions expect just that. They seem to think everyone holds their particular views on death.

To my horror, I once heard a lady say to a mother who had recently lost her child. "God needed another angel." For one thing, God doesn't need anything. An extreme sense of loss whatever the reason should be respected! And unless this happens to you, you cannot possibly know the pain. The less you say the better. And if you do have to say anything, at the very least, first try to imagine yourself in their shoes. Then maybe this verse will make sense:

"You did well: You communicated with my pain."
— Philippians 4:14

I just need to leave you with one more thing before I change the subject. According to the Bible Methuselah lived 900 years but what is even stranger than this, is a guy named Melchizedek. This character always reminds me of the character in Star Trek named "Q". Melchizedek (Hebrews 7:3) "...without father, without mother, without descent, having neither beginning of days nor end of life; but made like unto the Son of God: lives...continually." And interestingly it also says, "He was yet in the loins of his father, when Melchizedek met him (Jesus)." —Hebrews 7:10.

When I read about Melchizedek I was fascinated most preachers never mentioned him and I wondered why. The bible speaks of him thirteen times: once in Genesis, once in Psalms and the rest in Hebrews. He doesn't say or teach anything. He is simply there. Maybe he is teaching us about the possibilities of immortality? Yeah think?

Spiritual Death

"The most beautiful thing we can experience is the mysterious. It is the source of all true art and science. He to whom this emotion is a stranger, who can no longer pause to wonder and stand rapt in awe, is as good as dead: his eyes are closed." — Albert Einstein[34]

I think what Einstein is talking about here, is God. Personally I believe that if I don't believe in God I might be considered spiritually dead.

Jesus told a man:

"Let the dead bury the dead." — Luke 9:60

The man wanted to follow Jesus, but first wanted to bury his father. This seems rather harsh, but it is consistent with "warring after the flesh". Since the man was not dead, Jesus was speaking metaphorically.

"The flesh and the Spirit conflict: Choose."
— Galatians 5:17

In this verse I believe Jesus was saying we need to make God our first priority.

---

[34]The ABC's of the Mind Reader's Digest page 19.

The shortest verse in the bible is:

"Jesus wept."— John 11:35

Since Jesus wept, weeping in and of itself is okay. When we look at the two verses together they tell us it is okay to cry but we can't overdo the grieving. We have to keep going. We need to come to terms with what we have lost.

I was sitting next to a woman once and she was crying, I finally asked her why she was crying. She told me her husband had committed suicide.

"Oh," I said, "That's terrible. How long ago did he die?"

"Five years ago," She said.

It caught me off guard because she was crying in such a way, which seemed like it had just happened. At first I didn't know what to tell her. After a few moments to reflect, I told her, "I know what to do".

She looked up at me like I was the answer to her prayers.

"What?" She asked.

"You keep on crying, until you have finally get tired of it."

Everyone deals with loss differently, so you don't have to apologize to anyone. However, find some way to come to terms with it. Only you can do this. Only you can decide when you have finally had enough. But don't waste needless time and energy on something you cannot control. It might develop into a bad habit which can develop into a neurotic way to get sympathy, then later into an addiction. Instead, find peace, and find God.

"Let it be, God is with you." — I Samuel 10:7

"Let it be." — II Samuel 5:24

In one of my first psychology classes we were shown a clip from a documentary of a woman featured in The Three faces of Eve, but according to her account years later in a book called I'm Eve, Chris Costner Sizemore was diagnosed with 22 distinctive personalities.

In the book Sybil by Flora Schreiber Doctors diagnosed her with sixteen separate personalities.

Doctors have examined people like Chris and Sybil. The mind will try to make sense out of its surrounding and in extreme cases, it creates ingenious ways to deal with reality. Each different personality may have a physical condition such as high blood pressure, or the need for glasses etc., which the rest don't have.

This is an extreme case of the body identifying with the mind. The mind will continually try to come back to reality.

An identity crisis can happen when change comes too abruptly with no time to adjust. In an extreme cases a part of the mind in a personality cannot handle a situation so it creates another personality who can. The research points to higher than normal intelligence.

In the case of the lady whose husband committed suicide: She went from a wife and suddenly identified herself as a victim. So she cries to get sympathy from strangers. When this does not satisfy her she might turn to other distractions. These distraction are there to keep her from facing her problem. Which has its basis in fear and can take different forms: Guilt, financial stress, anger, etc.

The person can become depressed and with good reason. The mind will continue to struggle for a healthy resolution. After the Great Depression of 1929. Many businessmen could not cope with their financial losses and many committed suicide. It takes courage to face this kind of adversity.

I once had the great privilege of knowing a man, who was a millionaire then lost it all, and became homeless. He picked himself up, and once again became a millionaire. This same man became a minister, and wrote <u>Great Dramas of the Bible</u>. This man, Bill Cameron, baptized my son.

Minds may take extreme measures by denying what is happening and not dealing with the reality. I gave examples of this with creating blind spots. My advice is: Don't go up the river. We all know the river: "The Nile" (denial). Hopefully, you won't be able to deny what is happening to you nor be able to block it out.

If we take things to the extreme into a fantasy world: It simply means it will take us longer to get back to reality.

Things sometimes take an effort on our part. These is the vegetables in life, and not the dessert.

"Think not that I am come to send peace on earth: I came not to send peace, but a sword."— Matthew 10:34

"O Lord, thou gives us everything, at the price of an effort."— Leonardo Da Vinci

Help others without hurting yourself. Give others a smile and a kind word. These are gifts which won't cost you anything. Start there! I know from personal experience how painful life can sometimes become.

Careers and professions often become our only sense of identity. I remember I had lost another job, and my thoughts once again turned to suicide. But this time, I was determined to confront it head on, and finally get to the source. As I sat in the living room, I asked God to reveal the source.

I calmed down, and took three deep breaths to get my body relaxed. Then I breathed very calmly: Suddenly, I saw a memory from my past I had long forgotten.

My father and mother are in the kitchen talking,

and I casually overheard a conversation between the two. My father was searching for answers from my mother. In a desperate tone, my father pleaded, "What are we going to do? How are we going to feed all these kids?" Since I loved my father, the idea of suicide seemed like a viable solution. My child mind reasoned that if I ceased to exist it would mean my father would have one less mouth to feed. It never occurred to me it would cost a lot of money to bury me or even how badly it would make them feel. For a child it was a very fundamental answer to a very serious problem.

In coming back from the memory, I remember that day. It was the day my father lost his paycheck. I found myself back to the present day, confronting once again my jobless situation. I realized I was no longer a child. I was now a grown woman who could take control over what happens to me.

I remember when my teenage son was having a bad day in school. I suggested he be kind to people; open doors, say 'please' and 'thank you', and to just try it for one day. After school I asked him how his day went.

He lit up and said, "Oh mom, it was so great..."

Our spirit needs to be resurrected.

"Be not conformed to this world: but be transformed by the renewing of your mind, that you may prove what is the good and acceptable and the perfect will of God." — Romans 12:2

I learned that one way to get out of a depressive state, is to think of others. This I believe is the first step in healing the Spirit.

Watch your thoughts for they become words
Watch your words for they become actions
Watch your action for they become habits
Watch your habits for they become character

Watch your character
It becomes your destiny.
— Margaret Thatcher

What we think we become!

Once I was watching the TV game show, The Family Feud. The question Steve Harvey asked, "100 people were asked: What do we need to survive?"

Immediately I thought, *"Air, water, food, shelter."*

I didn't even come close. When the first contestant yelled out the top answer, "Phone." I thought to myself, *"Why can't I be normal like everyone else?"*

I now realize, I am glad I failed.

I am...well...different. I will always love the way Mr. Rogers use to tell me there was no one else in the world like me.

Depression

One of the most terrifying times in my life was when nothing I did worked. This was long after my divorce and the kids were gone. Everything had seemed to be going well:

- I had a house where I felt safe.
- There was no danger of being homeless.
- There was plenty of food in the refrigerator
- All my utilities were paid.
- There was steady money coming in.

I had even organized my house enough to be able to find things and have the luxury of a roll and a cup of tea in the mornings. I finally could look forward to enjoying the day. Suddenly, one morning, out of nowhere, I did not want to get out of bed. I tried everything I could to motivate myself to get up and get dressed. My internal dialog simply said, "*No.*"

I tried counting to three; or saying to myself, "*Just shake a little to get the blood pumping.*" My inner voice very calmly and stubbornly told me, "*No.*"

I told myself, "*You've worked hard and have been through so much. It's okay to get up and buy something nice for yourself.*" The answer was the same.

"*Get up and go buy anything you want, and don't worry about the money.*" But it was the same weak, "*No.*"

I finally gave up and told myself, "*It is okay.*" Besides I thought, "*You're going to have to get up sooner or later to go to the bathroom.*"

Eventually I did. But in a zombie like state, I went back to bed.

I lay there for hours. From my window, I watched it get dark. I lay there in the dark until I finally went to sleep. The next morning it was the same. I just didn't want to get up: Not even to eat.

I started to think it was getting dangerous but I didn't care.

All day long while lying there I could see myself just lying there dying, not lifting a finger to save myself. I thought no one would find me for days, and that no one really cared.

"*My kids would forget me and go on with their lives: This,*" I thought to myself, "*is as it should be.*"

I guess I just wanted to rest. I had been through so much abuse. I was tired of struggling and fighting and getting nowhere. It would never end. It was a one step forward two steps back type of existence.

The conversations and inner dialog went on. At noon I finally got angry with myself.

"*You worthless piece of shit: Everyone was right. You are pathetic.*"

I just listened to my angry inner voice without fighting back. "*All these books you've read. All these bibles and biographies of people who had it far worse than you: Martin Luther King, Gandhi...*" I kept naming book after book. I have over 2000 books in my library and hundreds are facing my bed. "*All of these books and you didn't learn anything. What a waste. You're pathetic! Where's your God now?*" I kept looking at the books. The topics ranged from anthropology to zoology. I had all the bibles; psychology books, and self-help books I had read over the years. The Conditions Of Learning, The Course in Miracles, The Secret of the Ages, How To Win Friends and Influence People, Master Mind, and so many others kept staring me in the face.

There were even my old college text books on motivation and I remembered how disappointed I was that what I had learned was not enough to motivate me to get out of bed. I kept reading and remembering titles. "*What a waste of time.*"

"*Okay*" I thought, "*I know this one will do it. Something to Live By.*" I remembered when I brought it. How could I forget? It had cost me a fortune. I brought it on a trip to Knott's Berry Farm. My mother loved taking us there. I remember touching the hardback book wrapped tightly in cellophane. Something to Live By. I could only read the front and back covers: "A book of help and comfort for all ages." The book cost $4.95, a fortune for a 12 year old. I remembered paying for the book, and ripping up the cellophane. On the inside cover it read: "When doctors told Dorothea Kopplin she would not live to bring up her children, she decided to write a book to serve as a substitute in their lives..." But unfortunately even this book did not seem to work. I just lay there, my mind was wanting what my body refused to give it. Finally, something seemed to strike a chord. Ever so slowly, I remembered a book I read years ago. It was written by a Priest. Or was it a book? I think it was something someone told me: A tiny spark which all of us possess. One tiny little spark within us which we can share with others. It was similar to the ancient Chinese saying:

"It is better to light a candle than to curse the darkness."

If I took this tiny spark I have in me and light a candle then another candle, the whole room would light up.

I realized this was all I had left: A tiny little spark which was getting smaller and smaller. I lost the anger, and calmed down. I saw in my mind I could go, and in a small way, help someone and maybe help light up a corner of my much dimmed world before my tiny spark got smaller.

Who knows why? Maybe I was finished resting. I saw myself get up and get dressed for first time in a day and a half. I decided to smile at the first person I saw. The person who smiled back, unknowingly saved my life.

We all make mistakes and I had made my share. Where had I gone wrong? I had always tried to do the right thing. What had taken me so far from the God I love? I had often been lost, addicted, and desperate. I had gone from one relationship to another, thinking it was going to solve all my problems. Yet all the time I seemed to be making decisions out of pure desperation.   The solutions for the fear I created were like the "love" I created. They both served the same purpose: Temporary distractions.

Although my healing began with a single thought, I could have so easily put a stronger label on what was going on. I could have reached for the drugs to "make myself feel better."

I was fortunate enough to have snapped out of it as quickly as I did. There had been an overload. I had to reset the computer. It had crashed. The years of garbage had finally caught up with me. And like Paul in Romans

7:19, I also seemed to be doing "the evil which I wish not to do..." Instead of dealing with my problems I covered them up.

I try to put God first. I am often lost and don't know how to stop the pain. I turn desperately to God hoping for another miracle. I want God to save me once again. Things get better then I make the same mistakes and the cycle repeats itself once again.

"How long will it take God?"

The answer comes, "As long as it takes."

I know how bad things can get: Especially when thoughts of suicide sometimes seemed the only way out.

Suicide

Any thought without God is suicide. God is unconditional love. A person sometimes thinks he is all alone and this brings with it, so much pain. Physical death seems the only way out. Don't they know they are going to die anyway? So why not postpone it?

Suicide is not the answer. There are too many people who will feel the loss and pain of this decision. It is even more tragic in young adults. They are often bullied, and worry more about what the bully is saying than how their parents will feel if any harm came to them.

Suicide has a very insidious nature. It is so often disguised in many forms. We don't need to try to find out how we got from point A to point D. We need to first find ways to stop it. We can then look for the source.

Sometimes people's thoughts can get caught in a loop. This is much like a computer which goes over and over until you pull the plug and tell it you have had enough. When the behavior escalates to the point where a person is thinking of doing physical harm to themselves or others, we as a society in general, have to find a way to help the person and stop them.

Take it from one who knows how absolutely bad it can get. Get them to talk and keep them talking about how they feel. Brainstorm for alternatives. They need a new way to see an old situation.

Even if you think they are doing it just to get attention: Do not leave them alone until you are sure they are safe. And if they want attention, help them to get it.

Whatever they think they can't handle, they need to be made to realize that this too will pass.

Maybe telling them something like will help:

You may be only one person in the world, but you may also be the world to one person.

Think of a time you were truly happy. Imagine yourself without a care in the world.

Reduce the part of your life you think can't change. This helps with the stress and mental torment. You might try what I did: When I was a little girl I pretended I died. I even imagined myself in a coffin and "saw" people saying kind words over me. In other words pretend you know longer exist. Take a page from the movie: It's A Wonderful Life.

If this doesn't give you a different perspective; do what I did and turn your life over to God. You don't want your life anyway, so why not turn it over to Him? No one needs to know.

Ask the Spirit within to tell you what to do. If it is Spirit, and not your ego: It will tell you to relax, and let you know you are safe and no one will hurt you, then do what it tells you to do.

You will know it is Spirit because you will get the feeling you no longer need to hurt anyone. The Spirit will get you out of the "mess" you think you are in.

At the very least, close your eyes, imagine Jesus,

---

or whatever you conceive God or life to be, and say these
two words: "Help me," Then relax.

"All parts matter however insignificant."
— I Corinthians 12:22

"No matter what a part says, it is part of the body."
— I Corinthians 12:15

The following is a poem I found in The Best Loved
Poems of the American People (Copyright 1936). Since
the Author is unknown, I feel I can include it here. I like
it because it says what I have be saying all along.

How to Be Happy

Are you almost disgusted with life, little man?
I'll tell you a wonderful trick
That will bring you contentment, if anything can,
Do something for somebody, quick!

Are you awfully tired with play, little girl?
Wearied, discouraged, and sick—
I'll tell you the loveliest game in the world,
Do something for somebody, quick!

Though it rains, like the rain of the flood, little man,
And the clouds are forbidding and thick,
You can make the sun shine in your soul, little man,
Do something for somebody, quick!

Though the stars are like brass over heard, little girl,
And the walks like a well-heated brick,
And our earthly affairs in a terrible whirl,
Do something for somebody, quick.
— Author Unknown

I do what most heathens do. I dance; wear makeup; consume animals for food; I kill rodents and other pests, (Samuel's job) and if push came to shove I would do anything to protect my family. I make my share of mistakes, and I certainly have not yet reached sainthood. (I will forever remain the eternal optimist!) I don't intend to go off to the Himalayas and become a monk, nor do I feel that I have to.

The great movie, The Razor's Edge, in my opinion, makes this point. Bill Murray's character, Larry, finally "gets it", and as he is leaving the monastery says, "...It is easy to be a holy man on top of a mountain." I guess what he was trying to say is that it is harder among the people. Or to view it from the bottom up: "It's hard to remember that you came to drain the swamp when you are up to your ass in alligators."

It is not about the body or whether it is on top of a mountain, a swamp, or in a concentration camp as in Wild Bill's case, it's all about the Spirit. The opposite of Spirit (love) is fear.

I ran across a paper I wrote on for one of my classes at WSU (Wichita State University): "Why Aren't You a Criminal?" Fear was one reason I gave, and then habits I have developed over the years, but mostly I wrote that I found it less of a hassle.

I want to tell the young people of today, especially ones that have broken the law. The only difference between them and me, is that somewhere along the way:

1. You felt so much fear and probably numbed it out of your system. I didn't.

2. You probably saw so much crime and thought it was normal. I didn't.

3. You probably saw so many people getting away with things they should not have gotten away with. I didn't.

4. You either thought one of two things:
   a. You actually thought you could get away with it.
   b. You just didn't care anymore.

I still care. The truth is, normal living also takes a great deal of courage. Life without crime is often harder. But I also know life is hard enough without the extra hassle. I know I don't have to worry about being afraid of cops; a drug deal gone bad; or worse—not feeling human; feeling dead inside; or feeling like an animal.
I want to tell young people of today. Stop lying to yourself: You are afraid; you do care; and it does hurt.
The wisdom that you learned, please teach it to others.

"Warn and teach all men wisdom." — Colossians 1:28

"If you stay within the law, you are living rightly."
— Proverbs 10:17

"Don't go in the path of the wicked and do not follow them." — Proverbs 4:14

"Be not overcome with evil; overcome evil with good."
— Romans 12:21

"Refuse the evil and choose the good." — Isaiah 7:15

And because, "Prevention is worth a pound of cure": These are my favorites:

"Avoid it, don't get near it, and keep away from evil."
— Proverbs 4:15

Let your Spirit of love guide you. Remember the war will always be about principalities so don't do anything stupid. We need to fight the war as Sun Tzu suggests, with "balance and stealth."

Don't be afraid to do the right thing. When we choose to do nothing, evil and corruption will get worse. We have to clean house before it gets so bad we get sick.

You don't have to believe in God, just turn in the direction of love. The (Holy) Spirit within will do the rest.

Many people have already learned they are responsible for what happens to their own bodies by way of their thoughts.

If you have perfect love there can be no fear. Can you confuse the two or have a little of both? Absolutely! This can be done only in the spirit (ego), because Spirit (God) is incapable of lying or being afraid even a little. If God is love then he can't be fear.

"... God...cannot lie..." —Titus 1:2

"God knows not man, but his Spirit."
— I Corinthians 2:11

When I first heard the following verse I was confused:

"God is no respecter of persons." — Acts 10:34
(Also in Romans 2:11, and in Leviticus 27:2)

I wondered: What else is there? How can God have no respect for people? However, if you take the verse in I Corinthians 2:11 mentioned above, not only is it consistent, but makes perfect sense. Throughout the bible, other verses are saying the same thing.

"Though you walk in the flesh, don't war after it."
— II Corinthians 10:3

"Stay absent in body, and present in God."
— II Corinthians 5:8

"You are more than a body." — Matthew 6:25

Hate and all the other negative emotions fall under fear. Anything you fear you hate. The fear is generated when there is a perceived loss of control.

"He that loves not knows not God; for God is love."
— I John 4:8

To me it is Spirit verses spirit. When I can't make sense out of all that is going on in the world, I refer to what Jesus said:

"What is that to thee? Follow thou me." — John 21:22.
Or
"I left all, rose up and followed God." — Luke 5:28

"It is not a fight about the flesh but principalities."
— Ephesians 6:12.

My son is Jewish, my daughter a Christian, and I was raised a Catholic. I guess if I had to put a label on my beliefs, I might say I was a monotheist because I believe in one God. I don't consider myself a deist, because I don't believe God created us then abandoned us. I am not an atheist, because I believe in a God. I am not searching for God so I am not an agnostic. But if I really think about it, because I believe God is in everything: I am what my "brother" is. So I guess this makes me all of the above and much more. But it does not matter. I'll take truth anyway I can get it. I love all the bibles.

I woke up this morning saying:

"Today is holy don't mourn or weep.
— Nehemiah 8:9

"Search the heart and you will know the mind of the Spirit." — Romans 8:27

What can I say? This stuff works! Others have said the same thing in different ways:

It feels good to wake up, especially at my age, where each day is indeed a blessing.

"The Spirit of the heavens brought me visions of God."
— Ezekiel 8:3

Part III

In The Beginning

"Tell your friends all the great things God has done for you." — Mark 5:19

My Early Years

At the age of ten, I had a vision of Jesus.

The incident with the lemons precipitated three days before my vision.

I had not eaten in a couple of days. I thought about the lemons. The orange trees had all been picked, but maybe the lemons would still be there. I knew it was wrong. Growing up in a very large, very religious Catholic family, had taught me well. And this would most definitely have been high on the "Don't-Even-Think About-It-list". And to be honest, when the idea came to me, I really didn't think about it being right or wrong.

It was as if an invisible string was pulling me toward the tree. I simply allowed myself to be pulled toward the forbidden fruit.

My plan was simple: I would walk down our property and along the edge of the orange trees; get to the estimated spot opposite the tree; run as fast as I could across the dirt road; hide in the trees on the other side; and then hurry to the tree in the middle of the neighbor's orchard.

And so I took off running. I looked both ways when I got to the dirt road. *"After all isn't that what you do before you cross any street? Oh, who was I kidding?"* It wasn't my safety I was concerned about. I couldn't even convince myself it was about safety. It was then I realized that what I had planned was a sin.

After crossing the dirt road, I ran and hid on the second row of orange trees. I loved to run. But it was sheer terror thinking I would get caught. I could see my blouse pulsate. I ran and hid behind every other tree. At each stop, I would listen for any sound. My ears strained to hear a voice or even the murmur of a tractor motor. When I didn't hear anything, I'd start running again. As I ran, I tried to think of something to say if someone was to see me. I could have asked permission, but deep down inside I knew I would never ask for the lemons. I guess this was too important to take a chance. They might say no and then I wouldn't even be able to pretend it was okay. Besides, I rationalized, it's just a game, and besides my mom did not like us to beg. I didn't even want to know what she would do to me if she knew I was stealing.

I kept running, it seemed like it was taking me forever. I didn't realize it was so far.

Finally there it was.

I was glad to see the fruit still on the tree. The bright yellow fruit looked like Christmas ornaments in the late afternoon sun. I thought to myself, *"Oh thank you God."* The word God must have triggered the voices, because that's when the nagging began.

"It's wrong to steal...You'll going to burn in hell....You're no good... You'll never be any good...God is going to punish you..."

"It's too late...this is the only time. I won't ever do it again...I promise..." Yet I didn't stop.

I quickly grabbed about five lemons. *"Not too large,"* I thought. *"I don't want to be greedy...just to stop my stomach from hurting."* I made a basket with my tattered dress and dropped the lemons onto the skirt. I headed back following my freshly make foot prints.

It was pure exhilaration when my bare toes grabbed the soft soil my dad had recently plowed. My mind yelled, *"S-s-s-A-A-F-E."* I felt as secure as a baseball player coming into home plate.

I had not planned any further than this and I was still scared.

Years later, someone would ask the age old question: "Why does a chicken cross the road?" I would remember the lemons.

The mental nagging got stronger. I knew I could not go near the house. I ended up at the edge of the alfalfa field on the top edge of our orange grove. The sun was setting when I swatted down to eat the lemons.

I felt like a little mouse nibbling on the sour fruit.

I noticed the sunset to my left. It was so beautiful, but it only made me think of God. This time the voice came back with greater force. *"You are a bad girl...You stole the lemons."* In the swatted position I turned my back toward the sunset. *"You can't turn your back on God. God sees everything...You'll burn in hell."*

The voice persisted. My conscience would not leave me alone. Suddenly out of nowhere. I turned around, stood up, held up my small, ten year old fist toward the sunset.

"Then send me hell! I'm just a little kid and I'm hungry. Why do I have to go hungry?" I yelled defiantly.

I waited for, what I felt sure was, certain death. I waited. Nothing happened, so I wiped away my tears.

A bit more sheepishly I added, "And besides, if you're so good. Why don't you give my family the money to feed me?"

I waited for the voice, but it didn't come. I buried the rinds in the soft dirt and started my walk toward the house. I walked into the house where everyone was sitting in front of the television. They looked up as if to say, *"Oh, it's only you,"* Then returned to face the television.

I was still hungry. *"You're always hungry."* I heard myself say. I had heard this more than once.

I walked into the kitchen in search of anything to eat. My sister was cleaning. And like so many times before, she was annoyed because it was her turn to clean the kitchen. She was angry and ran me out.

Already sensitive, this only added to my overburdened conscience. I ran crying to my room. But God was not yet done with me.

For three days I felt an enormous amount of guilt. This was a good thing however, because it took away my hunger. I had been in a stupor, for three days, wondering when God was going to punish me, and wishing he would get it over with.

I was watching television when my mom hollered at me to go and tell my sister Maggie she needed her for something. I thought she might be with a neighbor next door.

I walked lethargically across the dirt road, up to the green lawn. I said, "Hi" to their dog. He was always tied up. I guess I hoped the friendly gesture would win me some points with God. I walked up to their porch and knocked on the door. After a minute, Mrs. Rider walked up wiping her hands on her apron. She opened the door and motioned me to come in.

In my broken English, I told her my mother wanted my sister to come home and to please tell her. I turned and stepped down off the porch, not waiting to find out if Maggie was even there.

I don't know what possessed me, but instead of going back home I kept walking. I guess it was because I had permission to be there.

I was unusually calm, as I kept on walking. I must have been in a disassociated state, because I was so different from my usual self. Ever since I could remember my mind was constantly racing, yet this time I was unusually calm. I kept going further away from our house and found myself in the neighbor's orange grove far beyond, the now despised lemon tree which had caused me to sin.

I was just taking a nice stroll. "An adventure," I thought. "Just to see what I could find."

I now had an excuse, "I was looking for my sister. After all, Mrs. Rider hadn't really said one way or the other she was there."

After a time, I found myself at the edge or the orchard walking on the mound of dirt by the canal road.

The canal had deep sloping cement walls and was filled with water. I was strolling down the road along the right side of the canal.

The sun felt warm on my face and uncovered arms. I felt the fresh breeze. I had no worries. I was totally and completely aware of everything. I was totally in the "Now."

I looked up toward the top of the trees, and from the corner of my eye, I saw a very light blue, silver white, satin color shimmering. I turned to the right. Being fully aware of what I was looking at. I saw it was out of place. It started to take the shape of what appeared to be a curtain. It was so beautiful my eyes were fixed on this beautiful satin cloth waving like a curtain before me.

Magnetized, my eyes kept going up and up, higher and higher. The realization finally hit me. I was looking at Jesus. He wasn't smiling, he wasn't frowning, or sad or anything. He was just there with his arms showing me the scars on his hands. As I gazed in awe at his beautiful face, I could feel an overwhelming sense of love.

I felt a tap on my shoulder and a different more gentle voice said, *"Fear not, the angel of God is with you."* Suddenly in my mind, I saw an image of the guardian angel hovering in protection of two young children. The kids are walking precariously on a broken bridge. It was a picture which had been in my grandmother's house for as long as I can remember.

I remember I once had been with my mother in Sinton, Texas. I sat and played while she talked to my sister's father-in-law. I loved to listen to grownups tell their stories. On this particular day, Don Antonio was telling my mother what his dad had told him before he died. His dad had told Don Antonio that he had felt a tap on his shoulder, and recognized it as death. "La Muerte." Then added, that he had also felt the same tapping on his shoulder a few days before.

Don Antonio died a week later.

This, along with the idea, that no one sees God that does not die, had been planted in my head. Both ideas disrupted the indescribable and so incredible sense of love I was experiencing.

As soon as the thought of death hit me, I became very frightened. But as I kept looking up at the beautiful image of Jesus, it very gently faded away.

But once again I remembered what Don Antonio had said about death tapping him on his shoulder, and I ran hoping the running would wipe away what I had just seen. But how could I forget the way Jesus had looked at me, and the love I felt? I also knew I would never feel alone ever again.

I ran and kept on running as fast as I could. I wanted to erase what had happened. I ran to where the canal met the highway. I ran along the edge of the oranges trees by the highway. When I got to the dirt road going home I ran down it. I ran along the edge of the alfalfa field alongside our property. I looked down at the place I had buried the lemon rinds. I ran along the other edge of our property, through the trees.

"I did not want to die."

But I knew what I had seen. Not wanting to think. I ran and ran until I could run no more. I finally reached the house. My sister was sitting outside on a chair with a book in her hands. She was always reading something.

Out of breath I asked, "What if...what if...*Inhale...Exhale.*

Irritated at my interruption, she said, "Go away stupid."

"But," I persisted.

"What if someone saw God?"

"Can't you see I'm busy?"

"Okay." I said. Then I slowly walked away thinking, *"I'm going to die for stealing the lemons."*

Later on that night, I lay awake thinking of the incredible love I had felt for the first time in my life.

"At the very least, I will die knowing I had been truly loved."

I turned over and fell asleep.

As it turned out, however, I now had a direct line to the supernatural.

The Baby Picture

I was the fourteenth child born to Salud and Jose Chavez Fonseca.   It seems like from the beginning, my whole life has been clouded in doubt.

I was born in a corner room in my grandparents' farm house in Mathis Texas.   When I was christened a few days later, the baptismal certificate would read: Herminia Fonseca, with the date of birth being April 22.

My mother claimed I was born on April 21 at 2:00 in the morning: Emphatically arguing she had been there when I was born. My sister Mary also claiming she was also there, asserted that my mother went into labor on the 21st, but I was actually born at 2:00 in the morning on April 22nd.   Just to be on the safe side, I celebrate my birthday all week.

There is also some doubt as to how my last name is spelled.   Since my baptismal certificate spells my last name: Fonseca with an "s".   Years later I changed it to coincide with the certificate. The other members of my immediate family spell it "Fonceca".

On the night I was born, according to my mother, "The night was quiet.   Then, out of nowhere, lighting struck and thunder crashed." This all happened at exactly the same time they held me up by the ankles and spanked me.

My mother told me, "When you cried and took your first breath is when the storm came. It came as if out of nowhere. It was so loud it frightened everybody."

The first time she told me I scared everyone, I remember thinking, *"It serves 'em right for spanking me!"* Years later when watching Young Frankenstein, it would remind me, of what they told me about the events surrounding my birth. It makes me laugh even today.

At the age of about 8-9 months I was gravely ill, with a temperature of 105°. I had pneumonia when they rushed me in front of the camera before I died. They could have at least combed my hair. Except for the funny expression on my face, I was a cute kid.[35]

Ironically it was the only baby picture of me. When I did or said anything which did not seem "normal" to my siblings, they would tell me over the course of my lifetime it was because the fever had damaged my brain.

I never quite knew if there was a hidden message in my mom's voice. What exactly, was mom trying to convey to me. I never really found out. She would often imply something about me was not quite "normal". For years I wondered, if she meant I was Special or special.

My maternal grandmother tying me to the bed, (page 37) might have had something to do with my imagination. When one is physically restrained, the mind takes over. What I suspect happened to me, was that I was to discover another world inside me, where no one could hurt me. There were several times in my life where I would disassociate. Although it would be several years before I would be able to put a label on this condition.

I was surprised to learn from a Paul Harvey segment on his radio program, that Lucille Ball had a similar experience. Lucille Ball is the star of the I Love Lucy Show. Apparently her parents would tie her up to the tree in the back yard for hours. She would use her imagination to escape her ordeal and imagined she was rich and famous.

What I also think molded my character was my

---

[35] You can find the picture in the Spanish version of My Mother's Diary -1954, titled Los Fonseca.

surrogate mother, my sister. I mentioned her on page 139.

In a way, I compare my story to the story of King Solomon, but with a twist. As the story goes, two women wanted the same baby. Wise King Solomon decides to cut the baby in two. This is when the rightful mother gave up the right to the baby in order to save it.   King Solomon then reunited mother with her baby.

Such a happy ending.

Unfortunately, I was not that lucky.   My sister already had a baby of her own, and according to two of my sisters, Carmen was resentful and felt I was an intrusive competitor for my mother's love. This is understandable.   It is perfectly natural to want the love to go to her own baby. Furthermore, my mother also resented my intrusion on her freedom.

Since no one in my family rarely agrees, there is a long standing rule of thumb by which I rely: If two or more of my sisters agree, then it is probably true. So when two of my sisters told me Carmen was actually jealous of my mother's love toward me, it was hard to admit all this had a ring of truth.   But all of it became fairly obvious after reading my mother's diary. She clearly favored my niece.

My King Solomon story has a different ending.

Since both mothers resented my presence, King Solomon, (God) took me in.

The truth is, when it came to my family, I never fitted in. I unwittingly went through life not realizing this, and thinking it was somehow my fault, feeling lonely and abandoned but not being able to put a face to it until several years later.

Luckily along my life's highway, there were several people who took me under their wing.

In reality, I had a mother who had had one kid too many, and had a sister who conveniently happened to be breast feeding her own baby at the time.   And me, like an imprinted duckling, I simply followed the one who provided the food.

Somewhere along this time, (the age of ten) I gave up competing for my mother affection. In the meantime, my sister took care of me. And during these years, I was well fed and well dressed. At the age of seven, my world changed.

On the 30th of June in 1954, my surrogate mother left with her new husband to Texas.[36] Along with her, went my meal ticket. The rest of the family went about with their normal routines, and each assumed I was being cared for.

Having fourteenth siblings with some authority constantly over me, I think produced in me a way to read people, and helped hone my survival skills.

I felt lucky I found what I would later label "God's World."

At the age of five, after my bout with a mild case of chicken pox, I noticed that if I was to center myself and be very quiet, nothing would hurt me, either physically or mentally. I was fully aware someone was talking to me, but would manage to maintain my trance. I remember them walking away, calling me stupid, and going away totally disgusted with me.

"But it is so beautiful here," I remembered thinking.

It was difficult for me to let go of this beautiful state of mind. Understandably, this helped to reinforce my family's belief, my brain had somehow been damaged.

This coping mechanism was to be used periodically throughout my life. It would be both useful and problematic: A double edged sword.

My earliest memories were just bits and pieces.

I remember the flood where a lot of our farm animals died.

---

[36]According to my mother's diary.

After the flood waters receded, I remember to my horror, when my sister Mary reached around under the washing machine's tall legs. She was innocently retrieving some clothes which had found their way there.

Suddenly, she was bitten by a snake.

I think it was my dad who cut her finger to suck the blood out. They rushed her to the hospital, while we kids went and buried the badly beaten, dead snake.

As the car drove away I hoped Mary was okay and I remember how desperate and alone I felt.

About 20 minutes later, my dad suddenly and hysterically rushed through the door yelling at us.

"Where's the snake?" He kept yelling frantically, "Where's the snake?"

We showed him where we had buried it. He quickly dug it up. My dad rushed back to the hospital with the snake in a gunny sack. Apparently, they needed absolute proof it was in fact a rattle snake. The doctor would not give Mary the antidote until he was sure the antidote would match the bite. Once again it would be years before I found out why.

One memory I will always cherish was around the same time: The time of the flood. My dad took me by the hand and we walked to my grandmother's house.

I was always tagging along after my dad. My mother would get angry, but my dad would insist I could go. It was dark and I looked up for the first time and I saw the stars. I looked up and they were so beautiful. I pointed at a bright star and I said. "O o o o o o." My dad said, "You like it? I'll give it to you." *"Wow, my dad can do anything. My daddy loves me so much he gave me a star. And it's the biggest and brightest star. And it's mine, because my daddy said so."*

After I got over the initial awe of my vision, I came to believe the world was beautiful and all the people in it loving. This turned out nicely, since I came from a large family and I was mostly ignored, neglected, and barely eating (thus the vision). It was also nice because I could spend a great deal of time alone with God.

I was quite content living in a world I had come to create. I was introspective, and would make excuses for people's behaviors.

I thought for the most part, it was a wonderful world. Eventually this too would change. What I saw and felt, did not match up with the world I lived in. It was full of constant arguing, petty jealousies, and from my point of view, a great deal of suffering. Naively, in order to make sense out of the world, I simply came to the conclusion there must be two worlds: God's world and the people world.

I am truly fortunately my two worlds finally became one.

Strangely enough, I knew I was different, not from the vision I had of Jesus, but from the dreams afterwards.

Dreams and Miracles

"I have dreamed a dream, and my spirit was troubled..."
—Daniel 2:3

I look back and see the pattern which culminated in the writing of this book. I marvel at what I think is God's plan for me. I know something propels me to go forward with this book. For two years, I am continually drawn back to it.

I saw so much ignorance and sometimes plain stupidity on what some people think God is.

- Maybe I feel I have a duty to speak up.
- Maybe it is just things which have accumulated over the years, and the dam finally broke.
- Maybe it is just somethings I have always wanted to say about God.

I know there are people who feel the same way, because I have found them all over America.

- But maybe it can help someone to know they are not the only crazy one on this planet.
- Maybe, just maybe it can actually help someone.
- And maybe in my own way, I can fulfill a promise I made years ago on top of Snoqualamie Mountain.

There have been so many truly remarkable people who have helped me along the way.

Whatever happens, I feel I have no choice. I will try to do my best in conveying what I feel, and the rest is up to providence.

I have deleted: about 80 pages of writing. Mostly because I want to finish this book so I can get back to what I love: Reading!!

Originally I was going to delete this portion of the book (Dreams and Miracles). However, I have decided I would at least, attempt to clue you in, on how I got from A to M. And even though I didn't think I was qualified, it might answer why I wrote this book in the first place.

About a week after my vision, I was in a deep sleep, when suddenly, out of my control, I sat straight up in bed as if I were struck by lightning. I saw before me two small coffins. At exactly the same time, the phone rang. This made me conscious of where I was.

I heard my mother answering the phone. I could barely make out it was my sister.

Later that morning I heard my mother telling someone my oldest sister had had a miscarriage.

I Learned, the twins which she carried in her womb, had died. I did not even know she was pregnant.

Years later, my suspicious, skeptical, scientific, analytical, mind settled on that, "*I must have overheard it and it must have been in my subconscious somewhere.* "

Because of this and many other "dreams" and strange occurrences, I developed an interest in human behavior. My curious nature dictated I would try to find the source of my unusual condition.

My sister Lydia introduced me to handwriting analysis at a very early age. By the time I was twelve I was reading as many books as I could check out from the public library.

At the time, I thought handwriting analysis was a great parlor game. It was a way to appear "cool" among my school mates. According to them, I was surprisingly accurate.

I started taking it more seriously at the age of seventeen. It was around this time, when a neighbor named Mona Ehrlich took me to Alvarez Street.

Alvarez Street is still a popular tourist attraction in Los Angles California. Mona paid two dollars to have my handwriting analyzed. The lady said I didn't really play the piano but "banged" on it. I was amazed.

My sister Lupe had won a series of free accordion lessons. After the free lessons, along with my sister's lack of interest, my mother felt they were a waste of time. I, on the other hand would pick up the accordion, and attempted to, quite crudely, teach myself. Since my siblings complained about my playing. I would set up a chair in the middle of the orange grove, away from their sensitive ears. I would practice religiously. After the rental was returned, my parents bought me an accordion for $200. I was so proud of it. But unlike the rented instrument, it was more complicated. I did not have the discipline at the age of 12, to care about the rhythm, or pay to much attention to the counts on each note. I wrote of what became of the accordion in <u>My Mother's Diary -1954.</u>

About four years later, my mother bought an old piano that had been stored in a chicken coop. My mother asked the accordion teacher to see if it was worth the price. After getting the okay, she orchestrated, us kids to sand and varnish it. It turned out beautifully. I was proud of the work of art, and proud I was a part of its creation.

After my mother had the piano tuned, it sounded like an old player piano. Like the one you would find on Gun Smoke. (The TV series.)

The first complicated tune I played was my Dad's favorite. Over the years, I would often hear the tune when I would ride a merry-go-round.

I memorized all of five pages of Over the Waves. I felt it was easier to memorize the notes than to actually learn them. Especially since the left hand notes were more complicated on the piano than the accordion.

So yes, I did bang on the piano. How could the lady analyzing my handwriting know?

My interest into human behavior and psychology did not stop with analyzing handwriting. I started noticing patterns in people's general behavior, in people's facial features, and in their general appearances. I was amused at what people did without being aware they were doing it. I honestly wondered how on earth they could not see what was so blatantly obvious. Scars and tattoos were not the only things which were obvious. I noticed the way people stood next to each other, played with their money, or their wedding rings. My guesses got amazingly accurate. It might have been observation, intuition or my empathetic nature, but I suspect it was survival techniques I had developed at a very early age. There were seventeen people in my family whom it behooved me analyze quite rapidly. It was a good idea to anticipate how they were going to react toward me. Being able to "read" them might have helped in honing this particular talent.

It never ceased to amaze me how accurate I was with the smallest piece of information.

One day while waiting in a checkout line, I asked a

complete stranger if she had recently had an operation. "Yes, but how did you know?" She asked.

I had noticed a black dot in the iris of her eye similar to my sister's, and I simply took a chance. Later I would test my theory on others.

I found the tiniest wrinkle or facial expression fascinating. At first I thought it helpful to give people an insight into themselves: Gradually, wisdom set in, so I learned not to say anything.

It also became rather painful. People need and want somebody to listen to them, so many of them are crying out in pain.

"When a good man is hurt, all who would be called good must suffer with him."— Euripides

Years later in the Star Trek series, I identified with a character named Diane who also an extreme empath. I finally had a name for my condition and realized there were others.

At one time I became so obsessed, I started putting myself in the other person's place. The better I got, the more I could feel people's pain. With everything in my life, I took it to such an extreme it was hard for me to watch The Three Stooges.

As the years went by I realized I had a knack for reading people. The FBI calls it profiling. I latter realized what it really was: An invasion of privacy. I asked God to help me get rid of it.

It was only years later I realized that in and of itself the "gift" is not a bad thing. If everyone is connected, we should all be able to read each other. To some extent everyone has this gift. It is only the misuse which is wrong.

During the years I have had my share of epiphanies. However, at the age of twenty-seven, thinking what I had felt was God presence, it changed my life completely.

It was a morning, like any other morning, I went outside and I reached down for my morning paper. As I looked up, I saw the beautiful sunrise; the trees, the roof tops, and the grass all around me. I had no real thought one way or the other, about anything.

Suddenly, I became part of all of it. It was as if I became it and it became me. I was the universe. I could hold the sensation for only a split second, before I was once again stricken with fear, and then it was gone.

I tried to dismiss it as low blood pressure and thought maybe when I when down to pick up the paper the blood must have rushed to my head. However, in combination with a life time of experiences I could not escape the impression it had left.

This imagery took me into a journey which would last my lifetime.

After this sensation, I couldn't get enough of this thing I chose to call God. I went in search of God. This time I was not a sensitive, neglected kid. I was a fully conscious adult.

I realized I was not the only one who had been searching. The fact is, although it often goes by many names, this search is as common as the ages.

My approach, was to hone in on the main source.

It was like peeling away the parts of an onion: A reverse engineering of God. At first I found him in the strangest places. This gave meaning to my life. In later research, it was what Buddha discovered: He peeled away parts of himself.

In his book about the meaning of life, James Frankl, a Jewish holocaust survival writes that we create whatever meaning we choose for our lives. I believe this has a ring of truth.

We control our thoughts and give life meaning. No one else can. This basic responsibility never leaves our control.

I believe most people are like me. They are simply searching for answers. And maybe like me, simply trying to figure out how they can make their lives better.

My quest began with reading anything I could get my hands on. I wanted to learn anything which had to do with the subject.

I did not stop with the <u>King James version</u> of The Holy Bible, I kept reading: I read <u>The Dead sea scrolls,</u> <u>The Upanishads,</u> <u>The Vedas,</u> The <u>Bhagavad-Gita,</u> <u>The Quran</u> (Koran), <u>The Book Of Mormon,</u> The <u>I Ching,</u> The <u>Course in Miracles</u> and so many other too numerous to mention. I even read <u>The Zen of Motorcycle Maintenance</u>. (How was I supposed to know?)

I even had one book fall from a library shelf. I was walking through the Wichita Public Library aisles in the religious section asking myself, *"What do I read next?"*

Suddenly, without warning, a small book fell down from the top shelf and hit me on the head.

I grabbed it and went quickly around to the other side of the aisle to complain. But there was no one around. I went back around and realized the shelf was one sided. After I read the title, I thought it was some sort of cosmic joke.

I checked out the book which would have a profound influence on my life.

At that time in my life, things like these were normal. I would wish for something and it would appear, usually within three days.

The book which fell on my head was a prime example. I'm sorry to say I forgot the title and the author. And although I attempted to look it up in the internet I could not find one which dated that far back. There were others with the same theory, however. I remember it was a theory that God was dreaming us and when God woke up, we would be what our dreams become to us when we wake up.

I explained it to people this way:

Let's say you are dreaming of a bus, and there are six people on this bus. An old lady, and an old man, a teenager, a business man, and a woman with a small child. When you wake up, where did they all go?

And what I also want you to realize, and it makes Frankl's point nicely: When I mentioned the six people in the dream, it is you who decided what they would look like. Their unique features were created through your own experiences. These are created in much the same way you chose to wear what you are wearing today.

The premise of the book which fell on my head, fascinated me. Especially after I read: "Adam fell into a deep sleep but it never mentions Adam ever woke up."

This helped my perspective on how I saw the world.

My search took me from religion to psychology; from psychology to the mind; from the mind to what I was eating and back again.

My life took me to a wide variety of churches, religions, temples, and people from skid row bums to millionaires.

The most influential book I read was, an old black book, worn with age. This book was especially important to me, because it was written by my mother. It is a diary of a woman who could barely read or write, yet she was compelled to write it. I too have the compulsion to write about what I believed to be true. I am blessed to have had a mother who showed me the way.

I believe the bible is riddled with answers for so many of the questions for which people are searching.

I don't claim to be a bible scholar.

The Bible Project, as I decided to call it, was my way of:

1. Sharing what I found.
2. Sharing with others how much better I found it to live with "God".

3. And maybe add a little common sense into the mix.

The one thing which has always fascinated me was my dreams. I could account for being able to read people, but I could not account for the premonitions which I dreamt.

I would dream something and later it would happen. Was I picking up clues somewhere very deep in my subconscious? How would these clues be able to predict the future? Could I be causing them to happen? Were they only self-fulfilled prophecies?

I was not the only one whose dreams could predict the future. There was also Daniel in the bible. This comforted me. Maybe it was okay not be "normal."

For years I had had this recurring dream:

I was driving very fast over a hill and in order to avoid hitting a small child, I swerved into an embankment, lost control, and died. My body was lying on the sandy dirt. My sister and my niece, who lived in Texas, came to see me as I laid there on the side of the road.

When they saw me they started to cry.

"Here I am," I yelled at them, "See. I am here."

Realizing they could not see me, I blew at the dirt. I remember thinking this was enough to let them know I was there and to let them know I could hear them. But the only thing that happened, was they thought the wind was getting stronger and decided it was time to leave. As I looked down at my mangled body, I remembered thinking: "How did that wire get there?" I saw a wire. It somehow ended up through my cheek.

It seemed like the dream came every three years, then would go away.

I had always wanted to get braces, but I also knew I could not afford them. I had a habit of covering my mouth when I smiled.

Before I got married, I was going to college during the day, and working as a cocktail waitress at night, and on weekends.

One Saturday, I went to wait on my boss who was sitting with one of the regulars. I had seen him several times, but did not know anything about him. Then out of the blue, as if on an impulse, the man stood up, and told me to open my mouth.

"What?" I asked.

He once again said, "Open your mouth."

My boss told me it was okay. I felt like a dummy, but I did what they said.

He looked into my mouth without touching it, and said, "Be at my office first thing Monday morning."

Apparently, he was a dentist, who specialized in orthodontics.

"I can't afford it!" I protested.

"Yes you can," He said.

I could not believe my good luck when I learned he would periodically, provide his services at cost for people who could not afford it. I will never forget his kind generosity.

It was a miracle really, because it was something I had always wished I could do.

Within a month, my mouth was full of braces. Every few weeks he would tighten them. Then the day came to replace the braces with a retainer: A wire across the front. I had long since put the dream out of my mind.

One day, I heard from a family member my father had flown into the States and would be in Texas.

Without hesitation, I made arrangements to drive there. At the time, I was seven months pregnant with my son and working at a clinic. I would leave very early Saturday morning, drive thirteen hours, stay overnight and come back for work Monday morning.

I kissed my husband good-bye and off I went. I

had been driving for a long time in very little or no traffic.

At exactly 7:00 in the morning, as I came over an overpass, the morning rush hour hit with a vengeance!

I panicked at the sensation; I had been alone for so long, now suddenly there were all of these cars rushing in from the ramps. I managed to compose myself.

Once out of the city, traffic once again thinned out and so once again, I pumped it up to 75 miles per hour.

I was on a secondary road driving on a sloping hill at the point where I could see more horizon than road.

Maybe the first sensation triggered the second one, but I had what is called a déjávu.[37] Suddenly I remembered my dream. Miraculously it was enough to cause me to slow down. At this point I could not see the car.

As I drove over the sloping hill, I could see a car by the side of the road. The car had the driver's side, rear tire, off the ream. A man was taking a tire from the trunk. The mother had not noticed the small girl heading for the road. I honked my horn. The mother motioned toward the child. I slowed down more. In the seconds in which all this happened, it was just long enough to notice a sandy embankment along both sides of the road.

I have often told myself it was simply my body's way of protecting itself.

Although, this particular recurring dream stopped, there would be so many others.

I kept dreaming of hitting a blue car. Since the accident in my dream took place in a heavy snow every time it snowed I was hypersensitive. It would stop snowing then I would relax again. It was the strangest thing, in that year it snowed all the way into April.

---

[37]The sensation that you feel when you have already experienced the thing you are currently experiencing. The French words: déjá means "already" and vu means "seen".

During the week days it was fine, then on the weekends it would snow again. This repeated itself several times.

It was a mess.

It happened one day I let my girlfriend drive my car. Since in my dream I saw myself in the accident, I didn't see a problem.

At three in the morning I get a call telling me she had hit a car. The first thing that came out of my mouth was: "Was it a blue car?"

"How did you know?" She asked.

The truth is: except for the dream, I don't know how I knew.

These occurrences happened too frequently for them to be coincidences.

This gift or curse was simply there. I could not control it. All I could do was say, "Oh, that's interesting," and move on. I rationalized it as me being where I am supposed to be.

Years after I drew a picture of an oriental man in a barroom napkin. I saw that same man, a complete stranger, in the grocery store about four months ago.

What am I supposed to do with this information?

Should I have showed him the picture of himself drawn 40 years prior? Should I tell him it was drawn by a woman who did not know him and that it was drawn 40 year ago? I don't think so! He would have thought I was crazy.

Unless I am told differently, I will just continue to think I am where I'm supposed to be and leave it at that.

One thing I do know: God is so awesome. It's like electricity, I don't know exactly how it works, but it is nevertheless awesome. And to continue with that metaphor: I am barely learning where the light switch is.

One night I was in so much emotional pain, I just wanted to drive of a cliff. I remember I was in a Safeway store parking lot about 10:00 at night. I grabbed the steering wheel and screamed, "Help me!" It was simply a reflex in trying to keep myself from going over the deep end. You can only be tense for so long. After I screamed, I relaxed. I guess I was praying to God, because I felt like I was having a conversation with somebody.

I heard a voice say, "What do you need?" It was probably the first time I heard "The Voice".

"God's voice came to him." — Acts 7:31

It's hard to explain. Although I was conscious of it, I also felt that it was not really me. However, it was me, yet it was distinctly a man's voice. It spoke straight, without emotion.

Since I thought it was basically me, I answered to myself out loud, "I have a headache."

Again it questioned, "What do you need?"

I thought, "*I need an aspirin.*"

This is when I became aware that I was outside a grocery store. I thought, "*I need an aspirin and this is where you buy aspirin.*" I looked in my pocket and I had 29 cents. Years ago a person could buy a small one inch tin case with a few aspirin. This tin sold for 25 cents. So in I went.

This is where it gets weird, because as I stepped into the turnstile, I looked up and saw a huge sign in the back of the store which read: PHARMACY. The only way I can explain it is that I was drawn to the checkout counter. I had nothing in my hands! Why would I go there? Yet it all seemed so perfectly natural. Curiously the display case at the checkout was empty. Nothing was there except a large bottle of aspirin. It was clearly marked: 49¢ and I knew I only had 29 cents. I guess I was in shock or at least in a mild daze, because I picked up the bottle and turned toward the cashier and asked, "How much is this?" I thought, "*It 49 cents! It is clearly marked. What is wrong with me?*"

No sooner than that, I heard the cashier say, "Oh,

that's Thrifty Mart's. You can have it!"

I did not feel anything; I was still in a daze trying to make sense out of all of it.

I went outside and I didn't care who heard me. To the starry heavens I yelled out, "THANKS GOD!"

When Joyce Myers and others said, "God put it in my heart to say or do such and such; I picked up on it.

Instead of saying "God spoke to me" I decided this was a more sociably correct way to put it. I decided not to expound on the idea that I was hearing a voice.

I know what that implies.

This is how I came to figure out that it might be ego, or it might be the Spirit within.

"Give me an understanding heart to discern between good and evil." — II Kings 3:9

I am reminded of a story I read recently that reminded me of a memory long forgotten. It reminded me of my stupidity in regards to God. I have to admit sometimes it takes me a long time to learn. Here is the story:

***

Once Susia prayed to God: "Lord, I love you so much, but I do not fear you enough. Let me stand in awe of you as one of your angels, who are penetrated by your awe-filled name."

God heard his prayer, and His name penetrated the hidden heart of Susia, as it comes to pass with the angels. But at that Susia crawled under the bed like a little dog, an animal fear shook him until he howled:

"Lord, let me love you like Susia again."

And God heard him this time also.[38]

***

I was feeling very spiritual one day and I felt that I

---

[38] In Time and Eternity, A Jewish Reader, edited by Nahum N Glatzer (New York: Schocken Books, 1946)

was doing what God was asking of me: I was being kind to people and generally being, what I felt was, the kind of person God wanted me to be.

I remembered my vision I had at the age of ten, and decided that I wanted to have another vision.

I prayed, "I want to see you lord. After all," I argued, "I have been good." Then I stupidly added, "Not only do I want to see you, I demand to see you." Little did I realize what could happen!

I fell asleep, and I had another vision alright. I woke up wet in sweat. Just like Susia, I was scared with an animal fear. The following is a dream that taught me the valuable lesson:

I was on an island. It was very beautiful there. I could see the ocean beyond the beautiful lush green trees. I noticed what appeared to be sandals walking on the water coming toward me. I looked up and saw what appeared to be a huge very light blue, satin curtain. The closer the feet came toward me, the closer the curtain got. I kept looking up, and up and up trying to find a face.

I was so tiny compared to the man that was walking toward me. I felt like the sandals were going to crush me, so I yelled, "No! No!"

I woke up, and I was so relieved it was just a dream. "*That'll teach me,*" I thought, remembering what I had asked for.

There would be so many more trials that I would have to go through, before I would be able to come to terms with knowing peace.

Some miracles are subtle.

For example, I once had a friend by the name of Martha. Our friendship developed through the Sidetracked House Executives seminar mentioned earlier.

Martha and I would get together every Monday to encourage each other to change our bad housekeeping habits.

We were having so much fun, we decided that

others could benefit from some of our ideas. We decided to form a club: C.H.A.N.G.E (Creative Housewives Aiming for Neatness and Greater Efficiency.)

At one time there were nine active members.

Martha and I would take turns dressing up as 'house fairies'. We would take our magic wands and clip boards to visit member's houses for surprise visits.

We would give points for the very basics: Chairs cleared of books or papers; trash not running over the trash cans; and dishes washed.

At the end of the year we would have a ceremony in which our husbands were invited, and prizes were awarded for the most improved, and for the most points, etc.

The laughter, the joy, the tears, and the friendships were truly memorable.

"God showed wonders and signs great and small."
— Deuteronomy 6:22

How were we able to remove seven truckloads of 'junk' from one member's house? There were others member's with viable excuses: Cancer, depression, insomnia, etc., One member would average four good hours of sleep per week!!! She worked third shift and her family would not respect her need for sleep. They had lived this way for so long, no one bothered to question it.

On one particular meeting, we were busy chatting at one member's house. It was our first meeting held there. Suddenly, we turned around and became aware that the member was crying. I had no idea what this meant to her.

She was crying tears of joy.

Since her bout with cancer, she had let her house go. Although, she loved to entertain, she had not had anyone in her house for twenty years.

Were these miracles? If they were, these miracles did not just happen.

They had to 'find' us.
They had to 'let' us in.
They had to 'see' another way.
They had to have 'had' enough, and finally,
They had to 'do' it.

It was a privilege when a member allowed us to enter and help with clean up. Since I was the one in charge, I knew that we had to be respectful.

What seemed worthless to us, the person might still have strong feelings about. The things we might think useless they might still have a strong attachment to.

We had to be constantly aware and not forget that we were the invited guests. What we got rid of was totally up to them. We were serving simply as their minions.

There was a change in their expressions when they realized that they were in control. The fear of having us over was gone. I think it was at that point that they were free to get rid of even more things.

The miracle they saw in one house encouraged the others. Maybe it was an inner awareness that this opportunity would not come around again.

I was sensitive to the fact that to them it would be like amputating a leg. We had to convince them that it was decaying, and help them realize that it was indeed time for it to go. We helped each other get rid of judgments about the other members.

I knew that it would take three weeks to get used to the new feelings, and would read portions of <u>Psycho-cybernetics</u> at meetings. Our members would have to be supportive to this end.

There is not enough space and time to write about all God has given me and what it took to get me here. Maybe there is enough for another book. Right now it is like wanting another baby when I have not yet forgotten the pains of this one.

There is, however, one miracle that I want to share and it has to do with my son. It involved several people and different sequences to the final event.

I feel this is important for skeptics that say, It is just a coincidence." How many coincidences does it take to make it a miracle? You think of someone and they happen to call you: Is that a coincidence? What if you started doing it on purpose? At what point does it become visualization? How is it that 75% of people can be cured with placebos? Can we call this faith?

My son developed an interest into photography. After my son got his driver's license, he would oftentimes ask if he could borrow my car. Since I was the one that taught him how to drive, I knew he was a responsible driver.

I felt it would be more practical if I brought a second car. I also felt it would be a good investment for long trips if I brought a van. I knew I had good credit.

With this in mind, we went to a dealer where we had bought my little red Plymouth Horizon. It was Friday, and since I had purchased many other cars from that same dealer, he very generously let us drive the van on the weekend.

Monday morning we went back to the dealership, but to my surprise, my credit did not go through. "I don't understand it," I said, "You know me. Nothing has changed."

I saw the disappointed look on my son, and it did not sit well with me. "Look, I said, "I promised you a car and a car you shall have."

I had a friend who I knew would co-sign. He had worked for the Coleman Company for years, and I knew he had excellent credit. He said that there would be no problem and agreed to help me out.

I took my friend down to sign the papers, but once again the same thing happened. The credit did not go through. I could not believe it. What was going on?

Apparently, my friend had paid $100.00 out of his own pocket for a doctor bill. However, he was in the process of receiving a recent worker compensation claim, and there was a hitch, because of the $100.00 he had paid out of pocket. They were in the process of sorting everything out.

His credit was temporarily on hold.

Bad timing on my part.

I told my son that I would think of something else.

Sunday rolled around and I still was not able to get another vehicle. My son asked to borrow the car that Sunday. At about 3:00 in the afternoon, I get a call from a farmer close to Benton, Kansas.

"Don't worry," He said, "Your son is alright" "

"Who is this?" I questioned him as panic started to set in.

"Your son has been in an accident."

"What? Where is he? My son has been where? What are you saying? Can I talk to him?"

"Yes, just a moment."

As any parent knows, this can be the longest moment in history! As soon as I heard his voice I gave a sigh of relief.

"Mom, I totaled the car."

"Who cares about the car? Are you okay?"

"Yeah, Mom, but I'm sorry about the car?"

"David nothing else matters, as long as you are okay. Where are you exactly?"

I went to look at the accident. Apparently, he had lost control because of the gravel road. (Very dangerous even for an experienced driver.) I could not believe my eyes: He had knocked down a telephone pole and there were electrical wires around the car. Because of the height of the car, the wires had missed it. If he had been in a van the electrical wires would have electrocuted him. The left side of the car where the tank would be in the van was all smashed in. If he had been in the van, it would have exploded on impact. Driving the Horizon with the gas tank on the opposite side had saved his life.

I remember telling him, "David, God is not done with you yet!" I am truly grateful.

I called the insurance company, and Monday morning I was again back at the dealer. Before I could even open my mouth. He said, "After you left, I ran your credit through again, and it cleared, I don't know why it didn't go through the first time!"

Even though, I had never dreamt about it: This is a miracle. I don't care if anyone agrees or not. There were just too many coincidences. There are many others that have received these "miracles." I do know one thing. And that thing, I know that I know: No one, absolutely no one, in this world, or the next, can love my kids more than me.

"If I die today, I will die knowing I saw a rainbow of color in the atom from a tear drop that came from the love and pain of my children." — Herminia Fonseca

Random Acts of kindness

As I was driving this morning I heard a song on the radio, I think it is called "Joe". Joe performed an act of kindness and it was passed on, it reminded me of a story I once heard.

A man was on a bulldozer clearing some land.

He noticed a policeman's anxiety as he got out of his patrol car and paced back and forth. He asked the police officer if he could help. The policeman told him that he had received an emergency call and decided to take a shortcut. The shortcut however, was under construction. All he had to do was cross the road, and he didn't know what to do.

The man said, "Follow me" and created a road.

What they both found out the next day was that the call was made by the man's wife. The man saved his own son's life.

You can never know where an act of kindness will show up.

Miracle on Snoqualamie National Forest

I wanted to go home, when I realized that my marriage was not going to work. I suspected that I was pregnant, however, I just told him I wanted to go home for a while to think things through.

He didn't even try to stop me.

My last thought was that maybe he just got tired of losing at Pinochle.

The first time we played pinochle, it was a "fluff off" game so he could teach me. But he lost that one.

Unfortunately, for our marriage he would never win.

How I hated the game! But he kept insisting on playing it. Each time I would pray I would to lose. But as they say, "It was never in the cards."

I packed up a few of my things, threw them in my little red Corvair, left him a note telling how he could reach me and that I would be back as soon as I could.

I drove down State Route 97, then took Interstate 82, and headed across State Route 12. I got as far as the Snoqualamie National Forest.

At 2:00 in the morning, pregnant, with very little money, my car was out of oil.

When the car started knocking, I knew from previous experience, not to move the car any further or it would blow a rod. I did not ever want to hear that sound ever again. Once was enough!

I got out of the car, put the hood up, and walked around trying to decide what I should do. Instinctively, I knew that crying was not an option, especially since there would be no one to hear me. So I did what I always did, when I found myself in a difficult situation, I disassociated.

It was all so calm and quiet. There was a full moon, and not a car for miles and miles in either direction. The starlit sky was breathtaking. It reminded me of the field trip to the planetarium when I was twelve. The stars seemed so close I could almost touch them. My disassociate state was interrupted when I heard a wild animal, I had no idea or even a guess as to what it was. For all I know, it could have been "Big Foot". It certainly did not sound like anything I had ever heard even in my imagination.

I looked up into the sky. I pleaded with God, *"Please Dear God, Help me"*. Then more to myself than God, I thought, *"God, if you can get me out of this, you can get me out of anything."*

Almost as if on cue, a semi-truck came over the steep grade.

"...can't be scared," I kept repeating to myself over and over. I waved the truck down. I heard a loud switching sound as the big truck pulled to the side of the road, and turned on the blinking emergency lights that filled my eyes. I watched gratefully, as a tall heavy set man approached the car.

"Having trouble?"

"I think the car is out of oil," I answered.

"Car can't run without oil," He said as he lifted up the hood, and had me turn on the engine.

"Yep, it sure is," He motioned me to quickly turn off the engine.

The nearest town was twenty miles. He took me to get the oil, and generously paid for it, then he drove me back. He poured in the oil, but this time the car would still not start. So back to the town we went then handed me a twenty dollar bill, "... to help out," He said.

I offered to pay him back. "Every cent," I said.

"Write down your address," I said, scrambling around in my purse for a pen.

"No way. My wife would not understand."

"But, I insisted, "I will explain everything, and tell her how much you helped me. You have no idea...the wild animals...the dark..."

"Absolutely not. You don't know my wife."

"I wish there is something I can do for you to pay you back. You have no idea..." My voice trailing off.

He looked at me, and finally said, "I know what you can do: Help someone else. Pass it on."

"Thank you, I will." I said.

Writing this, reminded me of a time when someone called me an angel.

It was not the first time someone has called me an angel, and since there is no way I am an angel, every time this is said about me, for reasons known only to myself, it makes me chuckle.

On this day, it was very cold. It had been snowing for a couple of days, and because of the bitter wind, some cars would not start.

My car was one that did not start that particular morning. A neighbor realized what was happening, came over, lifted up the hood of the car, took the carburetor cap off, and pushed the butterfly[39] down, then told me to try to start the car. Miraculously the car started.

I thanked the neighbor and headed down the street, glad that I would get to work in plenty of time.

All of a sudden, the traffic slowed down.

Apparently, a car had stalled about five cars ahead of me. The five cars went around as the light turned green.

---

[39]The butterfly valve is composed of a small metal plate that hinges on a common spindle that acts as a throttle and permits flow in one direction.

To my discomfort, I saw an elderly white haired lady sitting in the stalled car in obvious distress. Without hesitating, I put on my flashers, set my brakes, got out of my car, and knocked on her car window. As I told her to pop the hood, I noticed the funny look on her face. I attributed this to the fact that I was a woman, I was dressed as a secretary not a mechanic, and in those days women mechanics were rare.

I proceeded to take off the top of the carburetor. I pushed the butterfly down and told her to try to start the car.

As the big smile of surprise appeared on her face, and by the time I got around to the window to tell her not to worry, I heard, "You're an angel."

I chucked, because I was just as surprised as she was. What she would never know is how the very same thing had just happened to me. The real angel was the neighbor that had helped me out.

My Mission

Years later, I remarried.

One day I was washing my dishes, I became in awe of my circumstances. I glanced at my husband reading the paper in his orange recliner; my baby boy was on the carpet playing contently with his Legos; and my little girl was sitting up straight practicing the piano.

I felt so much love! I went back to washing the dinner dishes and thought, "*I love you God. You have given me so much! I love you so much; I would even leave all this behind and feed the poor, or do whatever you ask of me.*" Just at the time, I heard The Voice say, "Wash the dishes."

I guess I must have repeated the words: "Wash the dishes" out loud, because just then, my husband had gotten up to go to the bathroom and curiously asked, "Wash the dishes? That what you are doing."

I couldn't explain to him about 'The Voice' so, I said, "Yeah, I guess that is what I am supposed to be doing."

About a week later, I received a brochure in the mail about a seminar. It was to be held at a Seven Day Adventist Church the following week. It was a series of bible lessons.

I decided to attend. I had finished studying with the Jehovah's Witnesses; I had attended a Lutheran Church, and so I thought, "*Why not?*"

It started out great, the people were amazing. Everyone seemed to enjoy each other's company.

I will never forget one particular lesson: I was sitting toward the front of the church. Some black ladies sat directly in back of me. We all sat basically in the same pews every week, so we became good friends. That particular week we were learning about what we could eat and not eat according to the bible.

With everything the preacher mentioned, from the ladies behind me, came a loud, "Amen!" The preacher would name something else, and once again I would hear another "Amen".

I turned around when I didn't hear an "Amen."

They were sheepishly quiet. We had to try hard to contain our laughter when we realized, what had happened. The preacher had gone just a little too far when he mentioned "catfish"!

When Lee, the younger preacher, preached it was more fun. The older one seemed more stoic and serious, and seemed to frown if we were having too much fun.

Toward the end of the series, the lesson was going to be on 666, and I was concerned that I would open my big mouth and contradict these wonderful people. I was at home, writing in the study guide, when I decided not to go.

That's when I heard 'The Voice' ask, "I thought you would do anything for me?"

I was sitting on the couch, with the study guide on my lap, I held out my arms, and said out loud, "Anything but that!"

When my arms fell, my hands pointed to large, bold face type letters: **GO AND TELL MY PEOPLE.** I could not have missed the message if I tried.

"Okay, okay, I'll go but I'm not going to say anything." I protested, vowing to myself that I was not going to say anything.

I got there and everything was going well. Lee was giving the lesson that day. So I thought everything would be alright. However, Lee made one mistake: With each word, Lee pounded on the lectern when he said, "When God says to do something, do it!"

My heart was pounding when I saw my hand pounding on my desk, and heard the words fly out of my mouth. "No sir!" I heard a gasp as everyone turned to look at me. I became flustered and realized I had to say something. Maybe it was because of my embarrassment, but it was as if something in me took over.

"Lee, didn't God tell Moses to go and tell his people: You know the part in the bible when Moses objected because he stuttered and wanted Aaron to speak? So Lee, if God tells you to do something, can't we question it like Moses did? Is that right Lee, or is that only a movie version of the Ten Commandments?"

Lee had to admit that sometimes it is right to question God. I would be many years later that it is not God we should question. It is our ego, trying to convince us, it is God.

Nevertheless, in that time and place, as the people nodded their head in agreement and once again looked up toward Lee, I felt like I had dodged a bullet.

I was thinking to myself that I was glad it was over. I was determined once again to not say another word. Yet once again, a power greater than me would take over: Lee said, "If your neighbor needs groceries, give him your groceries." I honestly can't remember if I raised my hand or just spoke. I felt that once again all eyes were on me, as I said, "Wait a minute Lee. The way I learned it is: "According to your faith be it unto you. "Now if I understand this right, if my neighbor needs groceries and I have a little faith, then I can give him bread, butter and milk. If I have a little more faith, then I can give him bread, butter, milk, and bananas. But if I know that God is my source, then I can give my neighbor all my groceries because I know that God will return it tenfold."

Lee told me, "You make a good point."

It surprised me that after the meeting several people went and patted me on the back approvingly.

I realized, however, that I was not as ready as I thought to be an ambassador for God. I just wanted to be normal! Unfortunately, I had no choice as to when God would use me again.

I was in a restaurant in Dodge City Kansas, reading a book on the Spirit of God. Once again my emotions and love for God got the best of me. I looked out the window and I remember thinking: "*God I need to go to church, I need to be close to you.*"

I especially remember that day, because as I stepped outside to go to my car, there was the most beautiful well defined double rainbow I have ever seen. Two perfect beautiful arches.

Everyone around me was looking at it and marveling at its beauty. This reinforced my plan to go to church, that Sunday morning. I didn't even care what church: After all, I thought "*God is God.*"

I went past this one church and quickly dismissed going there. I saw a lot of people with plates of food heading toward the door. Then something weird happened. My car went around a clump of trees, and I parked the car. I looked up and I realized I had parked in front of a church. "Well," I thought half way chuckling to myself, "I guess this is where God wants me to be."

I was greeted at the door, I gave them my name and I told them I was new to Dodge City. It was hard to get used to everyone calling me "sister". It was not something I was used to, however, thanks to my mother's upbringing, as a child, I was taught to be respectful of other people's beliefs.

I thought to myself that it would not be hard to put up with it for an hour.

Brother John, the preacher, introduced me to Sister Mary, who had me sit next to her.

She had me go first, which upset me a little, since I always prefer an aisle seat. But she directed me to the second seat, and then she sat in the aisle seat.

Sister Mary, was quite irritated and Brother Tom who had a huge deep scar running from his head to part of his forehead.

He turned around from where he sat, in the pew in front of me and started to talk.

He was all excited at seeing me and started rattling off about how he had gotten the scar working for the railroad; he was not married; told me how much money he made; and that he was glad I was there; and on and on. I tried to be as polite as I could considering that it was a very awkward situation for me.

But once again I reminded myself that in an hour it would all be over, and smiled politely at the experience.

Then the service began. Brother John wanted us to turn our bibles to Judges Chapter 4. I thought the book of Judges was a little extreme, but I thought, "*I only had to put up with it for an hour,*" And reminded myself to, "*Be respectful.*"

I could not anticipate what was about to happen.

He asked the congregation, "What happens if you clean a pig?" You can put nail polish and little pink ribbons on it, but after you let him go, it is still a pig. I guess his point was that he will go back to what it is used to doing. Which made sense.

But then he said something that caused my heart to start pounding. It was pounding so hard I could literally see my blouse move to the rhythm of my heart. I tried very hard to remain calm especially after I read the verse:

"She dwelt under the palm tree... and (they) came up to her for judgment." — Judges 4:5

The words kept playing tricks, I saw them going in and out on the page. I tried so hard to ignore everything.

I think Brother John started to notice that I was keeping my head down. He probably felt he was not getting enough of my attention. So I would look up periodically.

What caused my heart to start pounding was when he told us that soldiers in the old days would only give out their name, rank, and serial number, and die before they would tell secrets to the enemy. But they now would spill their guts at the least bit of torture. I continued to keep my head down, trying to be respectful.

But then he talked about his grandson, that's when I lost it.

He told about how one day the baby was learning to walk and he fell. Brother John went for the boy, but his son stopped him and told him that his grandson had to learn on his own.

That was enough! I had to leave! I was not going to be able to hold out for the whole hour. With the bible in my right hand, I got up, and tried as calmly as I could not to trip over Sister Mary's feet. She tried to stop me. But I politely ignored her as I pushed my way through. I would have been fine, if Brother John had not tried to shame me. "What's the matter sister? Don't you like what I am preaching?"

The only thing I remember at that time was

raising my bible up in my right arm, and turning around.

"Why not teach about the love of Jesus? There is so much love in this book!" I yelled as I walked toward him down the aisle holding up the bible. "And if a baby is learning to walk, hold his hand until he learns how to do it for himself." It was around that time that I became aware of my surrounding. "And God bless you!" I yelled as I turned around to walk out. Some were trying to saying something. I could not hear, all I was trying to do at that point, was walk out as quickly as I could.

I got to the parked car under the trees; it could not have been more prophetic if the elm trees had been palm trees. I opened the car door and threw the bible in the passenger seat, and said, "God, I'm not Jesus nor do I want to be. Please God, don't ever do that to me again" I was half smiling thinking, "*As if I could stop Him.*" I comforted myself on my way home, "Maybe it was something they needed to hear," and tried to put it all behind me. In the process of writing this book, I would read:

"Fear not. Be at peace and be strong."
— Daniel 10:19

"The Spirit will tell you what to say and how to say it."
— Matthew 10:19

I smiled and thought, "*Now you tell me.*" It appears that God has a sense of humor.

Communicating

When we talk about the physical it is easy. If I say table, and two people are in the same room. And there is a table in front of you. You can come close to what is meant then if one sees the table and the other doesn't.

If he speaks the same language, the odds increase even more. The two of you will at the very least be in the same ballpark as to what the other is talking about. The further physically you get the harder it is to get the same picture.

At any point in time we are influenced by our environment, our senses, and to what we are filtering out, in that specific time and place. For example if we are hard of hearing; dealing with a trauma that has just occurred; or if the rain outside is reminding us of a childhood experience. Our perception of what is going on at the time is being hijacked.

Physical things are easier when it comes to communicating. Although we can't get it exactly right. We can use our physical senses to come pretty close.

The problem comes with the abstract.

When we say God is love. You can feel the experience in some art form or human bond. You can kind of get the idea of love: Even though everyone's perception is different. But Can anyone proof there is a God? No. When we talk about God, we talk about the unknown: What we can't actually see.

Proof There's a God

"Love is not proof that we loved God, but that He loved us." — I John 4:10

If you dig deep enough nothing can be proven.

Faith is believing in what we cannot see. Can we proof God? No. Can we proof Science? No. Science like God is evidence of things not seen.

No one can see the things that science wants us to believe in. Very few can decipher their fancy equations. Many particles are only identifiable by the trails they leave behind.

In the justice system, we have to judge only by

the preponderance of the evidence. And the jury only has to prove that the defendant is guilty by a reasonable doubt; or by the conclusions of a "reasonable" person.

Nothing can be proven 100%: Even DNA is only 99% right.

Yet by the mere mention of any single word, we create something in our minds that we can agree on.

Take the word: Nothing. By merely mentioning it, it exists in some form.

The question is not that it exists. The question is: What is the truth? Where is the truth? Why does it exist and how do we use it for our betterment?

I think the answer is where the answer has been all along. Although ignorance and fear often tries to obscure or hide it. Ultimately, it will come out because it exists inside ourselves, and we will never find peace without it.

Sometimes all we have is a gut feeling. Nevertheless the truth is there.

"Faith is the substance of things hoped for, the evidence of things not seen." — Hebrews 11:1

I think this is worth repeating: Faith is a skill set, like all the rest, only this skill set is not seen, it is experienced.

There is a tribe I once read about: They would not believe anything unless the person was still alive, and could testify that he had seen it with his own eyes.

You can imagine how difficult this was for missionaries.

When we talk about God, we talk about the unknown. What we can't actually see.

Summary

In writing this book I reread many of my books.

The reason for reading all these books was because, at one time, I thought I could find out what was wrong with me.

What I really found out is that everyone is okay. We are all just going through our own spiritual journey. I also found out that what Matthew said was true.

"With God all things are possible." Matthew 19:26

I try to remember four things with life in general:

1. To know my limits.
2. Learn to wait.
3. To be persistent.
4. To keep working at it so hard that in the end I make it look easy.

"Not by might, or by power, but by my Spirit."
— Zechariah 4:6

I also learned that what I wanted to learn about myself I could not learn out of book. I not only had to read the books, study the books, but practice the books.

But I also had to realize some books were like some people ideas: They were not for me; I'm not there yet; I have outgrown them; or to me, in this space in time, completely worthless.

Some people want to be a concert pianist without touching a keyboard. And yet, some people make life look so easy, and others have no idea to the sacrifices it took to make their talents look easy.

See God and Good in all things, try not to hurt anyone, but when there is pain in whatever form, embarrassment etc., embrace the pain, it's trying to teach you something, find out what that something is, and move on. There will be others. Be easy on yourself. If your pain gets unbearable, get help. But don't forget,

YOU have to ultimately do the "work". You have to want to get rid of the pain.

The crucifixion of Jesus was a prime example of how innocent people will sometimes get hurt, because of ignorance, or fear. But always remember, that in the end of 'The Book', the 'Good Guy' wins.

To end our suffering:

- We have to get as much reliable information as we can.
- Look for motives, ignorance, and fears.
- Be aware that things can suddenly change.
- Be brutally honest with ourselves.

You have plenty of time. Take baby steps. If you don't get it right the first time it will keep coming back until you finally "get it". And this place you call hell, will mysteriously turn into the heaven you imagine. This is the truth that will finally set you free.

Love is the only thing that makes sense. God is LOVE. Survival is Love. Protect yourself by insuring your survival. God has its own agenda, you don't want to mess with it. You can't get in its way. It won't let you.

If you clean the lamp: the light will shine through. Which bring us full circle to Spirit.

What we want is at a deeper level. We want life not death. The reluctance to give up the future is sometimes more fearful then death.

Inside of us is a reservoir of being that never dies; is never exhausted; is unrestricted in consciousness; and is total bliss. THIS IS GOD! Yet as I once read, we are kings with amnesia living as paupers.

The real goal is to know God AND to have divinity on earth.

The moral responsibilities by way of the Ten Commandments: No injuries, no lying, stealing, self-control, etc., still apply.

We can find God in art, in music, in people, in dance and in laughter.

How should we live? The more important question is: How miserable do you want to be? What stage are you in? Have you out grown your toys? Are you afraid to let go? Dive into self-discovery? Let go and let God. If we are wrong at least we enjoyed our journey.

All religions are very interesting and rich in variety. Ramakrishna's said, "There are different names for water and God, but it is the same water and God. Follow your own path or religion. You cannot know God and hate the other religions."

I believe the world is a training ground. If you fail the boot camp don't worry about it, you will have to keep doing it over and over until you realize it was literally **in you**, all along.

The journey will be much easier if you remember that it was never about the flesh but the Spirit. Don't forget that it is a training ground in which our actions have consequences.

To some it is a spiritual experience and to others an intellectual one.

I have found it better to live with the belief that I have a protector, someone that loves me, and that will give me whatever I ask for, because He cares. I have a Friend, a Confident, something that gives me purpose.

My dear, atheist, I hope you have found as much.

"Put God first then do what you want." Saint Augustine

This training ground is like writing a book and knowing the characters are based on the writer imagination. In other words, people are only what you think they are, not what they actually are. (If that makes sense?)

We can eliminate unnecessary suffering if we know how we work and what we have to work with. And

I think the bibles holds so many of those answers. To want to find out these answers is an important choice and my idea of a miracle.

The following is a list a friend once send to me years ago and could be examples or good advice. I think people just kept adding to it over the years. Some have the same idea as others, but I thought they were fun to share:

1. Accept the fact that some days you're the windshield and sometimes you are the bug.
2. If you can't be kind, at least have the decency to be vague.
3. If you lend someone $20 and never see that person again, it was probably worth it.
4. It may be that your sole purpose in life is simply to serve as a warning to others.
5. Never buy a car you can't push.
6. Never put both feet in your mouth at the same time, because then you won't have a leg to stand on.
7. Nobody cares if you can't dance well. Just get up and dance.
8. Since it's the early worm that gets eaten by the bird, sleep late.
9. The second mouse gets the cheese.
10. You don't have to out run the bear, just outrun the guy running beside you.
11. When everything's coming your way, you're in the wrong lane.
12. Birthdays are good for you. The more you have, the longer you live.
13. Some mistakes are too much fun to make only once.
14. A truly happy person is one who can enjoy the scenery on a detour.
15. In order for a picture to be good it has to have both lights and shadows.
16. The true optimist is the guy that can fall off a twenty

story window, and as he passes each story repeats: "I'm doing okay so far."

Have fun and create your own to add to the list!

When I am going through some hard times, I try to remind myself that even pretty flowers that smell good, had to go through fertilizer to get to the sun.

Have you ever noticed, there always seems to be three sides to everything? There is heads, tails and the edge: There is hot, cold and lukewarm; Go, Stop, and slow; Males, females, and hermaphrodites now called transsexuals. Often these become controversial, yet:

"...there is no new thing under the sun."
—Ecclesiastes 1:9

I learned three very important rules with truck driving that I always try to remember.

1. Don't ever, ever forget you are driving.

2. Don't ever, ever take your eyes off the road. In others words: Stay focused. When you do, and because you will, then go to rule number three.

3. Don't get so close to others vehicles that you can't have time to correct any mistakes.

(a) Don't forget **you** are responsible.
(b) Don't lose sight of your goal.
(c) Pay attention to what you are doing.

"The Measure of success is not whether you have a tough problem to deal with, but whether it's the same problem you had last year." — John Foster Dulles

There are so many truly amazingly beautiful

people in the world. Don't let their appearance fool you, and above all, don't let a very few bad apples distort your view of this wonder world.

If this book helps a single person be more aware and of the need to pay attention to their actions, and not so much at the actions of others, I can truthfully say:

Mission Accomplished!

With this, I will end this book the way I started it:

"Whatsoever things are true, honest, just, pure, lovely, and of good report, if there is any virtue, or praise, think on these things. — Philippians 4:8

With The Holy Spirit's Help

Oh mind, cease your endless, futile thoughts and know.
Confusion from all sides may attempt to tear all good.
Relax in the quiet murmur of your heart.
    With its gentle poundings flow.
        To quiet streams of life and life beyond
        And to all life's source.
Release yourself, oh mind,
    That this may lift you to a Greater power
    And here on earth find rest![40]

---

[40] I wrote this prayer years ago, when I realized I had to calm down for God to work.

PART IV

The Physical Process

"The real voyage of discovery consists not in seeking new landscapes but in having new eyes." — Marcel Proust

How to Start Cross-Stitching Project

I first attempted using 18-gauge Aida cloth. I thought that with smaller squares, I could get more words in the square. But then I decided that it would work just as well with the 14-gauge and make it easier to see and count.

In the beginning I thought it would be nice to add a little color. However, the embroidered flowers I try were not only more expensive, but bulky. I settle for flower stickers.

I would change the process over the course of a year.

I went from the larger frames and finally settled for the 5x7 frames. I went from oatmeal colored Aida cloth to white sand and back to the oatmeal, which I think looks like marble. (The white sand was discontinued.) At one time, I tried butterflies, but they were harder to come by. Mainstays® frames at the beginning cost 84 cent each, but the price started creeping up. I feel that they can fit with any color scheme in a person's house because the verses pop in, and there is only a very thin frame line. The total cost for each finished verse comes out to approximately $1.25. That is if the labor is free.

After buying the frame, I use the cardboard back as a template. I use a pencil to draw the outline, and then I cut. If all the squares are cut with the same 5x7 template on 14-gauge cloth, there are 95 squares across and 65 square down.

I go through all the books of the bible, and place a book marker with the number of chapters in each of the 66 books. If your birthday falls on January 1, I look through all the book markers; read the verse for each book; and type only the ones I like into the computer. I go through all the months and keep eliminating book markers or put them to the bottom to indicate that there are no more days for that chapter. If your birthday is on December 31, I look through only the book markers that are left.

I pick a verse that I like; put it on a paper and start counting. For example:

"I left all, rose up, and followed Him."
— Lk. 5:28

The first line: I left all,

5 (4) 1 4 4 5 (4) 5 1 1 + 1 (,)

$5x3 = 15, 4x4 = 16 + 4x1=4$

$15 + 16 + 4 = 35$

I— l^{1}e^{1}f^{1}t —a^{1}l^{1}l^1,

6 spaces between the letters in left and all.

$6 + 35 = 41$

After counting the letters and spaces, subtract them from 95 and divide by 2. (95-41 = 54 ÷ 2 = 27). Square 27 is where you start the first line horizontally.

The second line: rose up, and

4 4 4 4 (4) 4 5 1 (4) 5 4 5

$4 x 7 = 28, 5x3=15 + 1$

$28 + 15 + 1 = 44$

r^{1}o^{1}se — u^{1}p^1, — a^{1}n^{1}d

5 spaces between rose up and the coma

$6 + 44 = 50$

Subtract 50 from 95 and divide by 2. (95-50 = 60 ÷ 2 = 22.) Count 22 squares horizontally. This will be where you start the second line horizontally.

The third line: followed Him.

4 4 1 1 4 6 4 5 (4) 5 1 6 1

$5X2=10, 4X5=20, 6x2=12, 1x4=4$

$10 + 20 + 12 + 4 = 46$

f^{1}o^1 l^1 l^{1}o^1 w^{1}e^{1}d —H^{1}i^{1}m^1.

10 spaces for between the letters in the 3rd line.

$10 + 46 = 56$

Subtract this amount from 95 and divide That by 2. (95-56 = 39 ÷ 2 = 19). Count 19 squares horizontally. This will be where you start the third line

---

The fourth line: — Lk. 5:28. This will start on the right side.

12 spaces for the flower sticker, 10 squares for: —,

Lk. 5:28.

$^4L^1k^1.\ ^4\ 5^{2:2}2^28$

22 + 4 = 26 spaces for the flower and the space before Lk.

4 + 4 + 1 + 4 +1 + 4 + 4 = 21 space for Lk. 5:28

4 + 1 + 1 + 4 + 2 + 2 + 2 = 16 spaces (small numbers.)

26 + 21 + 16 = 63

95 - 63 /2 = 16. This the numbers of square you Count from the right side.

For each line you need 13 vertical squares: 8 for the height of the letters, 4 if the verse has the letters, g, j, p, q, y, b, d, f, h, k, l, t and 1 for space between the lines

Count 4 squares down if the verse has 5 lines and start where the counts intersect.

In this example you start 27 across (see the 1st line above) and 9 down.

You will need more room for the lines if you have g, j, p, q, y, b, d, f, h, k, l, t. I will move up the lines when I have 5 lines.

Count 9 squares down, if you have 4 lines.

Count 13 squares down, if you have 3 lines.

Count 20 squares down, if you have 2 lines.

If there is a line with a low number. I align them in this way:

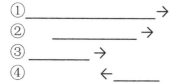

Notice That line one and 4 are aligned to the right.

The small script numbers on pages 37-48 are the number of cross stitching squares to count **across.**

Start on the square where the squares across and down converge.

When I finish the tall letters are 8 squares and the others are 4. (*See the Sampler.*)

I thread as many as ten needles at a time with three strands of black embroidery thread each, stick them on my stuffed sewing lady doll, set it beside my bed, along with a cup of tea, I turn on the TV, lay down, and pretend I am working very hard at sewing.

Abbreviations of the books of the bible
This is the way I abbreviated the chapters
They are listed in alphabetical order

Ac.	Acts	Jas.	James	Ne.	Nehemiah
Am.	Amos	Jer.	Jeremiah	Nu.	Numbers
I Ch.	I Chronicles	Job	Job	Ob.	Obadiah
II Ch.	II Chronicles	Joe.	Joel	I Pe.	I Peter
Col.	Colossians	Jo.	John	II Pe.	II Peter
I Co.	I Corinthians	I Jo.	II John	Ph'm.	Philemon
II Co.	II Corinthians	II Jo.	II John	Ph'p	Philippians
Da.	Daniel	III Jo.	III John	Pr.	Proverbs
De.	Deuteronomy	Jon.	Jonah	Ps.	Psalms
Ec.	Ecclesiastes	Jos.	Joshua	Re.	Revelation
Eph.	Ephesians	Jude	Jude	Ro.	Romans
Es.	Esther	J'g	Judges	Ru.	Ruth
Ex.	Exodus	I Ki.	I Kings	I Sa.	I Samuel
Ez.	Ezekiel	II Ki.	II Kings	II Sa.	II Samuel
Ezr.	Ezra	La.	Lamentations	S.S.	Songs/Solomon
Ga.	Galatians	Le.	Leviticus	I Th.	I Thessalonians
Ge.	Genesis	Lk.	Luke	IITh.	I Thessalonians
Hab.	Habakkuk	Mal.	Malachi	I Ti.	I Timothy
Hag.	Haggai	Mk	Mark	I Ti.	II Timothy
He.	Hebrews	Mt.	Matthew	Tit.	Titus
Ho.	Hosea	Mic.	Micah	Zec.	Zechariah
Isa.	Isaiah	Na.	Nahum	Zep.	Zephaniah

SAMPLER

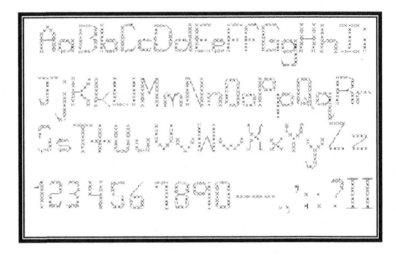

More Verses

January
1:3 Genesis – Let there be light and there was light.
1:4 III John – I have no greater joy than for my children.
1:18 Ecclesiastes – In much wisdom there is much grief.
1:22 Romans – Professing yourself to be wise you become foolish.
1:31 I Corinthians – He that is glorified: Let him glorify God.

February
2:1 Titus – Speak in sound doctrine.
2:2 II Timothy – Commit to teach what you have learned.
2:3 Philippians – Don't do anything through strife or vain glory.
2:6 Ezekiel – Don't be afraid of them, their words, or their
looks.
2:7 Jonah – When my soul fainted, I remembered God.

2:8 Joel – Everyone will walk his own path.

2:12 Song of Solomon – Flowers appear and birds are singing.

2:14 Philippians – Don't complain when doing anything.

2:15 I Peter – With well doing we silence, ignorant, foolish men.

2:18 Isaiah – Abolish all idols.

2:19 Jeremiah – Your own wickedness will correct you.

2:20 I Peter –It is good when you are criticized and take it patiently.

2:21 Galatians – If you are legalistic Jesus died in vain.

2:24 Deuteronomy – Rise up and take your journey.

2:25 II Timothy – In meekness (patience) instruct those that oppose themselves.

March
3:1 Ecclesiastes – To everything there is a season.

3:2 Titus – Speak no evil: Be gentle to all men.

3:4 Ezra – Do your duty according to this day as required.

3:9 I Kings – Help me to discern between good and evil.

3:15 Ecclesiastes – The past is now. God wants what is now.

April
4:1 I John – Don't believe every spirit, discern if they are of God.

4:4 I Timothy – Every creature of God is good.

4:6 Philippians – Let your requests be make known unto God.

4:10 Ecclesiastes – Don't be alone when you fall.

4:12 Mark – May you be ever seeing never perceiving.

4:14 Nehemiah – Fight for what is yours.

4:14 I Timothy – Don't neglect the gift which is in you.

4:15 Ruth – God restores life, and nourishes you in your old age.

4:17 Mark – Those that are not well grounded are easily offended.

4:18 Galatians – It is good to be zealously affected in a good thing.
4:20 I John – To say I love God, and hate your brother, is lying.
4:27 Ephesians – Don't give evil a foot hold.

May

5:1 Galatians – God has made us free. Don't be in bondage.
5:3 I Peter – Don't abuse power over people, but be a good example.
5:6 I Thessalonians – Be always aware.
5:11 Isaiah – Woe to them that rise up early for strong drink.
5:13 Luke – God wills that you be healed.
5:15 Romans –With grace by one many live.
5:16 Ecclesiastes – What profit is there in laboring for the wind?
5:17 Galatians – The flesh and the Spirit conflict: Choose.
5:24 Matthew – Make peace with your brother first, then offer your gift to God.
5:30 Numbers – When the spirit of jealousy comes on you, search for God.
5:30 Matthew – If anything offends you, cut yourself off from it.

June

6:3 Galatians – A man deceives himself when he thinks he is something when he is not.
6:4 Acts – Give yourself continually to prayer.
6:5 Galatians – Everyone will bear his own burden.
6:10 II Corinthians – Improve yourself.
6:11 Philippians – Put on the whole armor of God.
6:25 Proverbs – Don't lust after beauty.

July

7:3 Revelation – Do not hurt the earth, sea, or trees.

7:12 Ecclesiastes – The excellency of knowledge is that wisdom gives life to them that have it.

7:14 Luke – Young man, I say unto you: Arise.

7:25 Matthew – The destruction came, but the house did not fall, for it was built on a rock.

7:31 I Corinthians – Deal with this world but don't abuse it.

August

8:3 Jeremiah – Evil will choose death not life.

8:4 Ezekiel – The glory of God was in a vision I saw.

8:5 Hebrews – You make all things according to the pattern.

8:9 I Corinthians – Freedom can be a stumbling block if you are weak.

8:11 Nehemiah – Hold your peace, nor be sad, for the day is holy.

8:17 Zechariah – Let none of you imagine evil in your hearts.

8:25 Mark – He was restored, and saw every man clearly.

8:26 Matthew – Why are you so fearful? Oh you of little faith.

September

9:9 Proverbs – Teach a wise man: He will be wiser. Teach a just man, he will increase in learning.

9:11 Ecclesiastes – The race is not to the swift, nor the battle to the strong, but time and chance happens to all.

9:17 Acts – Receive your sight and be filled with the Holy Spirit.

9:20 Job – My own mouth will condemn me.

9:25 John – I was blind, now I see.

October

10:5 John – He knows not one stranger.

10:6 Hebrews – Sins have had no pleasure.

10:9 Proverbs – He that lives upright has confidence.

10:10 Ecclesiastes – If the blade is blunt, and you don't sharpen it, you have to use more force.

10:19 Deuteronomy – Love strangers, you were once a stranger.

10:19 Matthew–The Spirit will tell you what to say and how to say it.

November

11:2 Daniel – Now I will show you the truth.

11:6 Matthew – Blessed are you that are not offended by God.

11:9 Isaiah – The things that hurt will not hurt nor destroy.

11:19 Proverbs – The right-minded tends to life.

11:24 Proverbs – If you hold on to more than you make, it will lead to poverty.

December

12:2 Luke – All will be revealed: All will be known.

12:6 I Corinthians – There are diversities but it is the same God.

12:8 Ezekiel – God talks to me in the morning.

12:9 I Corinthians – One is given faith and another the gift of healing, by the same Spirit.

12:15 Proverbs – You are wise if you heed wise counsel.

12:16 Romans – Do not be condescending or conceited.

12:19 Romans – Don't avenge yourself, vengeance is God's.

12:25 Luke – Worry will not help you.

12:28 I Corinthians – God has set the ministries of miracles...

Made in the USA
Coppell, TX
15 December 2020

44896868R00157